KB262754

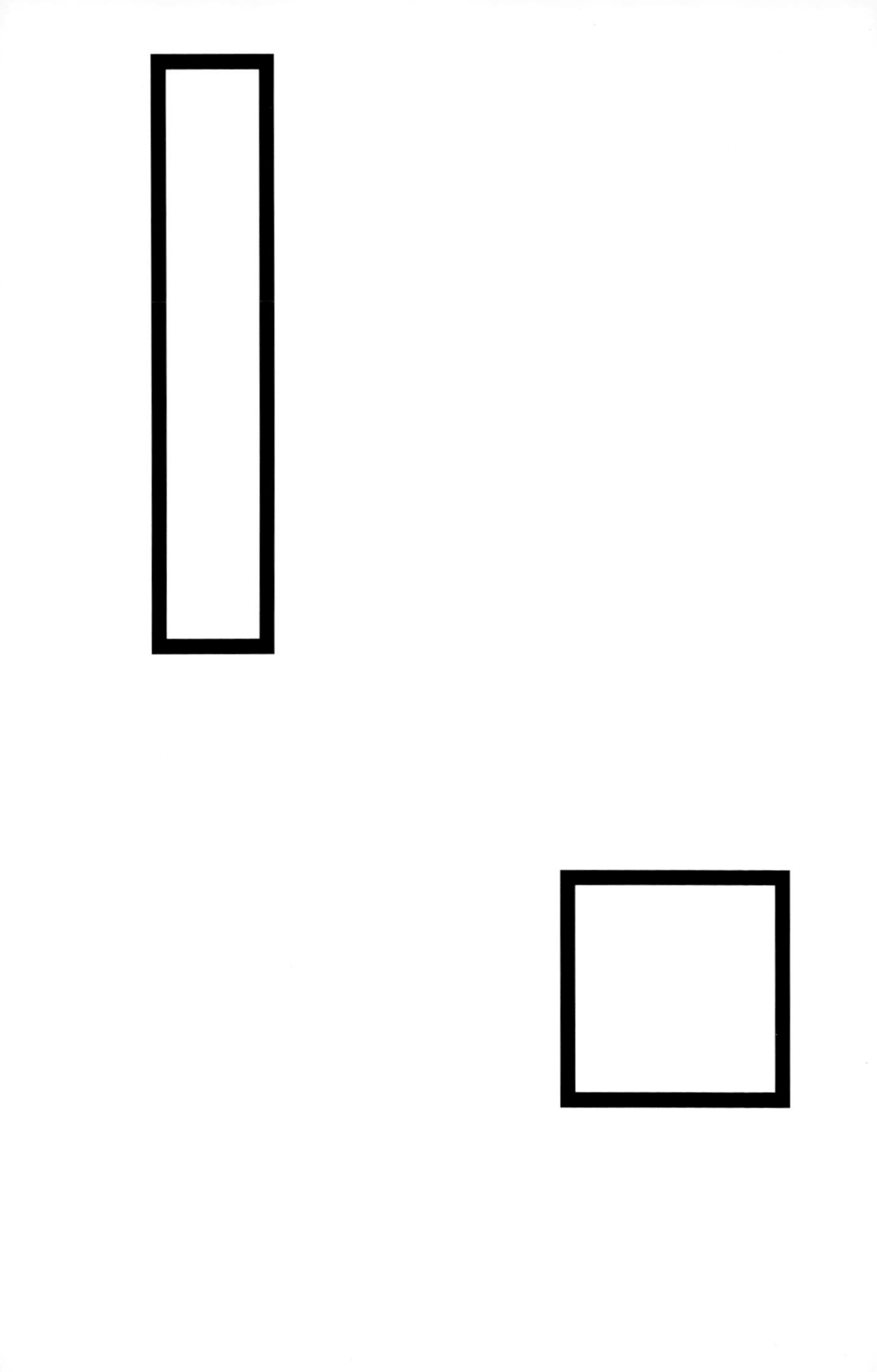

The 'meaning' of life is not to be found in anything other than that life itself.

삶의 '의미'는 다름 아닌 그 삶 자체에서만 발견할 수 있다.

Henri Lefebvre, *Critique of Everyday Life*

앙리 르페브르, ‹일상에 대한 비평›

Cook Folly

GD (Gwangju Dutch) Folly

see play eat walk

JAP SAM
BOOKS

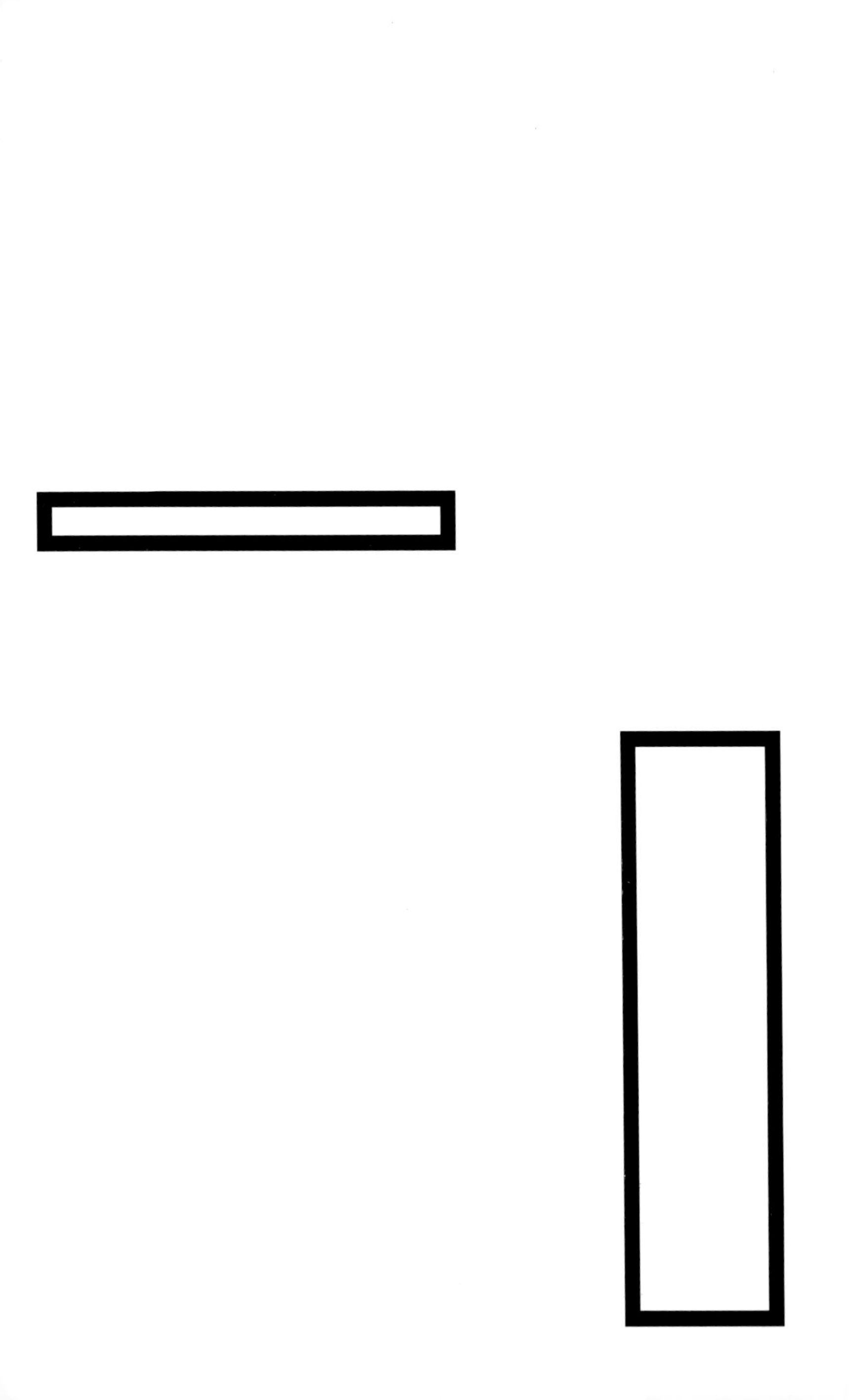

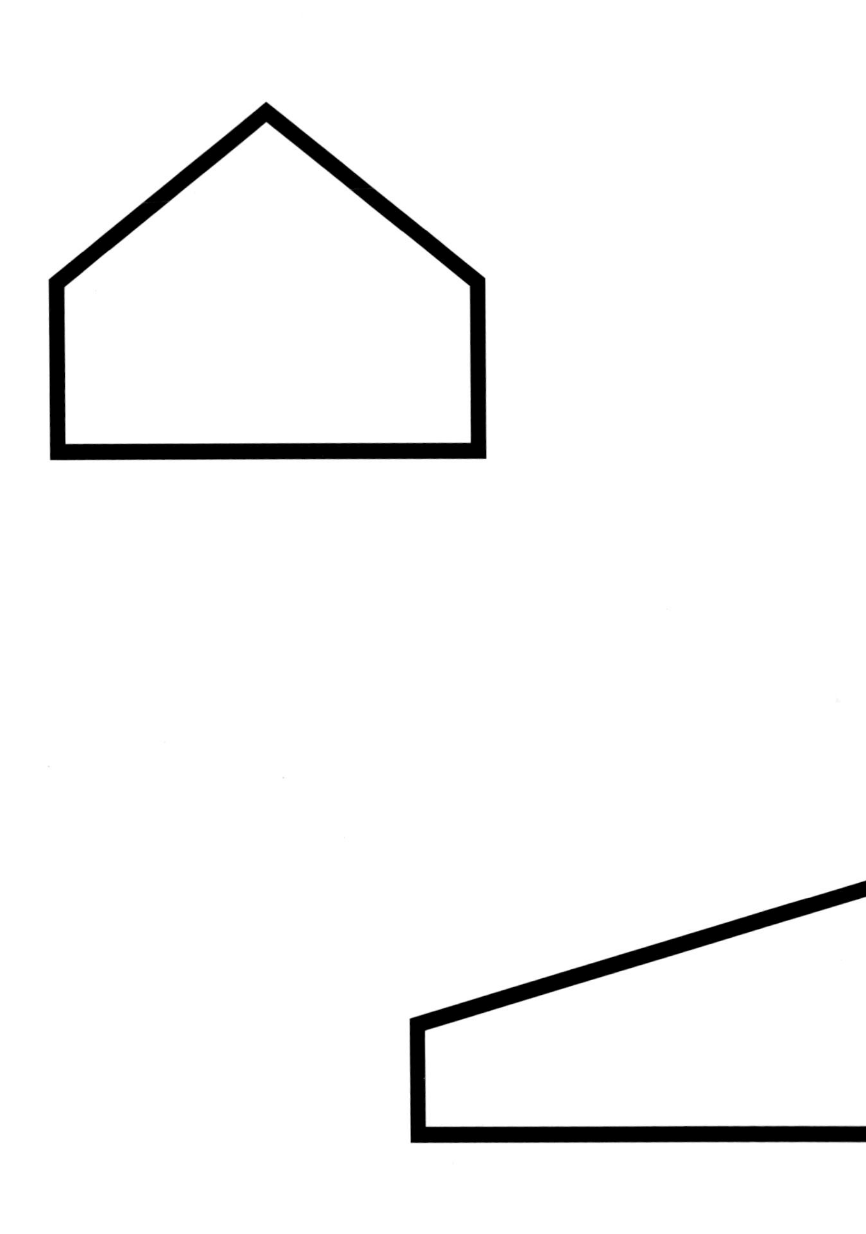

For the quest for satisfaction and the fact of being satisfied presuppose the fragmentation of 'being' into activities, intentions, needs, all of them well-defined, isolated, separable and separated from the Whole. Is this an art of living? A style? No. It is merely the result and the application to daily life of a management technique and a positive knowledge directed by market research.

만족에 대한 추구와 만족의 상태는 전체로부터 구분되고 분리되며 격리된, '존재'의 쪼개진 파편들을 전제한다. 즉, 분명하게 정의된 행위와 의도, 그리고 요구들인 것이다. 이것이 삶의 기술인가? 양식인가? 그렇지 않다. 이는 단지 결과이며 시장조사가 만들어낸 경영기술과 실증적 지식을 일상에 적용한 것에 불과하다.

Henri Lefebvre, *Critique of Everyday Life*
앙리 르페브르, ‹일상에 대한 비평›

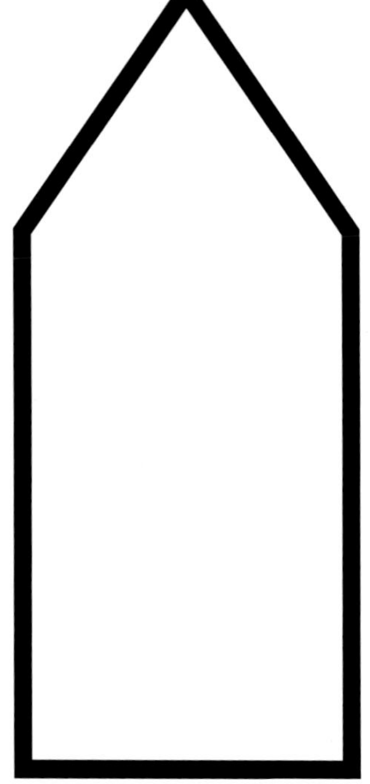

Against an economism void
of values other than
those of exchange, protest
stood for reuniting the festival
and daily life, for transforming
daily life into a site of desire
and pleasure. The protesters
were protesting against
the fact, simultaneously obvious
and ignored, that delight and
joy, pleasure and desire, desert
a society that is content
with satisfaction that is to say,
catalogued, created needs
that procure some particular
object and evaporate in it.

교환 가치 이외에는 어떠한 의미도 두지 않는 경제주의에 반해, 시위대는 축제와 일상을 재결합하고, 일상을 욕망과 즐거움의 장으로
바꾸기 위해 거리로 나섰다. 시위자들은 기쁨과 즐거움, 쾌락과 욕망이 만족스러운 사회를 유기한다는,
명백하고도 무시되어온 사실에 항의했다. 즉, 특정 대상만을 구하고 결국 그 안에서 증발해버리는, 만들어지고 목록화된 수요에 항의한 것이다.

Henri Lefebvre, *Critique of Everyday Life*
앙리 르페브르, ‹일상에 대한 비평›

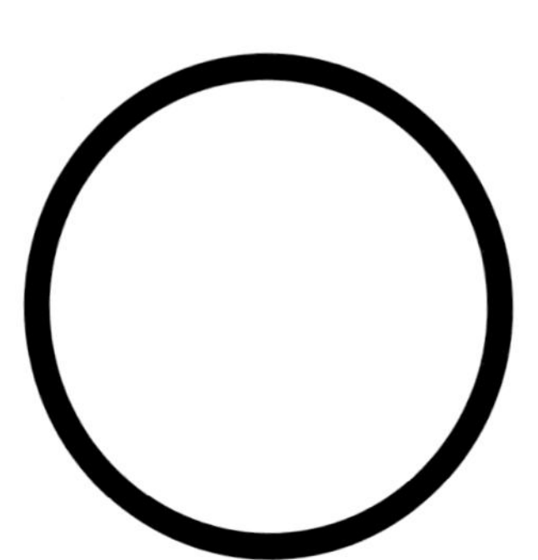

Chun, Eui-Young + Yoo, Uoo Sang + Wee, Jinbok

천의영 + 유우상 + 위진복

Small Urbanism with Gwangju Follies

광주폴리와 스몰 어바니즘

Place Reinventing

When considering the key terms that effectively conceptualise the evolution and the survival desire of cities, we come across such terms as "place marketing," "space marketing," "nation branding," "destination branding," "city branding," and "place branding." Despite their subtle differences in meaning, these concepts commonly refer to various forms of initiatives that bring more people to a particular place or make them want to live thereby providing positive experiences. More recently, the term "place branding" has been the subject of extensive attention. It was initially adopted to effectively increase the attractiveness of a particular place from a marketing perspective. In order to achieve this, it is vital to establish a core value and the spirit necessary for generating the unique identity of somewhere as well as a strategy to combine the potentiality and marketability of a particular place. In addition, to succeed in place branding, it is crucial to materialise distinctive value of the place to meet customer needs and, at the same time, to persistently maintain the process of "image generation," which improves such value. In the contemporary city, place branding can be

장소재창안
도시의 진화와 생존욕망을 가장 잘 정리한 핵심 개념어로는 플레이스 마케팅, 스페이스 마케팅, 도시 마케팅, 국가 브랜딩, 데스티네이션 브랜딩, 장소 브랜딩 등이 있다. 조금씩 차이는 있으나 기본적으로 더 많은 사람들로 하여금 특정 도시 또는 장소를 찾아오거나 거주하고 싶도록 하고, 이에 대한 긍정적인 인식을 만드는 다양한 종류의 노력을 통칭하는 것이다.
여러 용어 중 최근 가장 주목받고 있는 핵심 개념어는 장소 브랜딩(Place Branding)이다. 특정 장소의 매력을 상품적 관점에서 보다 체계적으로 증가시키고자 도입된 용어이다. 그러기 위해서는 장소의 잠재성을 상품성과 결합하여 그 장소의 매력도를 높이는 것 이외에도,

장소의 특별한 아이덴티티 구축을 위한 핵심 가치와 핵심정신을 만들어가는 재창안 전략이 중요해진다. 또한 특정 장소의 브랜딩이 성공하기 위해서는 그 장소의 독특한 가치들을 수요자들의 요구에 적절하게 맞추면서도 그 가치를 증대시키는 적극적인 '이미지 구축 과정'을 지속적으로 유지해 독특한 일관성을 만들어나가는 것이 중요하다. 또한 현대 도시에서 장소 브랜딩은 관련된 모든 전략적 요소들을 통합, 결집하여 만들어내는 '총체적 경쟁력 구축 과정(Holistic Competitiveness Building Process)'이라 볼 수 있다. 라이니스토 (Seppo K. Rainisto)는 이러한 장소 브랜딩을 성공적으로 진행하려면 리더십의 안정성과 계획가 그룹의 기획이 중요하다고 역설한다.

 Curatorial Team

viewed as a "holistic competitiveness-building process" that brings together all kinds of related strategies. To successfully implement this kind of place branding, Seppo K. Rainisto emphasises the significance of stable leadership as well as the importance of an excellent planning group.

Attempts to build urban competitiveness are currently occurring in the forms of public design, city design, community building, urban regeneration, the creation of pedestrian-friendly streets, and more. Each project can be categorised according to the lead organiser, whether privately led, government-led, or third-party-initiated. It can also be categorised according to implementation methods, such as a top-down or bottom-up approach. However, it always comes down to the question of setting up suitable methods for strengthening the creative competitiveness of the place and maintaining that strength. This is embodied by the term Amy Cortese coined, "locavesting"—the practice of encouraging participation and investment of local stakeholders both at the corporate

이러한 도시 경쟁력 구축 과정은 공공디자인, 도시디자인, 마을 만들기, 도시재생, 걷고 싶은 거리 등 다양한 방식과 유형으로 진행되고 있다. 누가 주도하느냐에 따라 민간주도, 관주도 또는 제3섹터에 의한 방식으로 나뉘고,

추진 형식에 따라 하향식과 상향식 등으로 분류할 수 있다. 그러나 본질은 각 장소의 창조적 경쟁력을 강화시킬 수 있는 적정한 수단을 어떻게 구축하고 그 힘을 지속적으로 유지하느냐의 문제로 압축된다. 최근 도시와 지역에서 캅스 앤 도너츠(Cops & Doughnuts)의 사례와 같이, 지역을 살리기 위해 창의적인 방식으로 기업과 개인의 참여를 유도하여 지역의 이해 관계자들이 직접 투자하는 '로카베스팅(Locavesting, Amy Cortese)'과 산업, 문화, 이벤트 등 다양한 요소와 결합하여 상향식으로 지역을 살리는 소규모 장소 재창안(Place Reinventing)이 새로운 대안으로 주목 받고 있다는 점이 흥미롭다. 세계 각지의 도시들과 유사하게 재능의 공유, 공간의 공유, 공구의 공유 등을 통해 지역

 Small Urbanism with Gwangju Follies

and individual level—as a creative way to revitalise an area, and something that was exemplified by the Cops & Doughnuts bakery initiative project in Clare, Michigan. Place reinventing, in which an area is regenerated in a bottom-up, small-scale approach by combining industry, culture, and events, is recognised as an important alternative solution. Similar to many other small village communities around the world, we are witnessing the emergence of both potential and practical examples where sharing talents, sharing workspace, and sharing used tools can revitalise any community within a region.

At the same time, a visitor exchange program can create emerging start-up companies in underutilised urban spaces through a global lodging and workplace exchange network while also stimulating ideas such as Berlin, Germany's Housepreneurs.

공동체가 활성화되는 가능성과 실제 사례들이 등장하고 있는 것이다. 또한 베를린의 '하우스프레누어(Housepreneurs)'와 같이 글로벌 숙박과 창업 교류 네트워크, 창의적인 아이디어를 통해 활용도가 낮은 도시 공간에 교류 방문 프로그램이 새로운 스타트업 기업을 만들어낼 수도 있다.

Fig.1

Success Diagram of Place Marketing by Seppo K. Rainisto
세포 K. 라이니스토(Seppo K. Rainisto)의 성공적인 장소브랜딩을 위한 요소 다이어그램

Store Urbanism

Gyeongridan-gil, Mangwon Market, and Dongjin Market in Yeonnam-dong are places where artists, architects, designers, and entrepreneurs initiated gradual urban regeneration by sharing rent-out spaces and setting up small creative shops rather than by carrying out public-led systematic planning. These kinds of local businesses allow people not only to experience the city in a new way, but also to increase sales through greater visitor flow, generating a so-called "store urbanism" whereby the urban regeneration phenomenon starts from smaller creative stores. Shoe Spot Seongsu was the project I participated into find solutions that strengthen the competitiveness of the handmade shoe industry, and help urban manufacturers survive in Seoul. The Shoe Spot project was driven by a collaboration between Seoul's Economic Policy Department, the Seoul Design Foundation, Seongdong-gu District Office, and the Seoul Business Agency. We all hoped the new stores under the Seongsu

Mangwon Market, Dongjin Market, Mapo-gu, 마포구 망원시장, 동진시장

The Shoe Spot Project, Seongsu-dong, Seongdong-gu 성동구 슈스팟 프로젝트

Seoul, Republic of Korea

Gyeongridan-gil, Yongsan-gu 용산구 경리단길

HAN RIVER

가게 어바니즘

경리단길, 망원시장, 연남동 동진시장, 어쩌다 가게 등은 공공에 의한 계획적 개발이 아닌 예술가, 건축가, 디자이너, 사업자들이 함께 기존 골목 건물을 개조하며 임대공간을 작게 나누고 여기에 창의적인 가게들이 입점하며 활력 있는 장소를 되살려낸 사례들이다. 이런 골목 상권 중심의 창조성은 그 도시의 경험적 측면을 새롭게 할 뿐 아니라, 방문객을 증가시켜 매출 상승으로 이어지는 소위 '가게 어바니즘(Store Urbanism)'이라는 가게 중심의 도시재생 현상을 만들고 있다.

    필자가 참여한 성수동의 '슈스팟 성수'는 서울시 경제정책실과 서울디자인재단, 성동구청 그리고 서울산업진흥원이 성수동을 중심으로 도심제조업인 수제화산업의 경쟁력을 만들어 내고자 여러 가지 노력을 하던 중 시작됐다. 성수역 매장은 물론 남쪽의 구두테마공원, 부자재 거리 등 특화거리와 함께 산업, 관광, 마을이 함께 연계되는 독특한 지역으로 거듭나길 기대한다. 핵심은 성수역 인근 직매장과 공동 브랜딩 매장을 통해 재고 감소와 가격인하라는 실질적 혜택이 생산장인들과 소비자들에게 돌아갈 수 있도록 한 점이다. 이와 함께 전철역의 통행공간을 활용해 작은 구두뮤지엄, 제화 도구 전시장과 탑승장 광고판 등을 만들어 보다 적극적으로 수제화산업을 홍보했다.

이제 성수동에는 제화산업뿐만 아니라 서울숲 인근의 카우앤독 등에 입주한 수많은 사회적 기업들과 카페 오르에르, 베란다 스튜디오, 수피,

subway station could connect people to Seongsu's shoe-
themed park, Yeonmujang leather market streets,
and other streets specialising in commercial goods of
one type or another as you head south, while also creating
a healthy network connecting the shoe industry, tourism,
and the local community. The key point of this project is that
both customers and shoemakers can actually benefit
from the reduced prices and lower rents with co-branding.
At the same time, the exhibition to publicise the project was
proceeded by utilising the subway passageway to create
a small shoe museum, display shoemaking tools, and
install advertisement boards to actively promote the handmade shoe industry. Currently, Seongsu-dong is not only
popular for its shoe industry, but for many of its creative
shops like Café Or Er, Veranda Studio, SU:PY, Column-Daelim
Warehouse, Zagmachi café serve as a creative core
community. Due to the fact that they created a close network,
the area soon led to an "industrial aesthetic" trend, and
it came to be known as the Brooklyn of Korea. Yet, as gentrification takes place, rents are increasing and it remains
to be seen how the local industry will maintain its competiti-

대림창고, 자그마치 등 다양한 카페들이 창조적
코어로 역할을 하고 있다. 이들이 선으로
연결되기 시작하면서 '산업적 미감(Industrial
Aesthetic)'의 트렌드를 선도해 성수동은
소위 한국의 브루클린이라고 불리게 되었다.
다만 지역의 고급화가 진행되며 지가와 임대료가
상승하는 젠트리피케이션이 진행되고 있고,
글로벌 제화산업의 재편에 따른 위기상황에서
어떻게 지역산업이 경쟁력을 유지해나갈지가
앞으로 향배의 중요한 관건이다.

이제까지 우리 도시는 '도시재생'이라는
화두로 여러 지자체에서 도시재정비사업을
진행해왔지만, 이는 주로 3종 주거지화의 지구
단위계획이 중심이 되는 공동주택개발에
편중되어 왔다. 특히 구제적 불황기에 사업자와
재개발 조합의 사업성과 이익을 고려하지 않을
수 없어 '슈퍼블록(Superblocks)'의 고층집합
주거단지가 들어서고, 도시경관이 획일화
된다는 위험이 있었다. 물론 대도시로의 성장은
고층화와 고밀도화를 피할 수 없다.

veness in a rapidly changing global shoe industry of the future.
        Up until now, numerous local governments have
initiated urban revitalisation projects under the pretext of
"urban regeneration," but the majority of the projects have
focused on building high-density residential areas at
the cost of demolishing small old houses and alleys. In particular, it seemed inevitable that high-rise residential buildings in so-called "superblocks" would be constructed when
considering the business model and profit value of redevelopment during any recession and the danger of maintaining monotonous residential cityscapes. Of course it is
nearly impossible to stop the development of global cities
from Manhattanisation and densification.

   Small Urbanism with Gwangju Follies

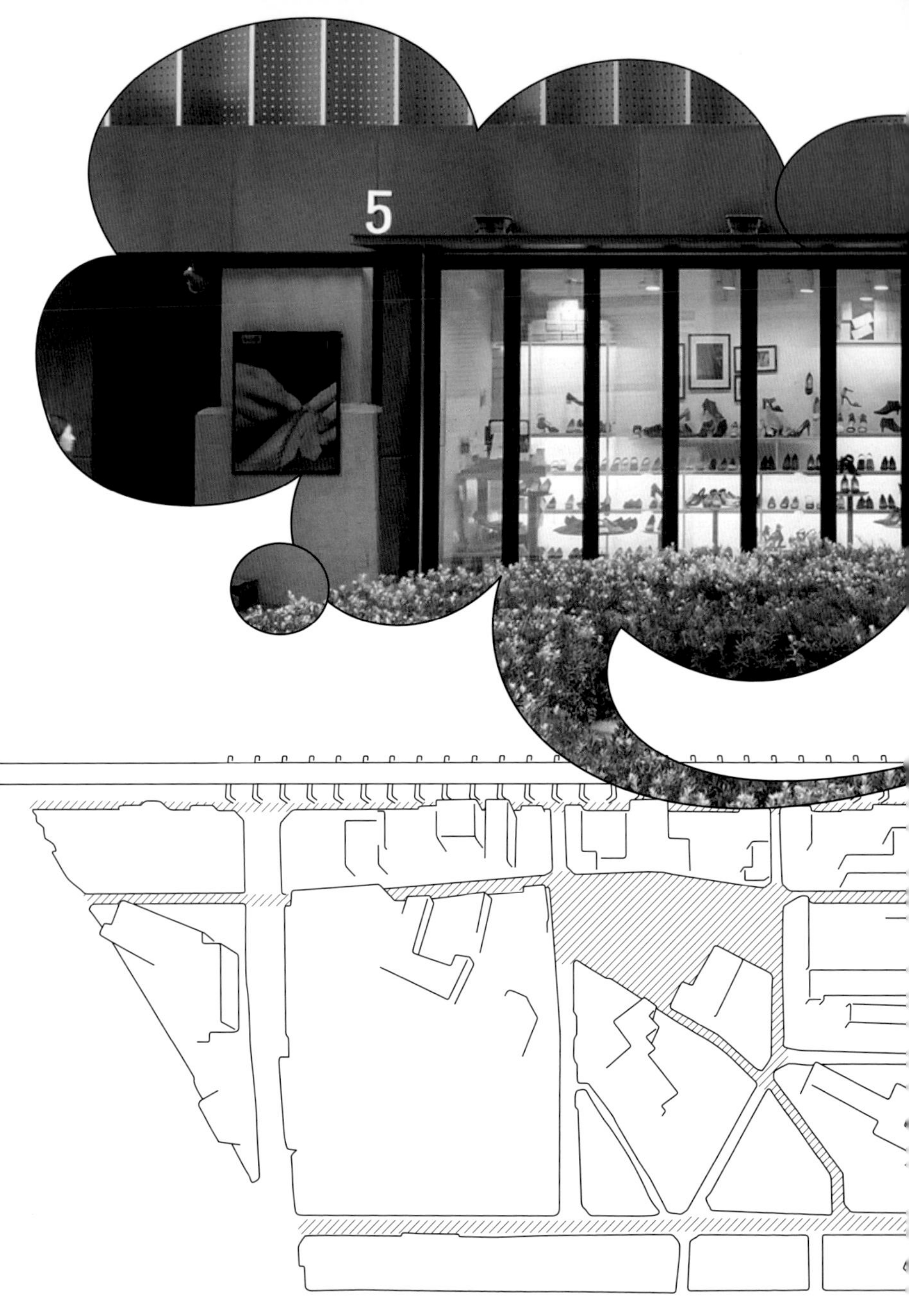

Curatorial Team

From SS
103, Achasan-ro, Seongdong-gu, Seoul, Republic of Korea
프롬SS, 대한민국 서울시 성동구 아차산로 103

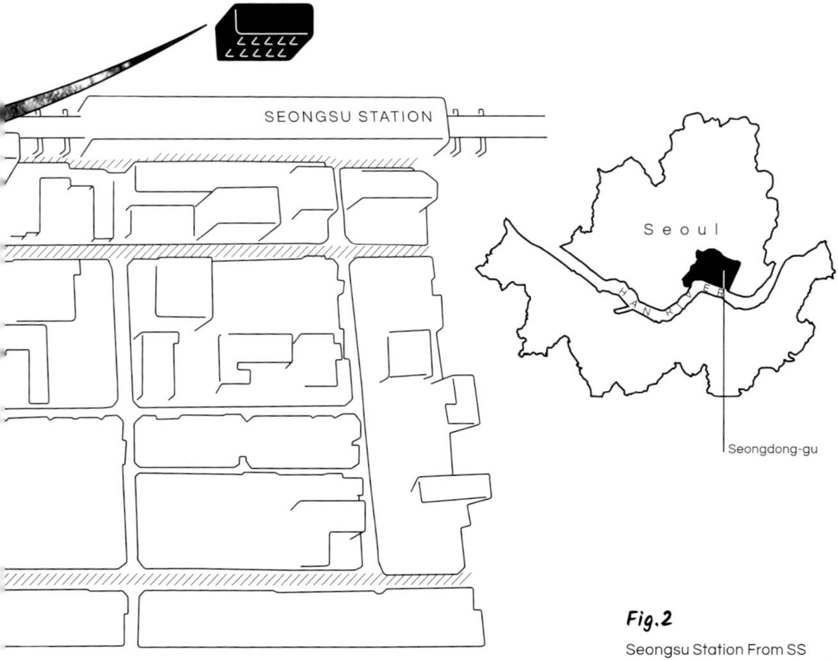

Fig.2

Seongsu Station From SS
the Public Handmade Shoe Stores
성수역 하부 수제화 공동매장 프롬SS

Small Urbanism with Gwangju Follies

However, we came to a point where the personal and historical traces of local people left in the back alleys of cities are
eradicated by the rise of uniform high-rise apartments
that dominate the skyline of a city through an increased FAR
(floor area ratio). A shared concern about such problems
hassled many cities to adopt place-specific, small-scale
participatory urban regeneration methods. Facing a period
of drastic decrease in urban population, many expect
that the construction of "hypercities" will be pursued in response to the restructuring of global cities. Korea should
eventually become a One City Nation, whereby every part of
the Korean peninsula can be reached within two hours
through high-speed circular trains. It is important to think
about how creative street shops of the cities that serve as connecting nods could become specialised cultural zones.
It is also crucial to consider how specialised zones evolving
around creative business programs, such as shared guest-
houses, unique restaurants and singular stores, could
be developed as a means to take part in desirable local-glob-
alisation and activate small-scale store urbanism campaigns.

그러나 도시에 살던 많은 사람들의 흔적과
도시의 뒷골목, 여기에 담긴 이야기와 역사성이
모두 사라지고 도시정비사업이라는 명목하에
용적률까지 상향하며 획일화된 아파트들이
도시경관을 지배하는 상황까지 발생하게 되었다.
이러한 문제의식들이 공유되며 작금의 여러
도시는 지역의 특성에 맞는 소규모의 점진적인
참여형 도시재생을 유도하고 있다. 이제 인구
감소의 시대를 직면하게 되는 우리 도시도
글로벌 도시구조의 재편에 맞추어 '하이퍼시티
(Hypercity)' 구조를 갖추며 한반도 전체가

동아시아의 새로운 허브 도시체제로 진화해야
하는 시점이다. 부연하자면 한반도 전체가
순환형 고속철도 교통체계로 2시간 이내에 연결
되는 하나의 도시국가(One City Nation)를
지향해야 한다. 여기에 연결 노드의 중심인
각 도시들이 지역의 골목에 주목하고, 창의적인
사업과 운영프로그램을 중심으로 게스트하우스,
이색식당, 매장, 그리고 문화공간 등에 특화된,
지역과 함께 국제화에 참여해가는 스몰 어바니즘
운동을 활성화해가는 것이 중요하다.

Gwangju Folly III

The word "folly" commonly refers to structures built without special uses in old gardens. Although follies were certainly built during times of famine in the past as a means to pay for labor, it was more common to refer to follies as non-functional buildings. Within the context of architecture, a folly can be defined in many different ways, and it is possible to be used as an open urban-architectural device. The contemporary notion of a folly became popular because of architect Bernard Tschumi, the man responsible for planning Parc de la Villette, which is situated in the 19 arrondissement of Paris, France. Tschumi also designed the so-called "symbols of non-representational structures" on a 120-meter grid. For the architectural competition, Tschumi aptly utilised the dualistic meaning of the homophone "folly," meaning whimsical structure, and "folie," meaning madness.

1) Folie Douce, 2) Folie Accueil-Information, 3) Entrée Cité de la Musique, 4) Folie Argonaute, 5) Folie Little Villette, 6) Petite Folie, 7) Folie Belvédère, 8) Folie Billetterie du Zénith, 9) Folie Café, 10) Folie de L'aventure, 11) Folie des Anges, 12) Folie de L'écluse, 13) Folie du Bout du Monde, 14) Folie Horloge, 15) Folie Information-Billetterie, 16) Folie Janvier, 17) Folie Kiosque, 18) Folie L2, 19) Folie des Fêtes, 20) Folie Philharmonie, 21) Folie Observatoire, 22) Folie Rond-point des Canaux, 23) Folie du Théâtre, 24) Folie des Vents et des Dunes, 25) Folie des Merveilles, 26) Trabendo

광주폴리 III

폴리란 일반적으로 오래전부터 정원에 지어진 비실용적인 구조물들을 의미한다. 물론, 기근 시에 노동대가를 주기 위한 폴리들이 만들어지기도 했지만 일반적으로는 실용적 기능 목적이 없이 지어진 작은 건축물을 일컫는 것이 보통이다. 하지만 건축분야에서 폴리는 다양한 방식으로 규정되거나 열린 도시건축장치로 사용될 수 있는 가능성이 있다. 현대적 의미의 폴리는 건축가 베르나르 추미가 프랑스 파리의 19구역에 라빌레트 공원을 설계하면서 120미터의 그리드로 무작위로 배치해놓은 소위 '비표상적 기표의 구조물들'로 널리 알려지기 시작했다. 추미는 현상설계공모를 통해 영어 '폴리(Folly)'와 발음이 같은 광기를 뜻하는

Small Urbanism with Gwangju Follies

The word commonly *folly* refers to structures built without special uses in gardens. Although follies were certainly built during times of famine in the past as a means to pay for labor, it was more common to refer to follies as non-functional buildings.

폴리란 일반적으로 오래전부터 정원에 지어진 비실용적인 구조물들을 의미한다.
물론, 기근 시에 노동대가를 주기 위한 폴리들이 만들어지기도 했지만 일반적으로는
실용적 기능목적이 없이 지어진 작은 건축물을 일컫는 것이 보통이다.

Fig.3

Fig.3
The Follies of Parc de
la Villette in Paris
파리에 있는 라빌레트 공원의 폴리

Curatorial Team

The park was created in the 1980s as an architectural device that transcended the conventional meanings of the urban context. In other words, Parc de la Villette exists within the structured urban space in relation to its historical context, but the unexpected introduction of the non-representational structures of follies enabled it to overcome the established historical context and create a new de-contextualised open meaning for urban revitalisation. Contemporary follies could therefore become part of some structure, but at the same time reject integration, revealing their creative potential beyond a certain context of a city. Many other follies have been designed even after Parc de la Villette. For instance, the Osaka Folly, the Groningen Folly (NL) and others have stimulated new ideas within urban contexts.

프랑스어 '폴리(Folie)'의 이중적 의미를 활용했다. 기존 도시가 가진 의미의 한계를 뛰어넘는 건축장치로 1980년대 공원을 해체철학의 틀을 도입해 새롭게 만든 것이다. 즉, 라빌레트 공원이 역사적 맥락에 의해 구조화된 도시공간에 놓여 있는 것은 분명하지만, 그러한 맥락을 뛰어 넘는 비구조화된 의외성의 도시 활성화 장치를 만들고자 한 것이다. 현대적 의미의 폴리는 도시구조의 일부분이지만 구조 안에 포함되기를 거부하는 새로운 맥락적 창조의 가능성을 갖는다는 의미로 해석될 수 있다. 라빌레트 공원 이후에도 폴리는 계속 등장해왔다. 오사카의 폴리나, 네덜란드 흐로닝언의 비디오 폴리 등 도시공간 내에 새로운 생각을 자극 시키는 다양한 건축적 시도들이 나타난 것이다.

현대의 폴리는 정원의 허튼 장식물로 시작되어 공원의 구조물, 그리고 기존 도심의 맥락을 뛰어 넘어 상업공간이나 주거공간에 서서히 침투하는 잠재태로 진화했다. 즉, 도시에 새로운 활력을 부여하는 장치나 기존 공간의 획일화된 위계적 배치를 탈피하는 공간, 또 공동주택의 획일적 한계를 극복하는 공유 공간과 커뮤니티 공간의 가능성을 열어주는 요소가 될 수 있다. 따라서 기존의 공간 구조에서 새로운 창의성을 유도하고 싶다면 작은 폴리를 만드는 것이 필요하다. 이를 통해 새로운 '비예측적 조우(Unexpected Encounter)'와 '잠재적 창의성(Latent Creativity)'의 발현이 가능하기 때문이다.

A contemporary folly has evolved from being an unnec-
essary decoration in a garden to a latent form which can
transcend existing urban contexts and gradually intervene
into spaces of commerce and dwellings. As a creative
potential that surpasses the established context, it can serve
as a stimulating device to redefine a space. Therefore, it
can become the space which can help to regenerate a city,
or escape from the existing hierarchy of contextualised
space, and open up the possibility of common and/or community spaces as alternatives against the uniformity of residential areas. In this regard, it is necessary to create a small
folly to generate creative solutions for existing spatial urban
context. By doing so, unexpected encounters and latent
creativity can emerge. This was the reason that Gwangju
Folly, an urban folly in the city of Gwangju, was founded in
2011 as a part of Gwangju Design Biennale. At the time,
11 urban follies had been created. The 3rd Gwangju Folly is
currently taking place, following the 2nd Gwangju Folly
of 2013, which resulted in eight follies. The 3rd Gwangju folly
has taken on the theme of "Folly & Everyday Life" as a
means to further develop the legacies of previous Gwangju
Folly editions and to achieve innovative creativeness.

이러한 의미에서 광주폴리는 2011년 광주디자인
비엔날레를 기회로 쇠퇴하는 기존 도심의
한계를 극복하고, 새로운 잠재성을 만들어내기
위해 2011년 11개의 어반폴리로 탄생했다.
2013년 8개의 2차 광주폴리에 이어 현재 3차
광주폴리가 진행되는 중이다. 3차 광주폴리는
1·2차 광주폴리의 과업들을 발전적으로
지향하면서도 혁신적 창조성을 만들어내기 위해
'도시의 일상성'을 핵심개념으로 설정했다.

                    Curatorial Team

Curator
Wee, Jinbok

View Folly
Moon, Hoon

FunPun Folly
Jin, Siyon

View Folly
realities:united,
Jan Edler

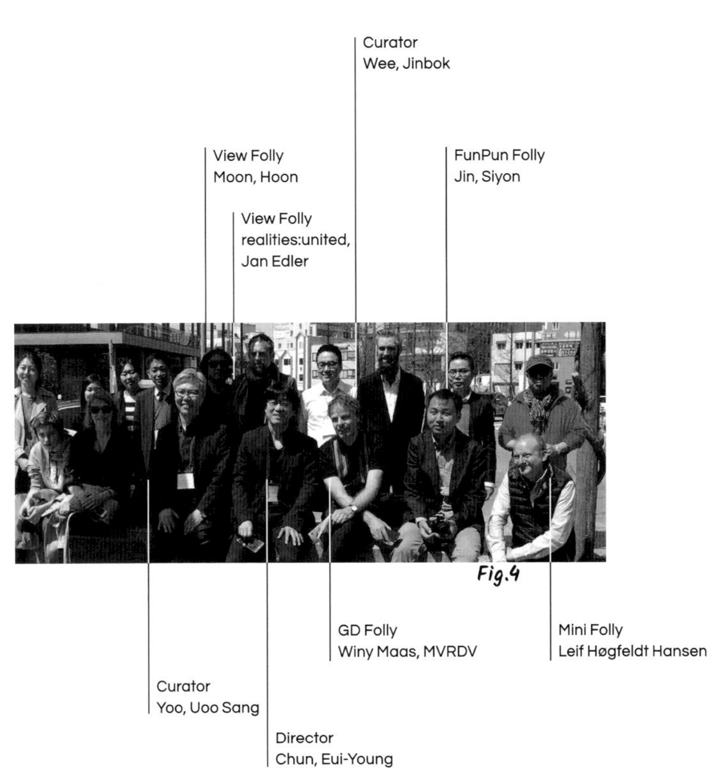

Curator
Yoo, Uoo Sang

Director
Chun, Eui-Young

GD Folly
Winy Maas, MVRDV

Mini Folly
Leif Høgfeldt Hansen

Fig.4

The Gwangju Folly III
a Workshop Site Visit
광주폴리 III 참여작가 워크샵 현장투어

   Small Urbanism with Gwangju Follies

Urban everydayness, as described by Henri Lefebvre, is where the abstract experience of the city and reality of daily life intersect. Through Gwangju Folly, we focused on the urban experience and social practice of producing a place, and then worked with the concept of "taste & beauty," which is considered a daily aspect when travelling through cities. As a result, the 3rd Gwangju Folly considers popularity, participation, and unexpectedness as three underlining principles, and maintains "taste & beauty" as a key concept to generate four types of action verbs—*see, walk, play, eat*—to experience city through "behavioral verb design." When described in more detail:

    1) The View Folly follows the verb *to see* of urban landscape over the Asia Culture Centre and Mt. Mudeungsan. Architect Moon, Hoon and Berlin-based artist group realities:united, Jan Edler & Tim Edler collaborated for the project. The vivid stairs and deck structure looking towards the mountain were designed by the architect and the metal

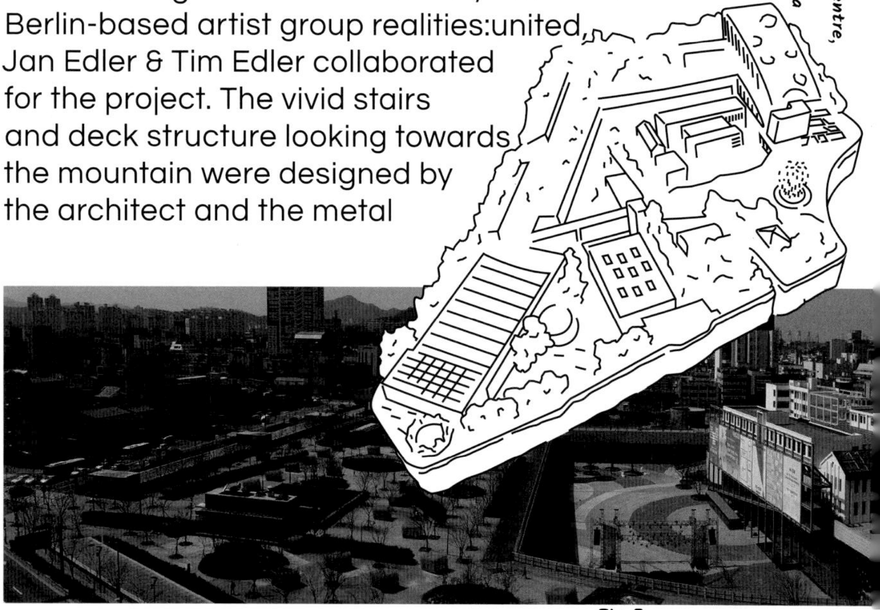

Fig.5

Fig.5

A View over the Asia Culture Centre from View Folly
뷰폴리에서 본 국립아시아문화전당 전망

 Curatorial Team

Trivision artwork with word "change" was designed by the artist. From the Trivision site, the sunken courtyard of the Asia Culture Centre can be seen quite nicely, while the observatory deck is a good place to rest with a view of a mountain.

    2) GD (Gwagngju Dutch) Folly, which encourages the experience of a neighbourhood that can be walked around, focuses on the verb *to walk*. It connects the View Folly near the Asia Culture Centre to the Cook Folly in Sansu-dong. It was initiated together with the Creative Industries Fund NL, which the name of the folly originated from. It is basically a playground for pedestrians and school kids. The Dutch architect group MVRDV and the Korean architect Cho, ByoungSoo agreed that Gwangju needed to be developed into a more pedestrian-oriented city.

    The folly kept the pedestrian-only street with the help of community organisations in front of Seoseok Primary School, thus symbolising the beginning of the transformation towards a walking city.

Fig.6

Fig.6

Urban Sketchbook Event with Seoseok Primary School Students at GD Folly (Sep. 18, 2017)
GD폴리 앞 서석초 어린이 거리칠판 행사 (2017.09.18)

    Small Urbanism with Gwangju Follies

3) FunPun Folly emerged from the verb *to play*, with media art on streets and alleys in the old city, which was started through a nationwide open call. Originally, P.U.N. was the acronym of Positive Urban Networking. The gate folly concept was the original idea, but it has developed as an urban regenerating device with media art in the alleys. The invited competition winner, architect Kim, Chanjoong and media artist Jin, Siyon worked together with urban research and site-specific media developments to finally create the unexpected folly.

4) Cook Folly invited young local entrepreneurs to start a restaurant business, inspired by the verb *to eat*, so that people could encounter the city through a dining experience. Meanwhile, the Cook Folly, which renovated an empty house and turned it into a café, was run by

Fig.7

도시의 일상성은 이미 앙리 르페브르가 '공간생산론'에서 이야기했듯 도시를 경험하는 추상성과 진실이 직면하는 교차점이다. 광주폴리를 통해 공간을 생산하는 사회적 과정과 도시적 체험에 주목하고자, 여행에서 도시를 경험하는 일상적인 요소들 가운데 하나인 '맛과 멋'을 보편적 화두로 삼아 작업을 진행하였다. 이에 따라 3차 광주폴리는 대중성(Popularity), 참여(Participation), 의외성(Unexpectedness)의 원칙을 바탕으로 도시의 일상성을 맛과 멋이라는 키워드를 통해 나타내고자 하였다. 또한 이들 키워드를 구체화하기 위해 도시의 체험을 단순화하여 보다(see), 걷다(walk), 먹다(eat), 놀다(play)라는 4가지의 행위동사를 중심으로 디자인하였다.

1) 뷰(View)폴리는 국립아시아문화전당과 무등산으로 이어지는 도심의 풍경을 조망하며 '본다'는 동사와 연계된다. 문훈과 베를린 기반의 작가 그룹 리얼리티즈:유나이티드의 협업으로 진행되었다. 선명히 드러나는 건물전면의 계단과 무등산을 조망하는 데크는 건축가가 설계했고, 단어 'change(변화)'를 사용한 메탈 트리비젼 작업은 베를린 작가들의 작품이다. 트리비젼이 있는 곳에서는 움푹 들어간 국립아시아문화전당의 전체와 선큰광장이 내다보이고, 데크에서는 광주의 정신이 깃든 무등산 전망을 바라보며 휴식을 취할 수 있다.

Fig.7

The Public Ideas Poster Contest
of FunPun Folly
뻔뻔폴리 대국민 아이디어 공모전 포스터

Curatorial Team

four carefully selected young local entrepreneurs who were trained for four months at Chang, Jinwoo Restaurant. These entrepreneurs then formed a cooperative and acted as principal managers. In other words, the folly combines urban regeneration and social issues. The participants now run old local favourites, namely Chungmijang and Congzib café, with 20 percent of its total profits being returned to the Gwangju Biennale Foundation as a way to support additional projects. Not surprisingly, Gwangju's Sansu-dong alleys have become a popular destination for people to visit.

The hope is that four different action verb types of Gwangju Folly, though a small step forward, will becomes creative urban devices for revitalisation, as well as a popular area for both local residents and visitors to take pictures.

Fig.8

Fig.8

Opening of the Cook Folly
(Jan. 10, 2017)
쿡폴리 오프닝, 콩집(2017.01.10)

Small Urbanism with Gwangju Follies

As we can see from the Shoe Spot Seongsu and Gwangju Follies, when urban spaces embrace small but attractive sites, they not only lead to increased visitor traffic but also the emergence and expansion of such urban spaces, almost like a popular app for a smartphone. One reason is because the developers' movement of space is geared towards customers who prefer unique experiences and tastes rather than readymade products favoured by the masses. This movement can be similarly understood as an initiative to provide so-called custom-made urban spaces for those who prefer various alleyways instead of the standardised large-scale flat complexes. Perhaps this is an important clue as to what can be called the shared economy society of public capitalism in the 4th industrial revolution age. Today, we are facing an era where everyone can participate as producers and makers of urban space with individual singularities, rather than as mere beneficiaries as we once were during the industrial revolution. We sincerely hope you will help contribute to this effort.

2) GD(Gwangju Dutch)폴리는 동사 '걷다'에 초점을 맞추며 보행자 친화적인 도시를 장려한다. 국립아시아문화전당 근처의 뷰폴리 부터 산수동의 쿡폴리를 잇는다. 함께 진행된 네덜란드창조산업기금에서 그 이름이 비롯되었다. 네덜란드의 건축가그룹 MVRDV가 설계한 '아이 러브 스트리트(THE I LOVE STREET)' 는 학생들과 보행자들을 위한 놀이터이자 거리 칠판을 이용한 셀피존이다. MVRDV의 협업 파트너로 산수동에 '꿈 집' 폴리를 설계한 한국의 건축가 조병수는 광주가 보다 보행자 중심적인 도시로 변화해야 한다는 데 의견을 같이했다. 지역시민단체와 서석초등학교 그리고 지자체의 노력과 도움으로 학교 앞 보행전용도로를 지켜낸 것은, 광주폴리가 걷는 도시로 변화하는 출발점이 되었다는 데 의의가 있다.

3) 쿡폴리는 경리단길 장진우골목으로 유명한 장진우 대표를 중심으로 지역의 젊은이 들을 선발해 식당을 창업하고 운영하도록 하여 사람들이 '먹다'라는 행위를 통해 도시를 경험 하는 방법을 고민했다. 엄선된 젊은이들은 서울의 장진우식당에서 4개월의 훈련을 거쳐 협동조합을 형성하여 과거에 빈집이던 곳을 개조한 식당과 카페를 운영하게 된다. 도시재생과 소셜 이슈를 결합한 모델이라 할 수 있다. 참가자들은 오랜 시간 지역의 사랑을 받았던 청미장 식당과 콩집 카페를 운영하며, 이를 통해 발생한 수익 의 20%는 기부되어 광주비엔날레 재단을 통해 추후 프로젝트를 지원하는 선순환을 이루도록 하였다. 기대했던 바와 같이 광주 산수동 골목길은 많은 이들이 찾는 곳이 되어가고 있다.

4) 대국민 아이디어 공모전에서 시작된 뻔뻔(FunPun)폴리는 구도심의 골목과 거리에서 미디어 아트와 함께 '놀다'라는 생각에서 출발했다. 원래 P.U.N.은 긍정적 도심 네트워킹 (Positive Urban Networking)의 두음 문자이나 여기서는 골목길 미디어아트를 통해 도시를 활성화하는 장치로서 개발되었다.

1차 대국민 아이디어 선발을 거쳐, 2차의 지명공모전에서 선발된 건축가 김찬중과 미디어 아티스트 진시영이 함께 충장로 도시골목을 탐구하며 장소특정적 미디어작업을 진행하여 '거북이 안경' 등 상가 골목의 틈새에 예상치 못한 미디어 폴리 작업을 만들어냈다.

슈스팟 성수와 광주폴리의 예에서 보듯 도시공간에 스마트폰의 앱처럼 작고 매력적인 공간들이 모일 수 있는 포용적인 구조와 방문자들의 트래픽이 점처럼 생겨나면, 이것이 선과 면으로 확대되고 창발하게 된다. 이는 제조자(메이커스, Makers)운동이 대중적 취향의 기성품 대신에 특별한 취향과 기호를 선호하는 맞춤형 소비자 시장인 것과 비슷하다. 스몰 어바니즘은 획일적인 대규모 아파트 도시공간에서 벗어나 다양한 골목길을 선호하는 일종의 맞춤형 도시공간 제조자운동인 것이다. 어쩌면 4차 산업혁명 시대의 공공자본주의적 공유경제 사회에 대한 중요한 단서가 여기에 있을지도 모를 일이다. 이전의 산업혁명에서처럼 단순한 수혜자가 아니라, 모두가 자신만의 창조적 특이점(Singularities)들로 기여하면서 도시공간의 기획자이자 제조자로 참여해야 하는 시대가 점점 다가오고 있다. 그리고 여기에 여러분 또한 동참해주기를 기대하고 있다.

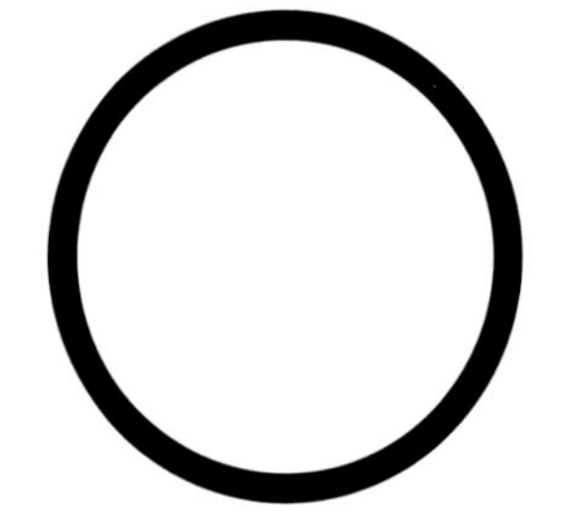

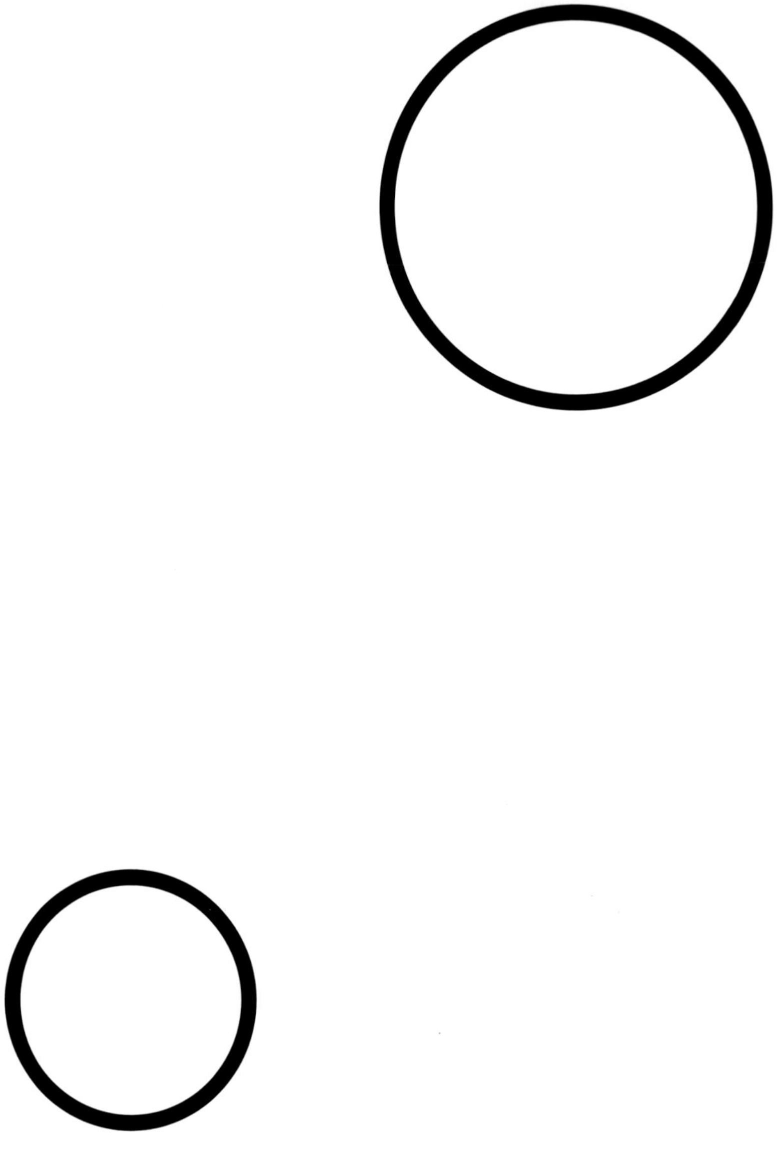

Gwangju Folly: Cultural Landscape and Place Marketing

문화경관과 장소마케팅 관점으로 본 광주폴리

This text is partially based on the manuscript submitted to the UIA Seoul Conference 2017. UIA 서울 컨퍼런스(2017)에 제출한 내용을 기본으로 작성되었다.

Folly as a Cultural Device for Revitalisation

To date, physical maintenance and development in urban regeneration have been given more weight than revitalising and reviving the area. Solutions focusing on improving the physical environment of run-down areas could not contribute to the invigoration of the region and exposed various issues. Considering the necessity of building a foundation for the city's sustainable growth, it is important to devise a new comprehensive system of urban regeneration. Thus, a type of urban regeneration that integrates culture has been stressed.

The reason why the 21st century is referred to as "an era of culture" is not only because culture is the complex whole that includes all the ways of life, but also because its presence is increasing in the value systems of both individuals and nations. The flow of culture policies is expanding from art to industry, life and to the urban realm. Moreover, culture policies have grown to include our overall lifestyle, from housing, welfare, leisure and traffic to ecology, parks and green spaces. The key term here is "everyday life," which is related to policies of cultural accessibility, activity, welfare and leisure. In addition, cultural policies are now

문화활성화 장치로서의 폴리

그동안 도시재생은 쇠퇴한 지역에 활력을 주고 부활하도록 하는 것을 목적으로 하기보다 정비와 개발을 한다는 물리적인 도시정비사업의 일환으로 진행되어왔다. 물리적 환경 개선에 초점이 맞추어진 처방은 실질적인 지역 활성화에 기여하지 못했고 사업의 추진 과정에서도 많은 문제가 드러났다. 따라서 도시의 지속가능한 성장기반을 확립하고자 한다면 도시재생에 대한 새로운 체계를 종합적으로 구상해볼 필요가 있다. 그에 대한 해답으로 문화를 접목한 도시 재생이 강조되기 시작했다.

21세기를 문화의 세기라고 부르는 것은 문화라는 용어가 모든 생활양식의 총체이며 개인 및 국가의 가치체계에서도 문화의 위상이 높아지고 있기 때문이다. 문화정책의 흐름은 '예술→ 산업→ 생활→ 도시'로 확대되고 있다. 이와 더불어 문화정책은 주거, 복지, 여가, 교통, 생태, 공원녹지 등 생활문화 전반으로 확대되었다. 여기에서 주목받는 키워드는 '일상성'으로, 문화향유, 문화활동, 문화복지, 여가문화 등이 중요한 정책 영역이다. 더 나아가 최근에는 문화도시와 도시문화, 도시재생, 도시 브랜딩과 장소 마케팅 등으로 문화정책의 영역이 도시 전반으로 확대되고 있다.

이때 주목받는 키워드는 '장소성'으로, 공간문화, 문화환경, 문화경관, 문화행정 등이 중요한 정책영역이라 할 수 있다. 도시재생 분야에선 특히 지역의 장소성과 문화를 눈여겨 볼 필요가 있다.

 Curatorial Team

expanding to the larger scope of the city, including culture cities (or urban culture), urban regeneration, city branding and venue marketing. Here, the keyword is "placeness" as it relates to policy sectors such as space culture, culture environment, cultural landscape and culture administration. It is important that urban regeneration focuses on placeness and culture. Only when their lives are changed through the creative practices and values embedded in culture and various contents that build up relations can a sustainable power of urban regeneration be secured. To this end, the city of Gwangju has installed small decorative structures, or Follies, throughout the city as cultural devices for revitalisation to create a new urban image. Gwangju Folly I was installed in 2011, Gwangju Folly II in 2013, and Gwangju Folly III is currently being installed.

Gwangju Folly

Gwangju Folly originally started as urban folly, combining references to the city and decorative architecture. It then adopted its own city's name, Gwangju, to highlight its identity. Since then it has been drawing attention from home

도시에서 문화란 공간에 구현된 도시민 삶의 시간성, 즉, 역사성을 내포한다. 문화가 갖는 고유의 속성인 창의적인 과정과 가치, 그리고 관계를 만들어내는 다양한 콘텐츠를 통해 도시민들의 삶이 변화될 때 그들의 생활이 문화가 되어 지속가능한 도시재생의 동력을 확보할 수 있다. 이에 광주광역시는 광주의 도시 이미지 창출을 위한 '문화 활성화 장치(Cultural Devices for Revitalisation)'로써 광주 시내 곳곳에 소형장식건축물인 '폴리'를 설치하였다. 2011년 1차 폴리가 설치된 이후 2013년 2차 폴리가 실행되었고 현재는 3차 폴리가 진행 중이다.

광주폴리

광주폴리는 그 명칭을 당초 도시를 상징하는 어반(Urban)과 장식용 건축물이라는 폴리(Folly)를 딴 어반폴리로 정했다가 광주의 정체성을 부여하기 위해 광주폴리라는 고유명사로 바꾸어 도시 정체성을 더해 국내외의 관심을 모았다. '광주폴리'는 광주광역시가 주최하고 광주비엔날레 재단이 주관하여 세계적 건축거장과 예술가들의 소형건축예술인 폴리 (Folly)를 설치하는 프로젝트이다. 도심재생과 도시브랜드 강화를 위해 2011년부터 추진 되었다. 폴리 프로젝트의 추진배경은 특색 없고 단조로운 도시경관을 폴리를 통해 '점'에서 '선'으로 연결하고 도심 전역을 '면'으로 확대하여 아름다운 예술도시로 탈바꿈시키고,

and abroad. Gwangju Folly is a project hosted by Gwangju Metropolitan City and organised by the Gwangju Biennale Foundation. It is done in collaboration with internationally renowned architects and artists to install small architectural artworks referred to as follies. To promote urban regeneration and the city's brand, it started in 2011 and is now seeing its third edition. By connecting "dots" to "lines" and then expanding to "surfaces" through follies in the featureless urban landscape, it aimed at transforming the city into an art city, building up a city brand of "Folly City," and becoming a tourist destination. Proceeding by phases, each one has different themes and focuses. In Gwangju Folly I, 10 Follies were installed along the remains of the old Gwangju Eupseong Town Wall, which shed light on the existence of the town wall, while connecting the past and present of the city. Gwangju Folly II, under the theme Human Rights and Public Space, addressed the potential of public spaces within the context of the "Gwangju Spirit" that the city of human rights embodies. Expanding beyond the historical limits of the city and to productively succeed the accomplishments of the previous editions, as well as create

도시브랜드로서 광주를 '폴리시티'로 자리매김하고 관광명소화하기 위한 것이다.

폴리 프로젝트는 단계별로 진행이 되는데 그에 따른 주제나 특징이 다르다. 광주폴리 I은 옛 광주읍성 터의 흔적을 따라 10개의 폴리가 설치되었고, 이는 과거 광주읍성의 존재를 일깨우며 광주의 과거와 현재를 잇는 기능을 한다.

광주폴리 II는 '인권과 공공공간'이라는 주제로, 인권도시 광주가 품고 있는 '광주정신'이라는 맥락 안에서 공공공간이 갖는 잠재성을 다양한 방식으로 풀어내고자 하였다.

광주폴리 III는 도시의 역사적 한계를 극복하고, 광주폴리 I, II의 과업들을 발전적으로 계승하는 동시에 새로운 대중성을 만들어 내고자 '도시의 일상성(Everyday Life of the City)'을 폴리의 새로운 핵심 개념으로 설정하였다.

광주폴리는 도시 안에서 단위개체로 작동하기보다는 군집되어 하나의 패턴을 형성하며 그 영향력을 발휘한다. 도시 안의 폴리들은 쇠퇴해가는 광주광역시 구도심 지역에 강력한 문화적 힘을 전달하며 도심재생을 이끌어낼 것이다.

Curatorial Team

greater accessibility, Gwangju Folly III has set "everyday life of the city" as its key concept. Rather than functioning in units within the realm of a city, Gwangju Folly will form a singular pattern that possesses great influence. Located throughout the city, follies will deliver a strong sense of cultural power to the declining old city centre area and lead the urban regeneration movement.

Lessons from Gwangju Folly I and II

Gwangju Folly I had positive effects such as introducing the concept of folly as an urban architectural facility and drawing attention to the city's history (town wall). Yet the sidewalks they were installed on did not allow much space for appreciation and participation. Also, there was a dearth of public consensus and support. On the other hand, Gwangju Folly II, titled "Human Rights & Public Space", shed light on the symbolic meaning Gwangju has in the context of humanrights, strengthening the city's brand that has been established through the May 18th Democratic Movement over the years. Folly II has also exhibited greater diversity in terms of the forms on display. Furthermore, the newly or-

<u>광주폴리 I, II가 주는 교훈</u>
1차 폴리는 폴리라는 도시건축적 시설물의 개념을 도입하여 실현하였고, 광주의 역사성 (읍성)의 화두를 쟁점화하는 긍정적인 효과를 가져왔으나 협소한 인도 위에 설치되어 감상과 참여를 위한 여유 공간이 부재했고 진행 과정에서는 시민과의 공감대 형성이 부족했다. 한편 '인권과 공공공간'을 주제로 한 2차 폴리는 인권도시 광주의 상징성을 부각하여 5·18 광주민주화운동에서 생겨난 광주의 대표적인 도시브랜드를 강화하였으며, 폴리의 형식적 면에서 다양성이 강화되었다. 또한 시민협의회가 참여하여 시민과의 소통이 강화되었다. 하지만 인권이라는 거대담론에 대한 일반 대중의 이해도가 부족했고 일부 폴리가 시민의 접근성이 어려운 위치에 설치되면서 폴리의 기능적 실효성이 문제로 지적되었다.

앞선 폴리들에서 얻은 교훈은 먼저, 소규모 시설인 폴리의 특성상 구조물 그 자체로는 집객 효과는 크지 않고, 둘째, 산발적인 소수의 폴리의 설치로는 도시 활성화 및 관광객 유치에 대한 획기적인 효과를 얻기에 부족하며, 셋째, 전문가의 상징적 의미는 일반 대중에게 전파되기 어렵다는 점이다. 일반 대중의 관심과 방문을 유도하는 랜드마크적 성격을 얻기는 힘든 것이다. 따라서 광주폴리 III는 구조물과 예술 또는 프로그램이 적절히 결합되며, 시민들의 삶과 일상을 파고들어 실질적 재미와 교감을 만들어야 한다는 데 주목하였다.

ganised Folly Citizens Committee strengthened its communication channel with citizens. However, in terms of effectiveness, it could be also pointed out that the public has a lack of understanding of the meta-discourse on human rights, as well as poor accessibility, as some of the follies were installed in places that were rather difficult to visit.

Lessons from the previous editions include the following: First, as small structures, follies are limited in the number of visitors they can attract on their own. Second, it is hard to achieve the effects of revitalising the city and attracting tourists with a small number of scattered follies. Third, it is difficult to target the general public with metaphoric and professional meanings, so they cannot become landmarks that attract people in great droves. Therefore, Gwangju Folly II focused on appropriately combining structure and art as well as creating an enjoyable and interactive folly that could permeate people's daily lives.

Directions and Types of Gwangju Folly III

To guarantee the key concept of Gwangju Folly III, 'Folly & Everyday life', and overcome the limits of Gwangju Folly I and II, we set five targets. An easy, eye-catching and fun public device, securing enough space to appreciate and experience, a folly beyond a subject to see but what visitors can participate in and interact with, that captures non-daily aspects through unexpected sites, physical forms and materials and modes of participation, and convergence that seeks the possibility of a new space device through creative encounters among architects and artists, professionals and general public, tradition and architectural structure and plastic art and media art and technology.

Four Main Follies and two Mini Follies were commissioned in Gwangju Folly III. Different from the previous editions, these Follies do not exist separately but are symbolically connected or are interlinked in different ways to present an experience where the daily and non-daily intersect with each other.

<u>광주폴리 III의 기본방향 및 구성유형</u>
광주폴리 III의 핵심 개념인 '도시의 일상성'을 확보하면서 광주폴리 I, II의 한계를 극복하기 위해 지향점을 5가지로 정리하였다. 쉽고 눈에 띄며 재미있게 이해되는 대중적 장치, 폴리를 감상하고 체험하기에 적정한 공간의 확보, 눈으로 보고 의미를 파악하는 것을 넘어 관객이 직접 참여하고 소통할 수 있는 폴리, 위치· 물리적 형태 및 재료·참여 방식의 의외성을 통한 비일상성의 확보, 그리고 건축가와 예술가, 전문가와 일반인, 전통적 건축구조물· 조형예술과 미디어 아트 및 테크놀로지의 창조적 만남을 통한 새로운 도시장치의 가능성을 추구하는 융복합이다.

광주폴리 III는 4개의 메인 폴리(Main Folly)와 2개의 미니폴리(Mini Folly)로 구성되었다. 메인폴리는 뷰폴리, GD폴리, 쿡폴리, 뻔뻔폴리로 이루어진다.

이들 폴리들은 이제까지와 같이 각기 따로 존재하는 것이 아니라, 서로 상징적으로 연결되거나 때로는 다양한 조합으로 결합되면서, 도시에서 일상성과 비일상성이 교차하는 색다른 체험을 선사하고자 했다.

V

View Folly & Art Installation "Architecture of Autonomy"

Moon, Hoon +
realities:united,
Jan Edler & Tim Edler
Gwangju Visual Content
Centre, 96 Jebong-ro,
Dong-gu, Gwangju,
Republic of Korea

뷰폴리 & 설치작업 '자율건축'

문훈 + 리얼리티즈:유나이티드,
얀 에들러 & 팀 에들러
대한민국 광주광역시 동구
제봉로 96 광주영상복합문화관

GD1

Dream House

Cho, ByoungSoo
23, Dongmyeong-ro,
67beon-gil, Gwangju,
Republic of Korea

꿈 집

조병수
대한민국 광주광역시 동구
동명로 67번길 23

GD2

THE I LOVE STREET

Winy Maas, MVRDV
Seoseok Primary School, 26,
82beon-gil, Jebong-ro,
Dong-gu, Gwangju,
Republic of Korea

아이 러브 스트리트

위니 마스, MVRDV
대한민국 광주광역시 동구 제봉로
82번길 26 서석초등학교

C1

Chungmijang

Chang, Jinwoo
16-19, Donggye-ro, Dong-gu,
Gwangju, Republic of Korea

청미장

장진우
대한민국 광주광역시 동구
동계로 16-19

C2

Congzib

Chang, Jinwoo
16-15, Donggye-ro, Dong-gu,
Gwangju, Republic of Korea

콩집

장진우
대한민국 광주광역시 동구
동계로 16-15

FP1

MEDIA CELL

Kim, Chanjoong + Jin, Siyon
38-2, Gwangsan-dong,
Dong-gu, Gwangju,
Republic of Korea

미디어 셀

김찬중 + 진시영
대한민국 광주광역시 동구
광산동 38-2

FP2

INFINITY LIGHT

Kim, Chanjoong + Jin, Siyon
45-2, Chungjang-ro,
Dong-gu, Gwangju,
Republic of Korea

무한의 빛

김찬중 + 진시영
대한민국 광주광역시 동구
충장로 45-2

FP3

MEDIA WALL

Kim, Chanjoong + Jin, Siyon
49, 5-ga, Chungjang-ro,
Dong-gu, Gwangju,
Republic of Korea

미디어 월

김찬중 + 진시영
대한민국 광주광역시 동구
충장로 5가 49

FP4

LIGHT PASSAGE

Kim, Chanjoong + Jin, Siyon
33-1, Chungjang-ro,
Dong-gu, Gwangju,
Republic of Korea

소통의 문

김찬중 + 진시영
대한민국 광주광역시 동구
충장로 33-1

M1

Infinite Elements

Kook, Hyoung-Gul +
Syn, Sue Gyeong
Movable

인피니트 엘리먼츠

국형걸 + 신수경
이동식

M2

SPECTRUM

Leif Høgfeldt Hansen
Movable

스펙트럼

라이프 호그펠트 한센
이동식

1

Gwangju River Reading Room

David Adjaye +
Taiye Selasi
Gwangju Social Welfare
Centre

광주천 독서실

데이비드 아자예 + 타이에 셀라시
광주사회복지사협회

2

The Roundabout Revolution

Eyal Weizman
In front of Gwangju Station

혁명의 교차로

에얄 와이즈만
광주역 앞

3

The Vote

Rem Koolhaas +
Ingo Niermann
Former Side Street of
Gwanju Student
Independence Movement
Memorial Hall

투표

렘 쿨하스 + 잉고 니어만
(구)광주학생독립
운동기념회관 옆

4

Power Toilets / Unesco

Superflex
Entrance of Gwangju Park

유네스코 화장실

수퍼플렉스
광주공원 입구

5

Memory Box

Go, SeokHong +
Kim, Mihee
Near Rendezvous
Plaza at Geumnam-ro
Underground
Shopping District

기억의 상자

고석홍 + 김미희
광주 동구 금남지하상가
만남의 광장 인근

In-Between Hotel

Suh, DoHo +
Suh Architects
Movable

틈새호텔

서도호
이동식

Cubic-Meter Food Cart

Ai Weiwei
Movable

포장마차

아이 웨이웨이
이동식

Autodidact's Transport

Raqs Media Collective
Movable
Gwangju Subway Trains

탐구자의 전철

락스 미디어 콜렉티브
이동식
광주지하철 객차

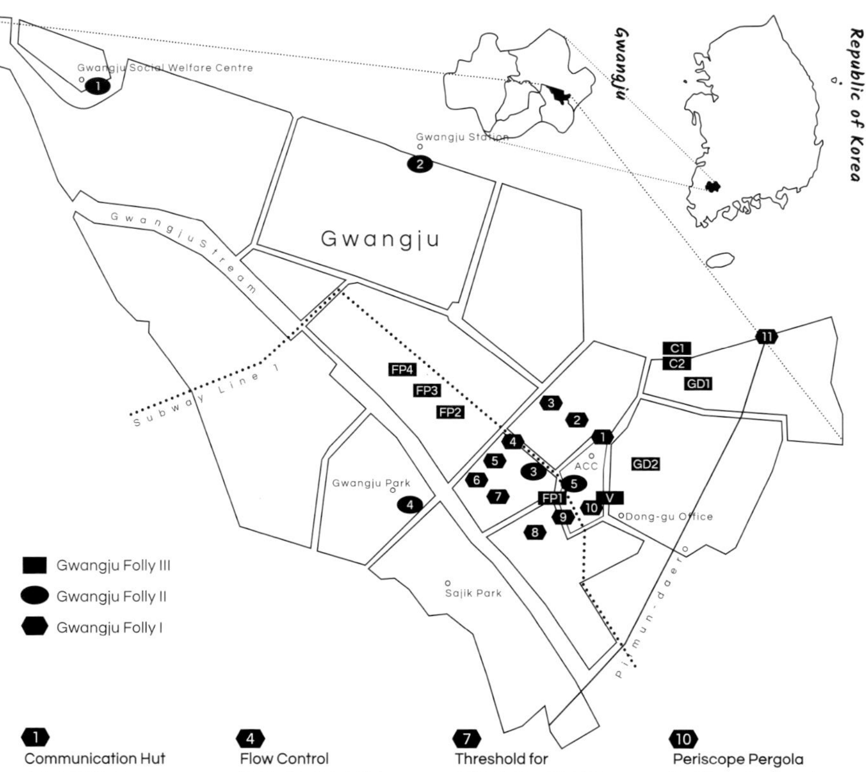

Gwangju Folly III
Gwangju Folly II
Gwangju Folly I

1

Communication Hut
Juan Herreros
Jang-dong Crossing
소통의 오두막
후안 헤레로스
장동로터리

2

Seowonmoon Lantern
Florian Beigel
Jebong-ro Sidewalk
서원문제등
플로리안 베이겔
김재규 경찰학원 앞

3

Gwangju Swarms
Nader Tehrani
Hanhwa Insurance
Crossing
광주사람들
나데르 테라니
한화생명사거리

4

Flow Control
Alejandro Zaera-Polo
Geumnam-ro Park
Crossing
유동성조절
알레한드로 자에라 폴로
금남근린공원

5

99 Kan
Peter Eisenman
Chungjang Police Station
99칸
피터 아이젠만
충장치안센터 앞

6

Open Wall
Jung, Sehoon + Kim, Sejin
Gwangju District
Tax Office Crossing
열린장벽
정세훈 + 김세진
광주세무서 앞

7

**Threshold for
Intimate Recollections**
Joh, Sungyong
Hwanggeum-ro
Crossing
기억의 현재화
조성룡
황금로 사거리

8

The Open Box
Dominique Perrault
Old City Hall Crossing
열린공간
도미니크 페로
구시청사거리

9

Public Room
Francisco Sanin
Sidewalk of
Asia Culture Centre
광주사랑방
프란시스코 산인
국립아시아문화전당 옆

10

Periscope Pergola
Yoshiharu Tsukamoto
Jebong-ro Sidewalk,
Daesung Academy
잠망경과 정자
요시하루 츠카모토
대성학원 앞

11

Ruined Steps & May Flower
Seung, H-Sang
Ruined Steps & May Flower
Farm Bridge
푸른길문화샘터
승효상
푸른길 농장다리

Gwangju Follies from a Place Marketing Perspective

Since 1995, with the advent of local governments in Korea, urban development strategies based on unique characteristics of local communities have become important. Place marketing strategy is a comprehensive, systematic, continuous, cultural, active urban development strategy that establishes a city's long-term identity based on an objective examination of the place, while also generating locally specific products by using marketing strategies. However, this strategy is possible only when a city's image and identity is distinct, when the city's economy is growing due to its unique cultural legacy, and when the quality of people's lives can be fully guaranteed so that a cooperative urban community can be generated. Place marketing begins with discovering a city's specific identity and developing its locality through a process of interpretation, curation and production. This is followed by the process of developing local contents, and then merchandising and branding them with specific marketing strategies. As discussed, the cultural objective of place marketing lies in developing a city's image based on three key concepts—site, cultural contents and marketing—

<u>장소마케팅 관점으로 본 광주폴리</u>
한국에서는 1995년 지방자치단체의 출범을 시작으로 그 지역만의 정체성을 중요시하는 도시개발전략이 부상하였다. 장소성에 대한 명확한 평가를 바탕으로 도시의 장기 비전과 정체성을 수립하고, 마케팅 전략 기법을 이용해 장소성에 기반한 도시 고유의 상품을 개발하는 장소 마케팅 전략은 포괄적, 체계적, 연계적, 문화적, 능동적인 도시발전 전략이다. 이는 도시 이미지와 정체성이 분명하고 도시 고유의 문화 자산을 바탕으로 도시경제가 활력을 띠며, 시민 개개인의 살의 질이 풍요롭고 다양하게 보장되고, 그를 통해 더불어 살아가는 도시공동체를 창출할 수 있을 때 가능하다. 장소 마케팅 전략의 출발은 장소의 정체성을 발견하고 해석,

기획, 생성하는 장소성 만들기 작업에서 시작한다. 그 후 장소성을 토대로 상품화 할 수 있는 지역의 문화적 콘텐츠를 기획, 개발하고 그것을 상품화, 브랜드화하는 구체적인 마케팅 전략과 프로그램이 추진된다. 이렇게 장소성, 문화콘텐츠, 마케팅 3가지 핵심 개념을 토대로 도시의 이미지와 정체성을 향상시키고 문화관광과 문화산업을 통한 경제적 파급효과를 창출하며, 삶의 질과 정체성이 묻어나는 도시커뮤니티를 창출하는 것이 장소 마케팅 전략의 문화적 의의라 할 수 있다.

이런 장소 마케팅 전략은 광주폴리 III의 기획개념과 실행전략에 깊숙이 관여하고 있다. 여기에서는 이무용(2006)이 제시한 장소마케팅 전략 모니터링 요소인 지속성,

                     Curatorial Team

so that it can generate culture tourism and a culture industry, facilitating economic growth and development of an urban community with a guaranteed high quality of life.

Place marketing strategies are closely related to the curatorial concept of Gwangju Folly III. In this essay, we will examine the third edition of Gwangju Folly based on five elements of place marketing: sustainability, authenticity, integrity, connectivity, and effectiveness.

1) Sustainability

Firstly, in terms of sustainability, Gwangju Folly III has inherited the direction and objective of the first edition of Gwangju Folly, which is to "rethink urban sustainability and cultural vitality." However, as a way to make the project more audience-friendly, the current project focused on people's daily experiences and introduced the theme of Taste & Beauty. The decision was based on Gwangju's branded reputation as a city of great art and food. In addition, the project led to active collaboration with media art, especially in light of the fact that Gwangju has been labeled a "media-creative city" by UNESCO. FunPun Folly, an open call folly, was the result of collaboration between an archi-

진정성, 통합성, 연계성, 효율성의 관점에서 광주폴리 III를 분석해본다.

1) 지속성

먼저 지속성 측면에서 광주폴리 III는 '도시재생과 문화적 활력 제고'라는 광주폴리 I의 기본방향과 목적을 이어받았다. 하지만 대중과의 더 쉬운 소통을 위해 도시를 경험하는 일상적 요소인 '맛과 멋'을 주제로 택했다. 이는 예술과 음식으로 유명한 광주의 도시브랜드를 반영한 결과다. 또한 유네스코가 선정한 '미디어 창의 도시'라는 광주의 정체성을 위해 미디어아트와 적극적인 협력을 추구하였다. 공모전 폴리인 뻔뻔폴리는 지역 출신의 미디어 작가가 건축가와 협업하여 폴리에 미디어아트 요소를 도입하였다.

2) 진정성

광주폴리 I, II가 어떤 형태를 띤 소형 공공 조형물이라면 폴리 III는 폴리가 가지는 물리적인 특성보다 기능적인 프로그램(to see, to eat, to play and walk)에 초점을 맞춘 새로운 유형의 폴리를 제안한다. 다양한 체험적 장치를 통해 방문객을 유치함으로써 도시이미지 향상에 직접적인 도움이 되기 때문이다. 뷰폴리는 주요 시선축이 수평적인 광주 도심에 위에서 아래로, 또 아래에서 위로 향하는 낯선 시선의 흐름을 도입한다. 이를 통해 광주 구도심의 문화 르네상스의 상징인 국립아시아문화전당과 구도심의 조감적 감상이 가능해진다.

tect and a media artist who integrated a media art element into the folly.

2) Authenticity

While the first and second follies were to serve in specific form as small public sculptures, Folly III suggests a new type of folly that focuses on a functional program (to see, to eat, to play, to walk) rather than physical properties. By attracting visitors through experiential and interactive devices, the follies also help develop the city image of Gwangju. View Folly, for instance, provides a vertical perspective of Gwangju—from above to below and vice versa—something that is rarely experienced in Gwangju where horizontal vistas are dominant. By doing so, the architecture of the Asia Culture Centre, which symbolises the cultural renaissance of Gwangju's old town, can be viewed from above.

3) Integrity

People throughout the community had both high hopes and concerns about Folly I due to the unfamiliarity of this structure called a "folly," and the lack of communication with the local community and citizens due to the urgency of the building schedule. On the other hand, Folly I gained

3) 통합성

폴리은 폴리라는 낯선 구조물이 갖는 이질감, 급한 일정에 따른 지역사회 및 시민과의 소통부족에 따른 기대와 걱정을 동시에 불러왔다. 대규모 스케일의 도시재생 사업이 아닌 소형 구조물의 설치로 주변 지역에 문화적, 경제적 활력을 증진시키려는 새로운 시도와 해외 유명 건축가의 참여는 긍정적인 평가를 얻었다. 한편 시민의 보행권 침해와 주변 환경과의 부조화, 인근 상점의 간판을 가리는 등 주민과의 소통이 부족했던 점은 부정적인 반응을 불러왔다. 이에 따라 광주비엔날레 재단은 2012년부터 폴리 도슨트와 함께하는 투어프로그램 및 지역 청소년과 문화예술 단체와 함께하는 프로그램 등을 운영하면서 시민들에게 문화향유 기회를 제공하고 있다. 폴리III는 시민이 작품 공모에서 선정, 운영에 이르기까지 전 과정에 참여하고 있다는 점에서 의의가 있다. 이런 크라우드 소싱 방식을 통하여 폴리의 위치, 형식, 프로그램 등 뻔뻔폴리 공모를 통해 제안하고 공모된 아이디어 중 선정된 안을 소셜미디어나 방송매체를 통해 공유하며 시민들의 참여를 유도한다. 또한 폴리 건립 후 운영관리 전반에 커뮤니티 비즈니스 형태로 시민이 직접 참여하기도 한다.

4) 연계성

광주디자인비엔날레의 일부로 추진된 폴리I 프로젝트는 지방정부의 공공주도형 도시재생에 가까웠다. 2차 폴리는 기획단계에서부터 시민, 사회단체가 작품별 운영 파트너로 참여하고 '폴리를 위한 시민협의회' 등을 꾸려 소통을

                    Curatorial Team

positive feedback, as it was a new attempt to promote the cultural and economic vitality of city centre Gwangju through the installation of small structures (not large-scale urban regeneration projects), and to realise the participation of famous architects from other countries as folly designers. However, the project's intrusion into pedestrian roads and the discord with the surrounding environment led to incidents where a folly would hide store signs, ultimately leading to dissatisfaction and ignorance among local citizens and degradation of the follies. Learning from this, the Gwangju Biennale Foundation initiated docent-led tours and programs involving local students and cultural organisations in 2012 to provide opportunities for diverse cultural experiences. In this regard, Folly II is meaningful in that local citizens have participated throughout the entire process of the open call selection and management. This time, citizen participation was encouraged through a method of crowdsourcing in that people were invited to suggest the location, format and program through FunPun Folly, and the selected ideas were then further communicated through social media or tradi-tional broadcast media. In addition, the overall management

시도하였다는 점에서 폴리 프로젝트가 점차 상향식, 커뮤니티 주도형 도시재생으로 발전하였다고 볼 수 있다. 폴리III는 쿡폴리에 참여하는 지역청년이 협동조합을 설립해 수익금의 일부를 폴리의 주 운영주체인 광주비엔날레 재단에 기부하는 등 유명 예술가만의 잔치가 아닌 일상속에서 시민과 함께하는 민관협력형으로 바뀌고 있다는 점에서 그 의의가 있다. 이 과정에 지역 청년창업단체가 개입하여 지역의 청년 조직과 네트워크를 형성하고자 한다. GD폴리는 시민단체, 학부모, 광주비엔날레 재단이 협력하여 도심, 특히 초등학교 정문 앞길의 보행권을 확보하는데 성공했다. 또한 GD폴리 설계에 초등학생의 아이디어가 반영되는 등 지역 주민과 디자이너, 폴리 추진조직이

적극적으로 네트워킹을 이루어냈다. 아울러 뻔뻔폴리는 처음으로 공적 영역이 아닌 사적 영역에 자리잡음으로써 민간 섹터와의 연계를 시작했다.

5) 효율성

1차 폴리는 해외 작가의 작품을 유치하여 구도심 재생과 광주의 문화자산 확충을 목표로 하였고, 어느 정도의 이슈화는 인정되었지만 지역경제에는 큰 도움이 되지 않았다. 2차 폴리에서 시민들과의 접점 다각화 노력은 '시민과 함께하는 도시 공공디자인 프로젝트'라는 이름으로 2014 대한민국경관대상 최우수상 수상의 원동력이 되었다. 지역문화예술단체와의 협업으로 진행하는 다양한 활성화 사업들은 새로운 도시 시민 문화를 창출하며 광주의 구도심에

of post-construction of the follies is managed by local residents through an adopting system of community businesses.

4) Connectivity

Folly I, which was initiated as part of the Gwangju Design Biennale, was closer to a government-led urban regeneration project. The second edition of folly could be viewed as a bottom-up, community-led urban development initiative, as local citizens and social organisations began to take part as management partners with each project, and the foundation organised a citizens committee for the folly project. In this context, Folly II is meaningful in that it initiated a cooperative with local youths to set up Cook Folly, the owners of which donated its profits to the Gwangju Biennale Foundation, thereby demonstrating a shift from an artist-centred event to a public-government cooperative project. In this process, a local youth start-up centre also intervened, attempting to generate a youth network and organisation for the city. GD Folly, on the other hand, succeeded in procuring the right to use a pedestrian road by the entrance of a primary school through effective cooperation among the community organisation, school parents and the Gwangju Biennale Foundation. Considering how primary

활력을 불어넣고 있다. 3차 폴리는 대중성과 참여성을 기반으로 사회적 이슈와 결부한 새로운 형태의 폴리로 지역경제 활성화에 영향을 미치고 있다. 뻔뻔폴리와 쿡폴리는 각각 쇠퇴하는 상업가로와 지역 골목상권 활성화를 위해 상업시설과 공공미술을 융합한 새로운 스몰어바니즘형 문화산업 재생 모델로 역할을 할 수 있을 것으로 기대된다. 또한 미니폴리는 이동성을 무기로 여러 지역에서 일상생활의 끊임없는 변화와 활동을 자극한다.

요소	광주폴리 I	광주폴리 II	광주폴리 III
지속성	장기계획 준비	목표집단 세분화	광주의 정체성과 연결
진정성	장소성	비장소성	탈장소성
통합성	장소성과 현실의 간극	소프트웨어 (교육, 투어 프로그램)	시민들의 적극적 참여
연계성	광주비엔날레행사와 연계	커뮤니티 주도형	민관협력형
효율성	해외작가의 작품유치	지역문화 예술단체와 협업	스몰어바니즘형 문화산업

Curatorial Team

school student ideas were integrated into the design of GD Folly, one could say that an active network among local residents, designers, and the Folly operations team was successfully accomplished. Folly III also signaled the beginning of a collaboration not just with the public, but also with the private sector for the first time.

5) Effectiveness

The first edition of folly was aimed at expanding Gwangju's cultural legacy and regenerating its old city centre through a collaboration with celebrity artists. Although it succeeded in establishing a discourse, it has not been successful in fostering a local economy. Alternatively, Folly II won the grand prize in the Korean Landscape Design Competition for its initiative titled "An urban public design project with the local community." Numerous regeneration projects established through collaboration with local culture organisations in Folly III have helped to develop the local economy. FunPun Folly and Cook Folly are expected to play an exemplary role as small urbanism-style cultural revitalisation programs that regenerate declining commercial streets and markets by combining commercial facilities with public art. Moreover, Mini Folly, through its mobility, is aimed at stimulating the continuous transformation and activity of everyday life.

Element	Gwangju Folly I	Gwangju Folly II	Gwangju Folly III
Sustainability	Preparations for longterm plan	Segmentation of purpose	Connection with Gwangju's identity
Authenticity	Locality	Non-locality	Trans-locality
Integrity	Gap between locality and reality	Software (Education, Tour program)	Active participation of local residents
Connectivity	Related to the Gwangju Biennale	Community-led	Private-public partnership
Effectiveness	Installations by international architects	Collaboration with local cultural organisations	Small urbanism-style culture industry

Gwangju Folly's Identity and Future

Gwangju Folly can be distinguished from follies in other cities in several different ways. First of all, Gwangju Folly is installed every two to three years on a continuous basis. From the conception, it is inevitable that it is approached in line with the previous editions and is influenced by reactions from the local community, citizens and professionals. It is similar to how design develops through the feedback process. Unlike follies elsewhere, this repeated process allows Gwangju Folly to gradually fit into the social, cultural and political geography.

Secondly, it is distinguished in that Gwangju Folly is necessarily connected with its previous editions in terms of space, context and function. As a device in an urban space intended to boost cultural vitality, Gwangju Folly becomes more efficient only when it is continuously pursued. It is critical to understand Gwangju Folly not as a completed project but one that endlessly changes and evolves. Only when it is culture and art which generates a relationship, entails creative processes, and values that it changes the lives of citizens—not fixed, completed objects or products

광주폴리의 정체성과 미래

광주폴리는 형태, 재료, 위치, 참여 방식의 의외성을 통한 비일상성을 제공하며, 건축과 예술의 창조적 만남을 통한 융복합을 추구하면서 새롭게 진화하고 있다. 하지만 광주폴리는 몇 가지 점에서 다른 도시의 폴리와 구별될 수 있다. 먼저, 광주폴리는 광주 도심에 2년 또는 3년 간격으로 연속적으로 구축된다는 점이다. 필연적으로 새로운 폴리를 구상할 때 선행 폴리의 연장선상에서 접근할 수밖에 없으며 지역 사회, 시민, 전문가들의 평가에 영향을 받는다. 이는 피드백 과정을 통한 디자인의 발전을 이루는 것과 같다. 이런 반복적인 프로세스는 일회성으로 끝나 버리는 많은 다른 도시의 폴리 건설과 다르게, 광주폴리가 광주의 사회·문화·정치적 지형에 맞춰져가는 기회를 제공한다.

둘째, 광주폴리는 필연적으로 이전의 폴리들과 공간적, 맥락적, 기능적으로 연결된다는 점이다. 도심 속 문화 활성화 장치로서의 광주폴리는 지속적으로 추진되어야 효과가 더욱 커진다. 폴리를 통해 문화가 생활영역에서 꽃피워 문화적 재생도시로 탈바꿈하기 위해서는 광주폴리를 하나의 완결체로 보지 않고 끊임없이 변화하며 성장하는 프로세스로 이해하는 것이 매우 중요하다. 고정된 것으로서, 대상으로서, 상품으로서, 완성된 결과물로서가 아닌 창의적인 과정과 가치, 그리고 관계를 만들어 내는 문화예술을 통해 도시민들의 삶이 변화될 때 도시는 재생된다. 사회에서 요구하는 문화 공간의 인프라를 조성하여 삶이 우선되고 생활이

—can the city be rejuvenated. Society gains cultural strength in an urban environment where life becomes the priority and culture itself is based on infrastructure for the cultural spaces that society requires.

Third, Gwangju Folly has become a receptor of a strong program. It is gradually moving away from the concept of the folly in Parc de la Villette, where it originated. In Paris it was offering indeterminately created coincidences and events. However, the follies installed in Gwangju consider all the social, cultural, and historical layers instead of the uncertainty of the site. In fact, the Gwangju Folly became more architectural where the messages of the artist or the functions it requires are programmed and inserted. With performances, readings, toilets, hotels, restaurants, cafés and an observatory, Gwangju Folly actively reflects historical, cultural messages, or the primer programs the artists or curators intended, under the umbrella of urban regeneration.

To contribute to creating a unique cultural landscape and regenerating the city, it should conceive of systematic guidelines based on these identities. First, urban planning departments in the city government and relevant

문화가 될 수 있는 도시환경의 질을 개선할 때 사회는 공간을 통해 문화적 힘을 확보한다.

셋째, 광주폴리는 강한 프로그램의 수용체가 되어간다. 현대 건축적 폴리의 시발이 된 라빌레트에서 시도되었던 비결정적으로 발생되는 우연과 사건 제공자라는 폴리의 개념에서 사건 발생자로서의 역할이 점차 강화되어 가는 것이다. 광주에 단계적으로 설치되는 폴리들은 현대 도시의 불확정성에 더해 장소가 가지는 사회적, 문화적, 역사적 시간의 켜를 고려하여 장소가 필요로 하는 기능 또는 작가가 전달하고자 하는 메시지가 프로그램화되어 삽입된, 더욱 건축적인 모습이 되었다. 광주폴리는 공연·독서·화장실·호텔·식당 및 카페· 전망대 등 그 장소의 역사·문화적 메시지를, 또는 작가와 기획진이 의도하는 도시재생 차원의 마중물 프로그램을 적극적으로 반영한다.

광주폴리가 광주광역시의 성공적인 문화 경관 형성과 도시재생에 기여하기 위해서는 위의 정체성을 토대로 체계적인 가이드라인을 마련해야 한다. 첫째, 광주시 도시계획 관련 부서와 이해 주체들 간의 유기적인 연계가 이루어질 필요가 있다. 광주시 도시기본계획, 경관기본계획, 공공디자인계획 등 도시재생 관련 계획과 연계하는 것이다. 둘째, 폴리 자체를 개별적으로 바라볼 것이 아니라 폴리 주변을 둘러싼환경과 다양한 인프라를 고려해 함께 조화롭게 발전할 수 있는 방향이 모색되어야 한다. 기존 폴리에 대한 시민들의 이용행태 분석을 통해 도시의 맥락을 찾고 후속 폴리들의 전략적

parties must establish an organic relationship. This should be considered in connection with basic urban planning, landscape planning, public design planning, and urban regeneration in general. Second, it should seek ways to harmonise with its surrounding environment and infrastructure instead of considering it something separated and independent. By analysing citizen use of existing follies, it should strategically position future follies and discover new programs. Third, for sustainable follies, citizens should be more actively engaging in their operation. Follies should be established as an urban regeneration point, maintained and monitored through the participation of citizens.

Gwangju Folly is strengthening its identity as a repetitive process, its building of interrelationships with one another through proximity, and its purpose as a practical structure with a strong program. At the same time, Gwangju Folly is an ongoing project that opens up new possibilities whenever new versions are introduced. Today, people are now curious how Gwangju Folly will change in the future, what will be added, and how it will move forward.

포지셔닝과 프로그램 발굴을 하는 것이 그 방법이 될 수 있다. 셋째, 지속가능한 폴리를 위해 주민들이 관리 주체로서의 역할을 보다 능동적으로 수행할 수 있어야 한다. 시민참여를 통한 모니터링과 유지관리가 가능해야 한다.

이와 같이 광주폴리는 반복적인 프로세스, 근접 공간에 삽입된 상호간 네트워크의 구축, 그리고 강한 프로그램이 적용된 실용적 구조물이라는 정체성을 확보해가고 있다. 동시에 새로운 버전이 도입될 때마다 새로운 가능성을 탐색하는 진행형 프로젝트이다. 광주폴리의 미래는 어떤 모습이 될지, 그리고 그것이 어떤 미래를 불러올지 궁금해지는 이유이다.

Moon, Hoon and
the Berlin-based artist group
realities:united
Jan Edler & Tim Edle
re-planned a building to allow
people **to observe**
Mt.Mudeungsan and the Asia
Culture Centre, which was
built in the old city centre area,
a major site of the May 18th
Democratic Movement.
In the urban context, the verb
to see is closely linked with
the conception of space that
varies in scale.

From **gazing** passersby at a café to those **watching** the scenery pass by and feeling the wind from a moving train to **viewing** the city from a higher place, all of these behaviours are that of perceiving where we objectify and de-objectify the subject based on the depth of the space.

Moon, Hoon offers beautiful staircases that have been made to stand out even more

with the architect's unique
use of brilliant colours
as well as a distinctive,
refreshing observatory deck
facing Mt.Mudeungsan.

On the other side,
the billboard designed by
realities:united, which
looks down at the old city
centre area, both invites and
interacts with visitors.
Penetrating through the socio-
political and cultural
context of the city, this all
becomes a new brand of
Gwangju.

문훈과 리얼리티즈:유나이티드
(realities:united)의
얀 에들러와 팀 에들러는 기존
건물 옥상을 재계획하였다.
5·18 광주민주화운동의 현장이자
광주 구도심에 새로 조성된
국립아시아문화전당 및 무등산을
전망할 수 있도록 한 것이다.

보는 행위see는 도시에서
매우 다양한 스케일을 갖는 공간적
단어이다. 카페에서 사람들
passers-by을 멍하니
바라보는 것gaze, 기차에서
속도감을 갖고 보는look 경관,
높은 곳에서 도시를 전망
view하는 행위 등은 공간의 깊이를
갖고 대상을 끊임없이 객체화,
탈객체화하는 인식행위이다.

지상에서 옥상까지 사람들을
유혹하는 문훈 특유의 화려한
색깔로 치장된 계단과 무등산을
바라보는 전망데크는 특별하며
생동감 있는 전망 공간을 제공한다.
문훈 작품 반대편에서 구도심을
바라보는 리얼리티즈:유나이티드의
빌보드는 시민들을 끌어들이고
상호 작용하는 참여형 폴리이며,
사회·정치·문화적 맥락을 관통하는
광주의 새로운 브랜드가 된다.

View Folly
& Art Inst 
"Architec
Autonomo
Gwangju Visual Content Centre, 96 Jebong-ro, Dong-gu, Gwangju, Republic of Korea
대한민국 광주광역시 동구 제봉로 96 광주영상복합문화관

뷰폴리 & 설치작업 '자율건축'
문훈 + 리얼리티즈:유나이티드, 얀 에들러 & 팀 에들러
allation
realities:united, Jan Edler & Tim Edler
CHANGE
ure of
"
Moon, Hoon

CHANGE
스마트 벤처플라자

CHANGE
광주영상콘텐츠융합센터
스마트 밴치캠퍼스
광주 콘텐츠 크리에랩

CHANGE
스마트 벤처플렉스
2017 광주
사운드파크 페스티벌
민주평
ACC Cult
ACC Ar

九州
大成學院
정보원
esearch
국립아시아문화전당
ASIA CULTURE CENTER
브라운지
Visitor Center
방문자센터
Welcome to ACC
멋 전

CHA
광주영상복합문화관

NGLE
스마트 벤처캠

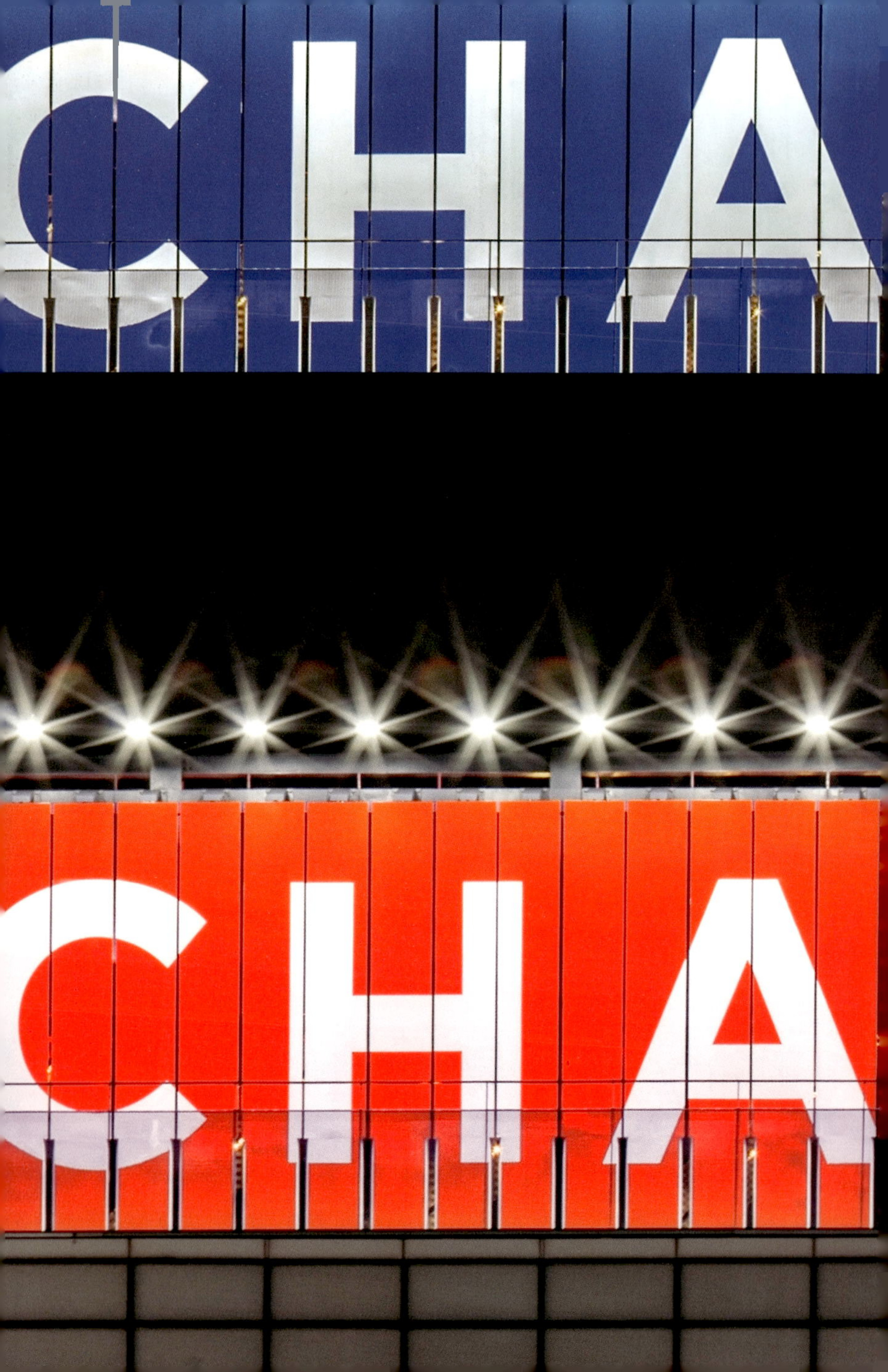

CGV
광주영상복지회관
2017 광주
사운드파크 페스티벌
9.2 9.3 @사직공원 일원
SOUNDPARK STAGE
광주콘텐츠코 어반자카파
9.3 SUN
브로콜리너마저 스윗소로우 옥상달빛
Polaris(일본) 바버렛츠 Sunset Rollercoaster(대만)
안예은 완태 신현희와김루트 예설
PEAKMUSIC STAGE
칵스 세이수미 구남과여라이딩스텔라
라이프앤타임 원보틀 센치한버스 이진우
아프로티켓 INTERPARK
50
마카로닉 테마파크

스마트 벤처캠퍼스

CHA

CHANGE

CHANGE
광주영상복합문화관
스마트

CHANGE

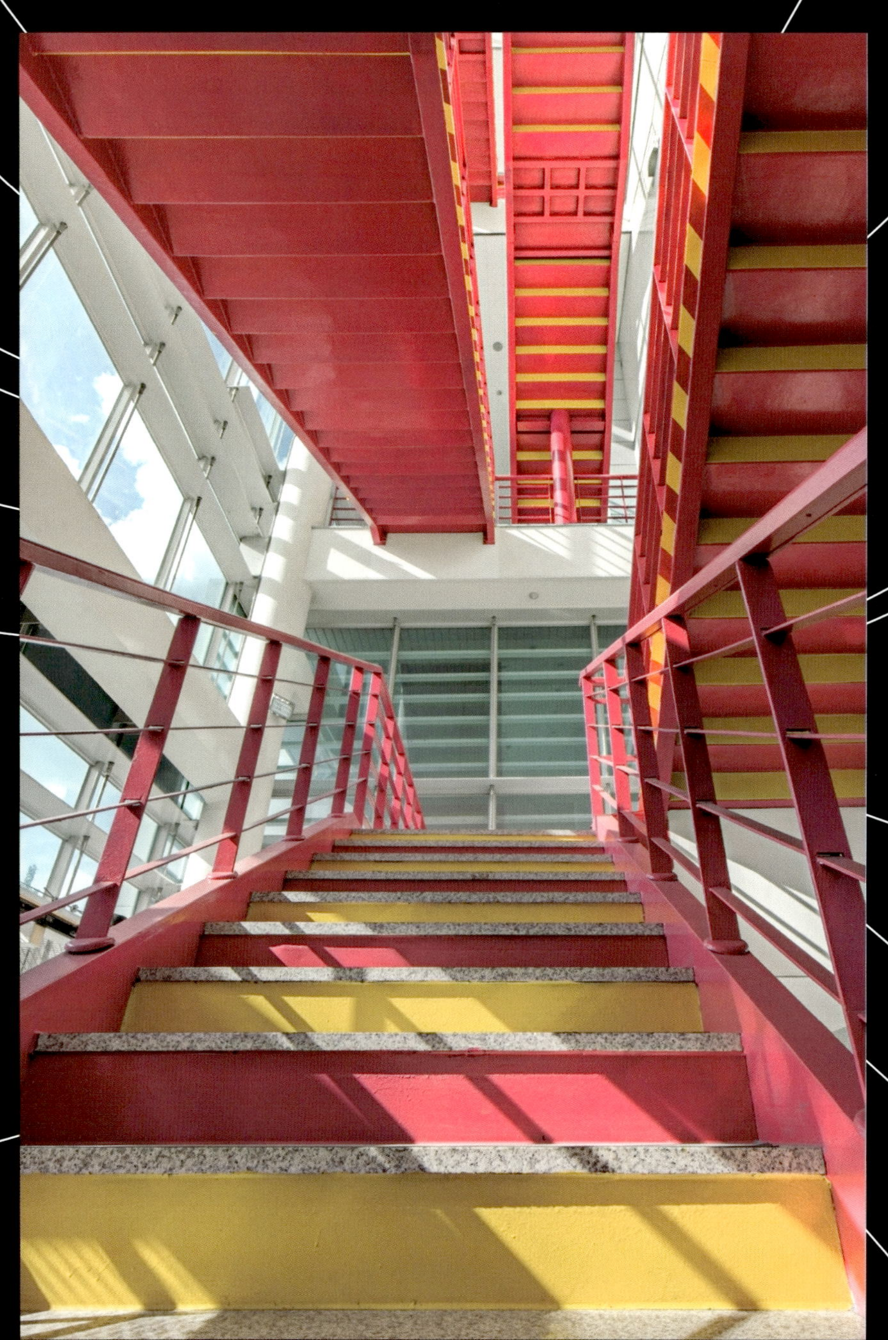

Project Name · 프로젝트 이름	View Folly & Art Installation "Architecture of Autonomy" 뷰폴리 & 설치작업 '자율건축'
Artist & Architect · 작가 & 건축가	Moon, Hoon · 문훈
Project Team · 프로젝트 팀	Kang, Changsu, Kim, Sookhee, Tomasz Kisilewicz, Cho, Guenyoung 강창수, 김숙희, 토마스 키실레비츠, 조근영
Location · 장소	Gwangju Visual Centre, 96, Jebong-ro, Dong-gu, Gwangju, Republic of Korea 대한민국 광주광역시 동구 제봉로 96 광주영상복합문화관
Site Area · 부지 면적	1595.68㎡
Building Area · 빌딩 면적	955.15㎡
Materialisation · 작품 구현	Steel, Wood · 철근, 목재
Construction · 시공사	CL Engineering, Green Wood Inc · 씨엘 엔지니어링㈜, 그린우드㈜
Building Scale · 건물 규모	6F · 6층
Gross Floor Area · 총 바닥 면적	6310.72㎡
Structure · 구조	Steel Frame Construction · 철골
Design Period · 디자인 기간	2016.02~2017.02
Construction Period · 공사 기간	2016.12~2017.06.30
Short Description of the Concept	Gwangju is the most suitable city representing CHANGE. Contrasting colours and alternating skin scaped projectiles boxed and directional sits on a calmly stepped podium surfaced with wood. As night appears the glimpse of festivity gently glows and the great romantic views of the Asia Culture Centre, Mt. Mudeungsan and Gwangju appears.
컨셉에 대한 간략 설명	광주는 변화를 가장 잘 상징할 만한 도시이다. 강렬한 대비를 이루는 색채, 잘 쌓여 방향에 따라 움직이며 전환되는 구조물이 고요히 자리한 목재 단상 위에 자리한다. 밤이 다가오면, 어렴풋한 축제의 기운이 부드럽게 빛나며 국립아시아문화전당, 무등산 그리고 광주의 낭만적 경관이 나타난다.

Project Name · 프로젝트 이름	View Folly & Art Installation "Architecture of Autonomy" 뷰폴리 & 설치작업 '자율건축'
Artist & Architect · 작가 & 건축가	realities:united, Jan Edler & Tim Edler 리얼리티즈:유나이티드, 얀 에들러 & 팀 에들러
Project Team · 프로젝트 팀	Johannes Fröhlich, Christopher Gramer, Paula Oster, Charlotte Popp 요하네스 프륄리히, 크리스토퍼 그레이머, 파울라 오스터, 샬롯 포프
Location · 장소	Gwangju Visual Centre, 96, Jebong-ro, Dong-gu, Gwangju, Republic of Korea 대한민국 광주광역시 동구 제봉로 96 광주영상복합문화관
Site Area · 부지 면적	1,595.68㎡
Building Area · 빌딩 면적	955.15㎡
Materialisation · 작품 구현	Steel · 철
Construction · 시공사	CL Engineering, Green Wood Inc · 씨엘 엔지니어링㈜, 그린우드㈜
Building Scale · 건물 규모	6F · 6층
Gross Floor Area · 총 바닥 면적	Surface: 92,7㎡ (one side) · 표면: 92.7㎡ (단면)
Structure · 구조	Steel Frame Construction · 철
Design Period · 디자인 기간	2016.02~2017.02
Construction Period · 공사 기간	2016.12~2017.07
Short Description of the Concept	"Architecture of Autonomy" is a dynamic public art piece which is closely with the View Folly installation by Moon, Hoon. "Architecture of Autonomy" forms space. "Architecture of Autonomy" questions the unity of fundamental aspects of architecture. "Architecture of Autonomy" is a call to the individual to get active.
컨셉에 대한 간략 설명	'자율건축'은 역동적인 공공예술작품으로 문훈의 뷰폴리와도 매우 긴밀히 연결되어 있다. '자율건축'은 공간을 만든다. '자율건축'은 건축의 가장 근본적인 측면들의 결합에 대해 묻는다. '자율건축'은 개개인의 활동을 촉구한다.

Gwangju View Folly

Moon, Hoon

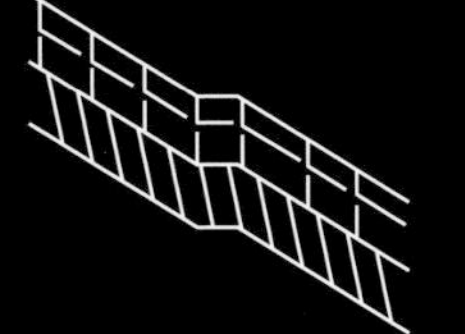

광주 뷰폴리
문훈

Prologue

By injecting a new and healthy virus media, View Folly, into the weakened host, Gwangju Visual Content Centre, we aimed at creating a space full of vitality and energy. The new land is the centre itself and its rooftop. As the term View Folly implies, it adds a device to a place you can view. Initially, the Jeonil Building and the Visual Content Centre were both considered as candidates, but for various reasons the centre was chosen. From the top of the building, everything can be seen—from the Asia Culture Centre all the way to Mt. Mudeungsan. This tract of land is exactly at the height where you can not only have a close-range view, but a distant one as well.

View Folly Drawing 1

View It is said that the act of looking down on a city landscape likely began with the construction of the Eiffel Tower. One of the largest attractions featuring an elevated view, the Eiffel Tower shows a complex man-made landscape to visitors. Here, too, the view is a city view, a general solution on the one hand, while a singular solution is also embedded. This is because it forms a directional relationship with the existing follies in Gwangju that are too far away to be seen when facing them, ultimately becoming a space that evokes imagination about those relationships.

Types of View There are two types of view. One is viewing through a specific frame, namely, the target view. The other is viewing from the deck, where one can freely look around without interruption. While comfortably sitting or leaning against a railing, visitors enjoy a drink as

see

they take in the view and appreciate all of this without any spatial or time restrictions.

Folly The origin of the word folly comes from something useless yet with a certain, temporary presence. This is also true of the follies at the Gwangju Biennale, which are seen and designed as devices or places that are more practical, accessible and sustainable.
Just as the Eiffel Tower, which was temporarily built for the 1889 World's Fair, has obtained permanence greater than any other structure in Paris, follies in Gwangju, including this View Folly, might well become truly grand one day. For the innate sense of tentativeness or the temporary— and it does not necessarily need to be functional—the materials and composition of View Folly are not very responsive to the weather. Also, the materials and form demonstrate tentative and temporary features. Nevertheless, this seems to be a slight contradiction, as View Folly could be baptised with a perpetuity that comes with vitality and is proportional to the commitment to and affection for sustainability.

View Folly Drawing 2

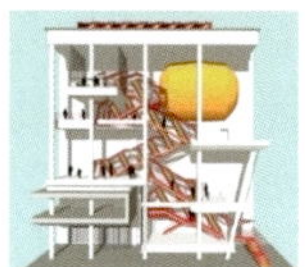

Ascent To reach the manmade tract of land on the top, one has to climb up. Existing staircases weren't often used in the past and did not connect all the floors. Thus, the fewest number of staircases were added to create a connection between all the floors.
Going up in an urban space is usually done by stairs or lifts. In this folly, the original idea was to create an ascent where one can experience space through the staircase, appreciate the view while climbing, and fully enjoy the scenery before reaching the final destination, which is the rooftop. As a result, having the curtain wall of the existing

building serve as the boundary, functional balconies of various sizes were designed to offer some rest for visitors
as they climbed up and experienced the continuity of the
indoors and outdoors, all the while exploring the theme
of landscape. Regretfully, due to the rigidity of legal interpretation and budgetary limits, this could not all be realised.

Rooftop Through the lift or the stair-
case, one reaches the inside of the View Folly. Following the
path, one then arrives at the rooftop. The Asia Culture
Centre unfolds beneath, while the media wall—a work done
by realities:united (Jan Edler & Tim Edler, both of whom collaboratively worked on this project)—stands to one's
left. The work that looks as if it is inspired by a Tibetan prayer
wheel, or perhaps intentionally, functionally resembling
an old-fashioned trivision billboard, awaits.
This offers great pleasure because you can rotate it as you
walk by, demonstrating the device's mechanic and analog
features instead of digital
media features that can
easily bore you. In addition,
it has a wide variety
of colours with an energetic
and ambiguous message.

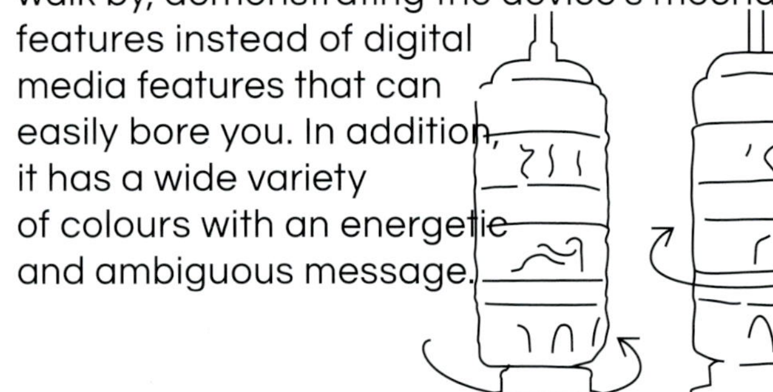

View Folly Drawing 3

Deck After experiencing the media
work, one arrives at a wide deck and scenery spread out
all the way to Mt. Mudeungsan. This is the space you
encounter before reentering the View Folly, where one can

                    see

walk all the way to the stepped boundaries or take a seat to quietly appreciate the city.

View Folly Drawing 4

View Folly Two differently sized squared cubes stretch out before you. One is long and horizontal, leaning against Jan & Tim Edlers' media work—almost as if it were a wall—and one faces Mt. Mudeungsan, pointing at the existing follies. The one parallel to the Edlers' work offers a relatively stable landscape together with a long built-in bench like an unmanned café. Among the three chains, two of them (not including the lift hall) unfold towards Mt. Mudeungsan and form an invisible relationship with the View Folly. The rather long and floating space on the left offers a frame on the existing landscape, adding further depth. Leaning on the small table connected to the handrail, one can view the scene from various perspectives through the space between the walls. The short, central space that meets the deck is a place where you can put a low bench, take a rest, and enjoy the view.

Blinker Space Blinkers are much darker than headlights, but are more easily recognisable. Plants with poison or zebras with stripes both unveil or hide themselves using such patterns. Taking advantage of their infinitely changing skin, cuttlefish capture their prey. The rhythm of alternating existence and absence, like dotted lines or crosswalks, are added on the entire outer skin of the View Folly. Entering the space is a layer showing a strong contrast of hot pink and lemon, in between which is empty space. Blinkering landscapes infiltrate through those gaps. In this blinkering space, even mundane landscapes that we would have otherwise been indifferent to become something new and different.

Epilogue

Under the main idea of Gwangju Folly, which is to enhance public accessibility, View Folly is based on the much more general function of observing the city. Still, it emits signals of festivals, non-daily or special events through blinkering spaces with splendid colours. The uniqueness of the space's ambience will be recognised by people over time, and the shared recognition will become the seed of new and different events that may happen here. It is our hope that this becomes an easy, light, and accessible site that can become the venue for creative practices that embody cultural and artistic activities, as well as different perspectives and a refreshing, entertaining playground.

→ 090 <u>**프롤로그**</u>

생명 에너지가 약해진 광주영상복합문화관을 숙주로 삼고 새로운 건강 바이러스인 미디어 뷰폴리를 투입하여, 새로운 활기와 에너지가 충만한 장소를 만들어보려 한다. 새로운 대지는 영상관 자체와 그 옥상이다. 뷰폴리라는 말이 이미 힌트를 내주듯, 무엇인가 바라볼 수 있는 장소에 장치를 더하는 것이다. 애초에는 전일빌딩과 광주영상복합문화관이 물망에 올랐으나 여러 가지 주변 상황에 의해 광주영상복합문화관으로 결정되었다. 오르면 가까이는 국립아시아문화전당이 멀리는 무등산이 눈에 들어온다. 광주의 근경과 원경이 들어오는 적정한 높이의 대지이다.

→ 090 **뷰** 아마도 에펠탑의 탄생과 더불어 도시전경, 혹은 도시를 내려다보는 행위가 시작되었을 거라는 말이 있다. 그 다양하고 복잡한 인공풍경을 거주자 혹은 방문자들에게 제공하는 것은 도시의 큰 매력 중 하나라고 할 수 있다. 여기서도 역시 뷰란 도시 전경을 '일반해'로써 제공하지만, 더불어 기존 광주에 있는 폴리들과 방향적 관계를 맺는 '특수해' 역시 품고 있는 것이다. 너무 멀리 떨어져 있어서 보이지는 않지만 그곳을 정확하게 향하고 있기에 그 관계들에 대한 상상을 불러일으킬 수 있는 장소가 된다.

뷰의 종류 타겟 뷰(target view)를 통해 어떤 특정한 프레임을 통해 바라보는 방식이 있고, 아무런 제약 없이 두리번거릴 수 있는 장소인 데크에서 바라보는 뷰의 방식이 있다. 멀리 보이는 풍경을 안주 삼아 가벼운 맥주로 목마름을 달랠 수 있고, 공간이나 시간의 제약에서 벗어나 자유롭게 바라볼 수 있기도 하다. 다만 조금 더 편안하게, 앉아서 혹은

기대서 바라볼 수 있는 것이다.

→ 091 **폴리** 폴리의 어원을 살펴보면 '쓰잘머리 없는, 그러면서도 동시에 어떤 존재감을 잠시 동안 지니는 그 무엇'일 터인데, 광주비엔날레에서의 폴리는 보다 실용적이고, 시민과 가깝고, 게다가 지속가능성이 있는 어떤 장치 혹은 장소의 측면에서 기획되고 있는 것이 사실이다. 마치 만국박람회용 일시적 폴리인 거대한 에펠탑이 파리의 어떠한 건축물보다 강력한 영속적 존재의 가능성을 획득하였듯, 광주의 폴리들, 그리고 이번 뷰폴리 또한 그러한 반열에 속하게 되는지도 모르겠다. 임시적, 혹은 일시적이라는 뜻과 특히 기능적이어야 할 필요가 없어도 되는 장치라는 뉘앙스와 의미를 내포하고 있기에, 뷰폴리의 재료와 그 구성 또한 날씨에 대한 대응력이 떨어지는 것이 사실이고 그 재료나 형상이 더욱 더 임시성, 일시성을 도드라지게 드러내게 된다. 그럼에도 불구한 지속가능성에 대한 의지와 애정에 비례하는 생명력의 가능성에 대해 영속성을 세례받을 수 있으니 이 또한 가벼운 모순이 아닌가 싶다.

오름 높은 인공대지에 다다르기 위해서는 오르는 행위가 수반되는데, 기존 건물의 잘 쓰이지 않는 계단 공간에 더불어 모든 층을 연결하지는 않지만 최소한의 계단만을 신설함으로써 전 층의 연결을 보장했다. 도심지에서의 오름은 대부분 계단 혹은 엘리베이터를 통해 이루어진다. 이번 폴리에서는 계단을 통해 공간을 경험하고, 오르면서도 바깥 풍경을 바라보는, 그래서 최종 목적지인 옥상에 다다르지 않아도 충분히 풍경을 만끽할 수 있는 오름을 만드는 것이 최초의 의도였다. 그래서 기존건물의 커튼월을 경계로 하여 안팎으로 통하는 다양한 크기의 기능성 발코니들을 만들어 오름이라는 행위 중 쉼을 제공하고, 풍경이라는 주제로 내·

외부 공간을 연속적으로 느낄 수 있도록 계획하였으나, 법규적인 해석의 경직성과 전체 예산의 한계로 모두 삭제되어 매우 안타까운 심정이다.

→ 092 **옥상** 계단 혹은 엘리베이터를 통해 오르면 뷰폴리 본체의 내부 공간에 도착하고, 지정된 동선을 따라 움직이면 외부 옥상으로 인도된다. 국립아시아문화전당이 아래 풍경으로 펼쳐지는 동시에, 이번 협업 팀인 리얼리티즈:유나이티드의 얀 에들러와 팀 에들러의 작업인 미디어월을 좌측 편으로 맞이하게 된다. 마치 티벳에 있는 기도 바퀴(prayer wheel)에서 영감을 받은 듯한, 혹은 의도적으로 유행이 지난 트리비전 광고판과 기능적으로 닮도록 한 작업이 기다리고 있다. 이 작업은 걸어가면서 손으로 돌려볼 수 있는 즐거움을 주는데, 아주 쉽게 지루해져버리는 디지털미디어아트가 아닌 기계적이고 아날로그적인 특징이 잘 표현된 작품이며 보너스로 다양한 컬러와 힘차고 중의적인 메시지도 볼 수 있다.

데크 미디어작품의 체험이 끝나고 나면 넓은 데크가 나타나고 무등산 방향의 풍경이 펼쳐진다. 뷰폴리에 재진입하기 전에 펼쳐지는 공간인데, 단이 져 있는 공간의 경계까지 활보하거나 걸터앉아서 느린 속도로 도시를 바라볼 수 있다.

→ 093 **뷰폴리** 얀과 팀의 미디어작업을 벽처럼 기대고 평행한 긴 박스 형태의 공간과, 무등산을 바라보며 기존 광주폴리의 방향을 가리키는 2개의 다른 크기 박스공간들이 펼쳐져 있다. 에들러 형제의 작업과 평행한 공간은 마치 무인카페라도 되는 것처럼 기다란 빌트인 벤치와 더불어 어느 정도 안정적인 풍경을 제공한다. 여기서 연결되어 있는 3개의 고리 중 엘리베이터 홀 공간을 제외한 나머지 두 공간은 무등산 방향을 향해, 보이지 않는 기존의 뷰폴리와의 관계 속에 쭉 뻗어 있다. 왼쪽의 다소 길고 허공에 떠 있는 듯한 공간은 기존 풍경에 프레임을 마련하면서 동시에 깊이감을 선사한다. 난간과 연결된 작은 테이블에 기대어 벽체의 벌어진 틈들을 통해 다양한 시선과 풍경을 구경할 수 있다. 다소 짧고 데크와 충돌해 있는 공간 가운데에는 적당한 크기의 평상을 두어 앉아서 휴식하며 풍경을 바라볼 수 있도록 했다.

→ 093 **깜빡 공간** 깜빡등이 전조등보다 훨씬 어둡지만 눈에 쉽게 띈다. 독을 품은 식물과 스트라이프 무늬의 얼룩말들은 그 패턴들을 이용해 자신을 드러내기도 혹은 감추기도 한다. 갑오징어는 무한하게 변화하는 표피의 변화를 이용해 자신의 먹이를 환희로 보내버린다. 있는 것과 없는 것이 교차하는, 마치 점선 혹은 횡단보도 같은 리듬을 뷰폴리 안팎 전체의 표피에 입힌다. 공간에 들어서면 핫핑크와 레몬색의 대비가 세트로 이루어진 스킨 사이사이로 표피가 비어져 있다. 그 사이로 다양한 도시풍경들이 깜빡깜빡하고 들어온다. 평소에 보았던 너무나 익숙하고 그래서 무관심했던 풍경마저 이렇게 깜빡이는 공간에 의해 다르게, 혹은 신선하게 느껴질 수 있는 것이다. 술에 취하지 않았는데도 불구하고 마음이 울렁거리는 작은 환희를 느껴볼 수 있는 공간이 될 것이다.

→ 094 **에필로그**
보다 시민에게 가까워지려는 폴리 전체의 기획하에 준비된 뷰폴리는 우선 도심조망이라는 아주 보편적인 기능을 기본으로 담고 있지만, 그에 더불어 화려한 컬러의 깜빡 공간을 이용하여 축제 혹은 비일상 혹은 특별한 이벤트의 신호를 뿜어내고 있다. 이러한 분위기는 시간이 지날수록 그 고유의 장소성으로 시민들에게 인식되고, 그렇게 공유된 인식에너지는 그 장소에서 일어날 수 있는 새롭고 다양한 이벤트의 씨앗들이 될 것이다. 참으로 많은 문화예술 활동 혹은 새로운 시각을 담은 창조적 행위들이 일어나는 가볍고도 만만한 공간인 동시에, 신선하고 재미있는 놀이 생산의 터가 되었으면 하는 바람이다.

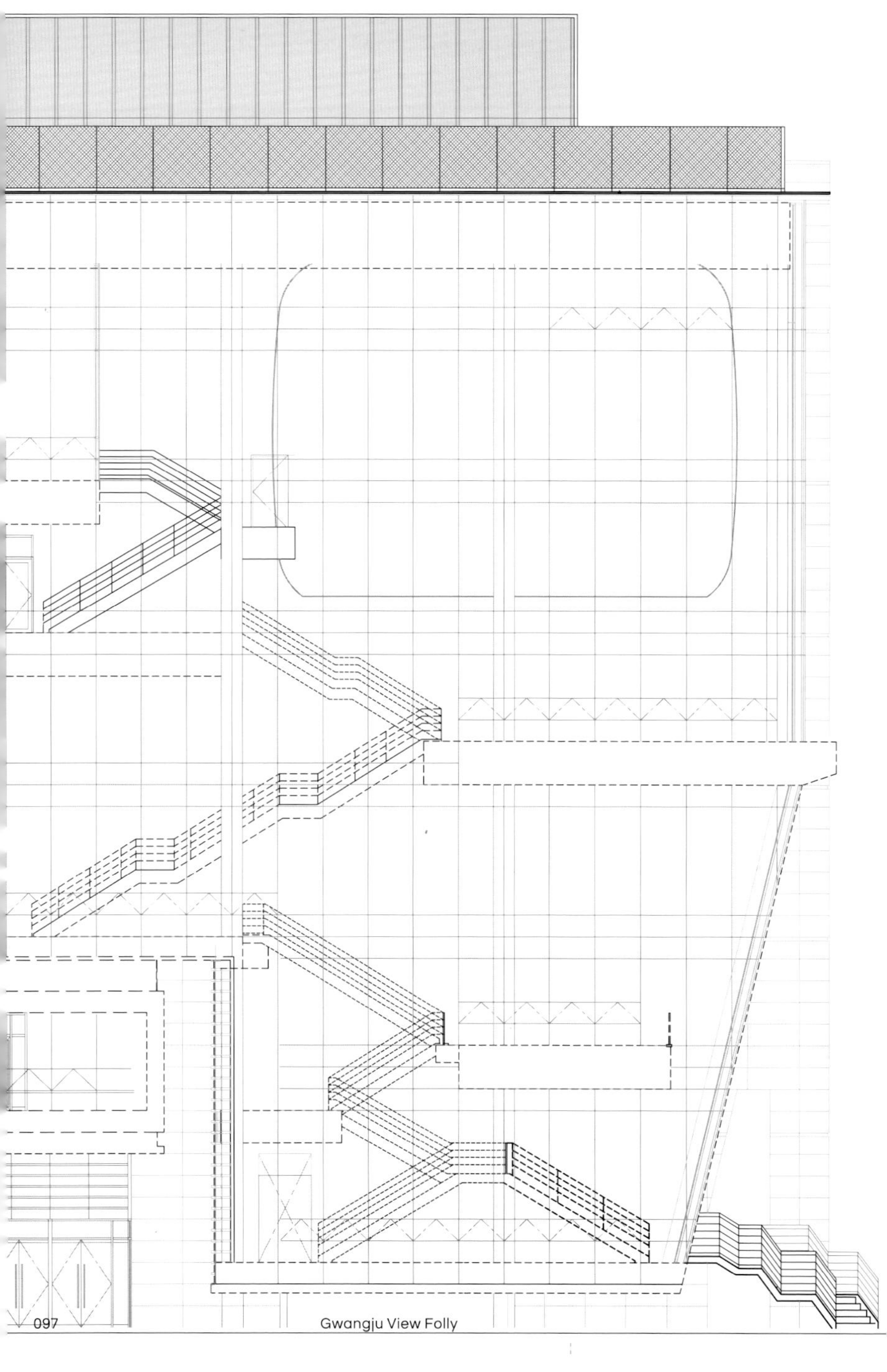

Gwangju View Folly

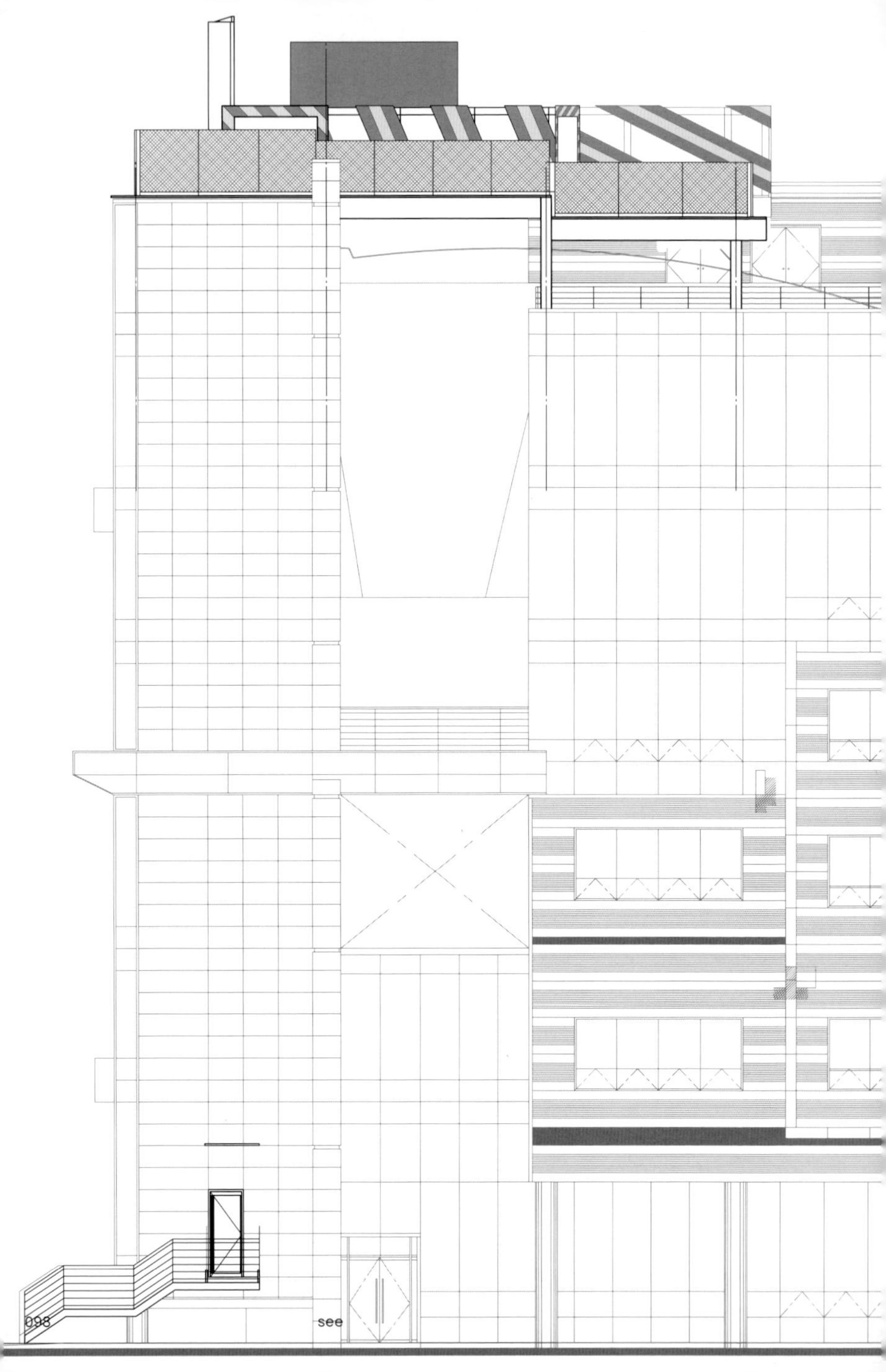

see

Gwangju View Folly

see

Gwangju View Folly

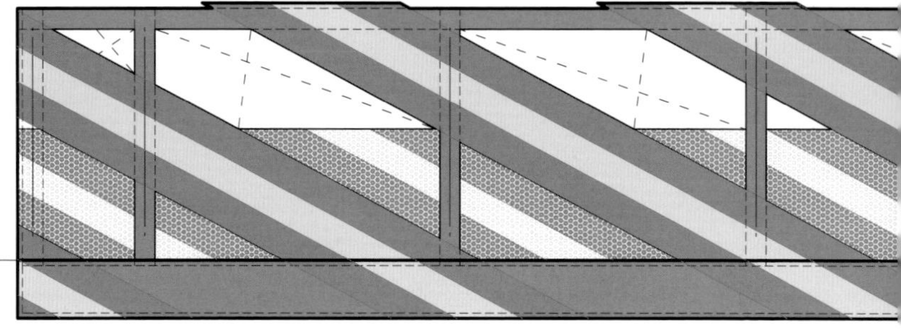

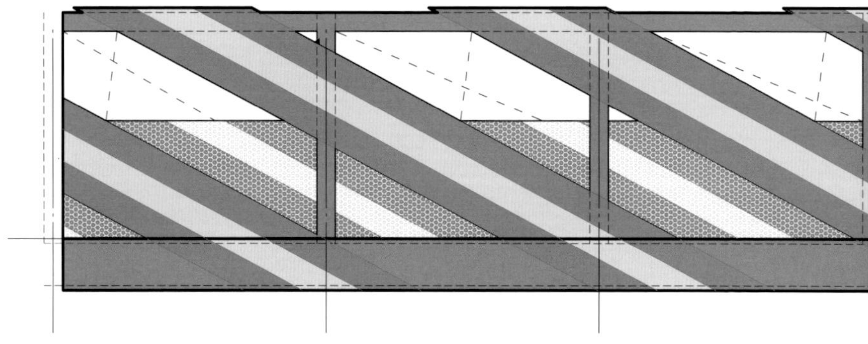

see

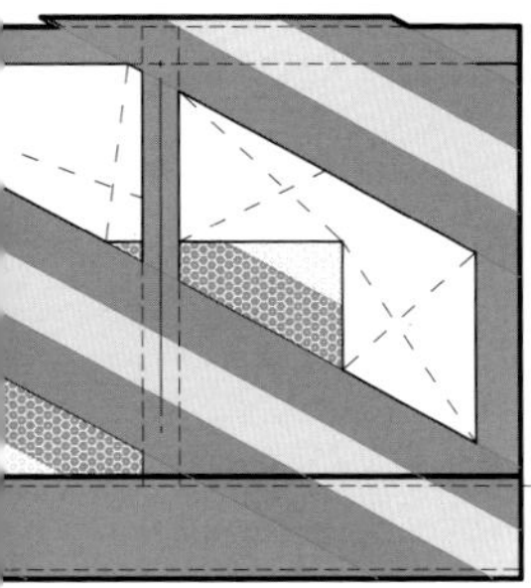

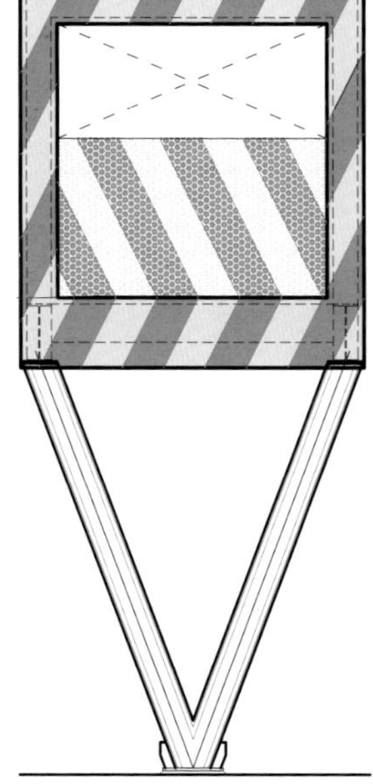

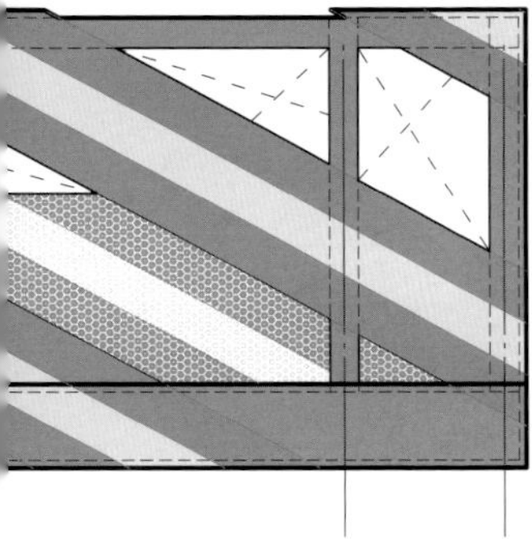

Gwangju View Folly

see

Architecture of Autonomy

realities:united, Jan Edler & Tim Edler

자율건축

리얼리티즈:유나이티드, 얀 에들러 & 팀 에들러

The installation *Architecture of Autonomy* by the Berlin-based artist group realities:united is closely connected with the installation *View Folly* by Seoul-based architect Moon, Hoon. *Architecture of Autonomy* is an installation that forms space. It defines a front and a rear side, or an external surface, and the resulting usable interior space. The themes of surface (or façade) and space, or what is involved in the relationship between these two main aspects of architecture, is the theme of the *Architecture of Autonomy* project.

On various levels, the unity of these two aspects is questioned or dissected in this project. External surface and interior space are treated as loosely connected, independent players. No longer are they organically and absolutely connected; rather, they form a kind of strategic or symbiotic alliance, whose members only contingently cooperate in the framework of a precisely negotiated subscription, thereby pursuing their own goals.

Accordingly, there is a clear separation of conceptual and design responsibility between realities:united for the exterior surface and Moon, Hoon for the usable space behind it. The exterior shell externally objectifies the interior space and gives it a visual identity, or "address," which is recognisable from afar. At the same time, the initially invisible "actual" space on the adjoining rear roof surface supplements the visitors' (ultimately) rather simple experience of the external "interactive" installation, *Architecture of Autonomy*. This shift in the reference level between *Architecture of Autonomy* as "superficial attraction," which presumably was a primary motivation to climb to this remote site, and the "usable level" behind it is an aspect of the experience of the overall ensemble. It is also a principal component of the overall concept: The initially perceived functions and meanings of the individual components move and, on closer inspection, begin to blur. Upon closer inspection, the installation *Architecture of Autonomy*,

see

which from afar appears to be the goal of the climb, transforms into a kind of interim component or passage way
to another, initially unknown experience behind it.

The two initially dominant aspects of
the exterior surface are, first, its effect as a typically
authoritarian *propaganda instrument* whose message is
broadcast to the city from a secure height, and, second,
its "interactivity" and expression of the individual person's
will to design, both of which are set in motion as soon
as one contemplates it more intensely.

The term "change," visible from afar,
is a central metaphor of our time. Simultaneously, its
meaning is completely indeterminate or self-contradictory.
In 2008, it became the trademark slogan of Barack Obama's
presidential campaign, but it is also clearly inscribed in
his successor's presidency as a kind of negative afterimage.
Today, the term is at the centre of attention between
the political forces of emancipation and democratisation,
on the one hand, and those of old and new authoritarianism, on the other. For example, "change" is supposed to
lead to equality and the elimination
of differences between people— CHANGE
or to a return to structures, classes, castes,
and nations that make it possible to avoid
contact with what is different.
But it is precisely the idea of "change" that
divides society and creates differences.
There are those who consider change
vitally important and those whom it frightens.
Many want a radical change in the
political system and the entirety of our political
or philosophical thinking, but pursue
the goal of ultimately preserving nature
or society unchanged, with the explanation that continuing
the current process of change will otherwise lead

to a dystopian *final* steady state, one in which nothing more can be changed.

The term "change," however, also describes the un*chang*ing process of the world that happens anyway, and which currently is once again involved in far-reaching change, for example, through the complete digitisation of every conceivable aspect of life. This, too, is accompanied by the euphoric expectation of an unprecedented empowerment of all people, on the one hand, and, on the other, by fear of an abstract, psycho-technological authoritarian system whose capacities for control and manipulation could grow practically without limit for the first time.

Architecture of Autonomy:
Behaviour
Rotating the 33 triangular columns
allows visitors to create
their individual colour code.

Architecture of Autonomy:
Interaction
Visitors entering the roof rotate
columns individually.

see

As far as we can see today, involving every individual in purported decision-making processes is part of the strategies of societal control. "Change" as a call to the individual to become (himself or herself, and autonomously) active does not essentially differ from the call to collaborate or even to be subjugated.

Ultimately, it all depends on whether the possibilities to change also include changing the system of action. The boundary is fluid between open interaction in the sense of genuine possibilities of development and codetermination, and a guided collaboration that in some cases is set up for control or exploitation and that behaves "interactively" and "voluntarily," but ultimately turns every aspect of the person, down to his innermost wishes and motives, into a trade good. In between these poles lie, in all shades of gray, various systems of social self-occupation that actually feel like participating and collaborating.

The installation *Architecture of Autonomy* similarly combines the summons character of the slogan "change," with an opportunity to interact, that in return makes the display wall itself the object of change; it can actually be configured to an unimaginable number of different colour patterns. Compared with the norms of commercial advertising, in which every nuance of colour, every form, and simply all content is subjected to a strict, market-specific precept, this offers a substantial possibility to intervene. However, the original slogan text is preserved in every colour variant. The colour pattern is thus changeable, but the central text message, calling for action, is not. The user cannot alter the system and its central message, which seems a latent paradox, because in this special case the question arises whether it is possible for the user to fulfill the summons successfully. The question is left unresolved whether enabling and simultaneously absorbing a moderate interactive intervention doesn't primarily

 Architecture of Autonomy

serve the existing hierarchical system by not only binding the populace's latent revolutionary energy, but also by making it possible to interpret people's interactive voluntary collaboration as a sign of approval, in the sense of rein-forcing the legitimation of the propaganda.

Not only within the installation *Architecture of Autonomy*, but also in the combined instal-lation consisting of *Architecture of Autonomy* and *View Folly*, there is a situation in which a conventional distinction bet-ween means and end leads to no clear result. The effective meaning of this communicating façade and its message increases through the "liveliness" breathed into it by inter-action or through its perception as a societal site. This is why enticing visitors and inducing them to remain on the rear ter-race after a short phase of "interaction" can be seen as means subordinated to this end. The alternative consists in understanding this relationship between the communi-cative or attractive level and the effective place to stay and spend time (behind the former) as a symbiotic relation-ship, like a flower that "pays" in nectar to the participating insect for spreading or transporting its genetic **message**.

With this, we return to the idea formul-ated at the beginning: a complex, symbiotic "contractual relationship" between façade and space forms a sub-stitute for the conventional idea in which the (exterior) wall serves to delimit the manmade architectural space from the environment, that is, in which erecting the wall is subor-dinate to the goal of creating space.

Thinking about this is motivated by the process of economic change in the modern city, driven primarily by digital transformation. Through it, not only individual construction and design components are losing their traditional function, but so, too, is the city itself. Due to digitisation, after the production of goods, now the trade in goods and many central service functions are

 see

no longer tied to the urban space. The increasing possibility that the city will be defunctionalised, however, does not lead to its disappearance (in the sense of diffusing into the landscape), but to a concentration on the importance of the city as a psychological or sometimes ritual framework for living together: the city as stage or backdrop for social interaction or as a space of affirmation in which the role of architecture must be written entirely anew, one in which buildings become effective essentially through their external appearance or their cultural or social associations. See: realities:united, *Museum X* (2006).

Museum X
An urban mise–en-scène art installation, Mönchengladbach, Germany, 2006-2008
Using printed façade panels and other components, the hull of the city's centrally located and unused Mönchengladbach. Theatre building was transformed into an imaginary museum building, designed in distinctive post-war Modernist style. This clearly discernable illusion of a cultural building, conceived as an "urban status symbol," is detailed all the way to an actual entrance foyer, staffed with museum personnel for the 18-month project duration. This is a hybrid between a billboard, urban revitalisation project, and art sculpture.

In the past, realities:united implemented a number of works broadly concerned with the "new" relationship between architectural façade and interior or urban space. The differentiation between space and façade is carried forward in the dealings between the material and the media, or message, aspect of the façade.

With its first façade work *BIX* in 2003, realities:united produced a hybrid that eludes the conventions of a classical façade, but equally the newly emerging conventions for media façades as propaganda or message surfaces. This and other projects in subsequent years, like the works *Crystal Mesh* (2009) and *C3A* (2012), are part of the research and development of the original form of medial or changeable architecture. What this means is, for example, that media message surfaces on buildings can

     Architecture of Autonomy

and should be understood first as an aspect of dynamically changeable architecture and only secondarily as
platforms for external advertisements that appropriate or
co-opt the viewer.

BIX
A Communicative display skin for
Kunsthaus Graz, Austria, 2003
(in cooperation with Peter Cook and
Colin Fournier Architects)
Using conventional fluorescent lights
as super-large pixels, *BIX* proposes
a new model for a "media façade"
regarding both its scale
and high degree of abstraction.

Crystal Mesh
Media façade for the ILUMA Urban
Entertainment Centre,
Singapore, 2010 (in cooperation
with WOHA Architects)
Crystal Mesh consists of a tessel-
lated pattern made of 3,000 modules
of deep-drawn polycarbonates
that cover a façade-area of
more than 5,000 m². Its function
and design brings to mind historical
ventilation façades, the modular
façade designs of the 1960s,

and 1970s, and the analog light-
bulb aesthetic in the entertainment
districts of the 20th century.
At the same time, it also contains
the "futuristic" concept of the

monitor as a complete substitute
for the conventional façade
construction—the façade as
digital medium.

C3A
An Artistic multi-resolution,
multi- scale light-and media façade
for the Centre of Contemporary Art,
Cordoba, Spain, 2012/2016
(in cooperation with Nieto Sobejano
Architects)
The architectural motif is translated
to form a characteristic outer topo-
graphy on the façade. The surface
shows a system of irregularly
shaped indentations of varying den-
sity and size. Those "bowls", which

are geometrically derived from the
building's floor plan, are individually
lit to become "pixels" of a large
display system. Transforming the
façade into a light and media display

without fundamentally changing its
solid appearance as envisioned
by Nieto Sobejano turned out to be
the biggest challenge in the project.

This approach also explains realities:
united's affinity for exploring technological formats from the
field of advertising that are repatriated into the field of
architecture, or are now appropriated in the other direction.
The installation *2x5 (brothers)* from 2012 uses the technology of "scrolling billboards" to produce surfaces that change
colour in the foyer of the Perry and Marty Granoff Centre
for the Creative Arts building in Providence, Rhode Island

                    see

(Diller Scofidio Renfro Architects), and thus to create an extremely slow pictorial choreography that takes months in the "pace and scale" of architecture. The façade *BIGGA* for *The Khalifa Park Art Souq* in Abu Dhabi (a competition entry in cooperation with BIG architects) is one of the first designs displaying the transmission of the likewise advertising-associated Trivision format on a scale that can relate to architecture in terms of size and speed of behaviour, and that transforms the whole building into a dynamic spatial sculpture of surfaces whose colours change.

2x5 (brothers)
A kinetic building site art installation,
Brown University,
Providence, USA, 2012
2x5 (brothers) is a time-based work and makes use of an established commercial technical format well known within the advertising industry. Instead of displaying a series of images, the two apparatuses in the building's entrance are used to show full-surface monochromatic-coloured prints. With one to four changes per day, the frequency of the change is so negligible that visitors initially experience the installation mostly as static in the respective configuration.

BIGGA
A competition entry for
The Khalifa Park Art Souq,
Abu Dhabi UAE, 2008
(in cooperation with BIG Architects, Denmark)
The façade features rotating triangular tubes, or *Trivision*, which allow the display of three different colours or materials. Stretched over 60 percent of the façade, this system sufficiently evokes the impression of an unlimited variability in utterly changing the building's surface. The effect caused by this slow change is dramatic; large changing fields of colour or material appear and disappear, giving the building a permanently changing face and fundamental expression.

Architecture of Autonomy

→ 106　베를린에 기반하는 작가 그룹 리얼리티즈:유나이티드의 설치작업 '자율건축(Architecture of Autonomy)'은 서울을 중심으로 활동하는 건축가 문훈의 뷰폴리와 긴밀하게 연결되어 있다. '자율건축'은 공간을 형성하는 작업으로, 전면과 후면 또는 외부 면을 규정하면서 사용 가능한 내부 공간을 만들어낸다. '자율건축' 프로젝트는 평면(또는 파사드)과 공간, 그리고 건축의 주요 요소인 이들 사이의 관계에 대해 묻는다.

　　　　이 프로젝트는 두 요소의 결합을 다양한 층위에서 논의하고 해부한다. 외부 면과 내부 공간은 느슨하게 연결된 독립적 주체들로 간주된다. 즉, 유기적으로 완벽하게 연결된 것이 아니라 적확하게 합의된 골조에 한정지어 협력하여 그것들의 목표를 좇는, 일종의 전략적이고 상징적인 동맹을 만든다.

　　　　따라서 외부 면을 담당한 리얼리티즈:유나이티드와 그 뒤편의 사용 가능한 공간을 담당한 문훈 간에는 개념과 디자인적 책임의 명확한 구분이 있다. 외부 벽은 내부의 공간을 표면적으로 대상화하고 그것에 시각적 정체성이나 멀리서도 인식 가능한 '주소'를 부여한다. 반대로 뒤쪽 지붕과 맞닿는, 처음엔 보이지 않았던 '실질적인' 공간은 외부의 '상호작용적', '자율건축' 설치작품이라는 단순한 경험을 보완한다. 이 외딴 곳을 오르게 할 주된 동기인 '외형적 요소'로서의 '자율건축'에서 참조할만한 변화는 전체적인 앙상블의 한 측면이다. 그 변화는 자율건축 이면의 '실용적 층위' 사이에서 발생한다. 또한 이것은 전체적인 개념에 있어서도 주요한 요소이다. 처음 인식되었던 개별 요소들의 기능과 의미는 이동하다가, 보다 자세히 들여다보면 점차 지워지기 시작한다. '자율건축'은 멀리서는 등반의 목적지 같아 보이지만 가까이에서는 일종의 임시적인 것으로, 그 뒤엔 알 수 없는 경험으로의 연결통로로 변화한다.

→ 107　애초에 지배적으로 드러나는 외벽의 두 가지 특징 —즉, 안전한 높이에서 도시에 메시지를 전달하는 전형적으로 권위적인 프로파간다적 도구로서의 역할, 그리고 '상호작용 가능성'과 디자인에 대한 개인적 의지의 표현— 은 당신이 고민하면 할수록 눈앞에 드러난다.

　　　　멀리서 보이는 '변화'라는 용어는 우리 시대의 주요한 메타포이다. 동시에 그 의미는 완전히 부정형이거나 자기모순적이다. 2008년 버락 오바마의 대선 캠페인의 슬로건이면서 동시에 후임 대통령에게는 어떤 부정적 잔상으로 새겨져 있기 때문이다. 오늘날 이 용어는 한편으로 민주주의와 해방을 추구하는 이들, 다른 한편으로는 오래되거나 새롭게 등장한 권위주의자들의 관심을 받는다. 예를 들어 '변화'란 사람들 간의 차이를 제거하고 평등으로 이끌거나, 다름과의 접촉 자체를 피하기 위한 국가와 구조, 계층, 신분으로의 회귀로 이어진다. '변화'의 개념은 사회를 분열시키고 차이를 만들어낸다. 변화를 필수적으로 생각하는 사람들과 변화를 두려워하는 사람들이 있다. 많은 이들이 정치시스템과 우리의 정치철학적 사유 전체에 근본적인 변화를 원한다. 그러나 궁극적으로는 자연과 사회를 변함없이 보호하고자 한다. 그렇지 않다면 이 지속적인 변화가 더 이상 아무것도 변화될 것 없는 디스토피아적 상태에 다다를 것이라 이들은 주장한다.

→ 108　그렇지만 어찌됐건 이 '변화'라는 용어는 현재 일어나고 있는 '변화가 없는' 과정 또한 담고 있다. 예를 들면 우리가 인지할 수 있는 삶의 모든 면면들이 완벽히 디지털화되는 것은 광범위한 변화에 속하기도 한다. 또한 한편으로는 전례 없이 모든 이들이 권한을 나눠 갖는다는 기쁜 기대감이나, 추상적이고 심리공학적이며 권위적인 힘이 무한정 통제와 조작을 키워간다는 공포가 따른다.

→ 108　천의영, 문훈, 위진복
　　　　자율건축 앞에서

→ 108　자율건축: 행동
　　　　회전하는 서른 세 개의 삼각기둥을 회전시킴으로써 관객들은 그들만의 색의 조합을 만들어 낼 수 있다.

→ 108　자율건축: 교감
　　　　옥상에 들어선 관람객들이 기둥을 회전시키고 있다.

→ 109　오늘날 우리가 보듯, 모든 개인을 의사결정과정에 관련시키는 것은 사회제어전략의 부분이다. 능동적으로 활동하라(자기 자신이 되어라, 자율적이 되어라)는 점을 요구하는 '변화'는 협동하라는 요구, 심지어 지배당하라는 요구와도 본질적으로 다르지 않다. 결국 모든 것은 변화의 가능성이 행위체계의 변화까지도 포함하는지에 달려있는 것이다. 발전과 공동결정의 진정한 가능성을 가진 열려있는 상호작용, 그리고 제어와 착취를 위해 의도되고 궁극적으로 개인의 모든 면면을 그의 내밀한 욕망과 동기로 바꾸고 교환수단으로 만드는 '상호작용적', '자발적'인 의도된 협동 사이의 경계는 유동적이다. 이 2개의 극단 사이에 마치 참여와 협동인 양하는 사회적 자기지배의 어둡고 다양한 시스템의 그림자가 놓여 있는 것이다.

　　　　이와 유사하게 '자율건축'은 '변화'라는 슬로건이 지니는 '소환적' 특징을 상호작용의 기회, 즉 전광판 자체를 변화의 대상으로 만들며 결합시킨다. 전광판은 무수하게 많은 각기 다른 컬러 패턴을 설정할 수 있다. 모든 색채와 형태, 간단히 말해 모든 콘텐츠가 엄격한 특정 시장규칙에 지배되는 일반적인 상업광고와 비교했을 때, 이는 상당히 대립적이다. 그러나 원래의 슬로건 텍스트는 모든 색채 변화에 보존되어 있다. 따라서 컬러 패턴은 가변적이지만, 행동을 요구하는 중심 텍스트 메시지는 고정적이다. 사용자는 잠재된 역설로 보이는 시스템과 그 중심메시지를 바꿀 수 없다. 왜냐하면 이런 특별한 경우에는 사용자가 성공적으로 그 부름을 수행하는 것이 가능한지 질문이 생겨나기 때문이다. 또한 대중의 잠재적인 혁명 에너지를 결합할 뿐 아니라 사람들의 상호보완적이고 자발적인 협동을 프로파간다의 정당화를 보완하는 기호로 설명할 수 있게 함으로써, 그 질문은 기존의 계급제도를 돕지 않는 중간 상호작용적 개입을 흡수하는지 해결하지 못한 채 남겨진다. → 110 '자율건축'뿐 아니라 '자율건축'과 뷰폴리를 구성하는 결합된 설치작업에서도, 의미 사이의 관습적인 구분이 있으며 그것은 명확한 결과 없이 끝을 맺는다. 이 소통적 파사드와 그것이 주는 메시지의 유효한 의미는, 상호작용에 의해 숨 쉬는 생명력 혹은 사회적 위치로서의 인식 때문에 증가한다. 이것이 관람객을 매혹시키고 그 끝에 종속된 의미로 보이는 '상호작용'이라는 짧은 문장 뒤의 테라스에 그들을 남겨두기 위해 포섭하는 이유이다. 대안은 소통적 혹은 매력적 층위와, 상징적 관계로서 시간을 보내고 머무르는 유효한 공간 사이의 이러한 관계를 이해하는 데 있다. 이것은 마치 꽃이 그것의 유전자 메시지를 퍼뜨리기 위해 벌레를 끌어들이며 꿀을 '지불'하는 것과 같다.

여기서 초반의 개념으로 다시 돌아가보자. 파사드와 공간 사이의 복잡하고 상징적인 '계약관계'는 [외부]의 벽이 자연으로부터 인간이 만든 건축적 공간의 구획을 나누는 것을 돕는다는 관습적인 개념을 대체한다. 즉 벽을 세운다는 것은 공간을 창조하는 목적에 따르는 것이다. 이는 주로 디지털적 변화에서 기인하는, 근대도시의 경제적 변화에 때문에 활성화된다. 이를 통해 개별적 건축물과 디자인 요소, 도시의 부분 또한 전통적 기능을 잃는다. 디지털화 때문에 재화의 교환과 중심 서비스 기능들이 더 이상 도심지역에 국한되지 않는다. 도시가 기능을 잃어갈 가능성은 증대되지만, 그것이 도시의 소멸(풍경 속으로 희미해진다는 의미)이 아닌 공생에 대한 심리적이거나 종교 의식적인 뼈대로서 도시가 갖는 중요성이 강해지는 것으로 이어진다. 사회적 상호관계의 무대 혹은 배경으로서, 혹은 건축의 역할이 완전히 새로 쓰이는 확언의 공간으로서 건물들이 그들의 외관이나, 문화적, 사회적 연대를 통해 본질적으로 유효해지는 지점인 것이다. 리얼리티즈:유나이티드의 Museum X(2006)를 보자.

→ 111　리얼리티즈:유나이티드는 과거 건축적 파사드, 인테리어와 도심공간 사이의 '새로운' 관계를 자주 다루었다. 공간과 파사드 간의 구별은 재료와 파사드의 메시지적 측면의 문제로 옮겨갔다. 첫 번째 파사드 작업인 BIX(2003)에서, 리얼리티즈:유나이티드는 고전적 파사드의 관습뿐 아니라 동시에 프로파간다 혹은 메세지적 껍데기로 새롭게 등장한 관습을 모두 피하는 일종의 하이브리드를 생산했다. Crystal Mesh(2009)와 C3A(2012) 같이, 뒤따르는 몇 년간의 다른 프로젝트들은 내측적 혹은 가변적 건축의 고유형태에 대한 발전과 리서치의 일부이다. 이의 의미는 건물 표면의 미디어 메시지들이 우선 역동적으로 변화하는 건축으로 이해된 다음에야 부수적으로 관객의 시선을 끌어들이

는 외부 광고 플랫폼으로 인식되어야 한다는 것이다. 이러한 접근법은 그와 방향성이 다른 광고 영역에서 기술적인 형식을 탐험한 후 이를 다시 건축이나 그 외 분야에 사용했던 리얼리티즈:유나이티드의 활동을 잘 설명한다. 2012년의 2x5(brothers) 설치작업에서는 미국 프로비덴스(딜러 스코피디오 렌프로)에 있는 크리에비티브 아트 빌딩의 페리 앤 마티 그라노프 센터 현관에 색깔을 바꾸는 벽을 만들기 위해 '스크롤링 광고판' 기술을 사용, 건축의 '속도와 규모'에서 몇 달이 걸리는 극도로 느린 그림 안무를 만들어냈다. 아부다비의 칼리파 공원 예술시장의 파사드인 BIGGA는 행위의 크기와 속도 측면에서의 건축과 연결 지을 수 있는 규모로 트리비전 광고형식을 보여준 첫 디자인 중 하나이다. 여기에서는 전체 건물의 색채가 변화하는 역동적인 공간 조각으로 건축물을 전환시켰다.

→ 111　Museum X
도심 미장센 설치 작업, 뮌헨글라드바흐, 독일, 2006-2008
파사드 인화 패널 등 각종 요소들을 활용해 도시 한가운데 위치한 극장의 외관을 전후 모더니즘 특유의 스타일로 디자인된 가상의 박물관으로 탈바꿈시킨 작업. '도시적 위치의 상징'으로서 구상된, 눈에 그대로 보이는 이 문화 공간의 환영은 일 년 반 동안 이루어질 프로젝트를 위해 박물관 직원들을 배치하는 등 홀 입구까지 매우 세세하게 구성되어 있다. 옥외 간판, 도심 재활성화 프로젝트, 그리고 예술 조각이 모두 뒤섞인 하이브리드형 작업이다.

→ 112　BIX
오스트리아 쿤스트하우스 그라츠 소통의 외피 전경, 2003
(피터 쿡, 콜린 포니어 건축사무소 협업)
평범한 형광 조명을 거대한 픽셀로 활용한 BIX는 규모 그리고 고도의 추상성이라는 두 가지 측면에서 새로운 '미디어 파사드' 모델을 제시했다.

→ 112   Crystal Mesh
ILUMA 도심 엔터테인먼스 센터
미디어 파사드, 싱가포르, 2010
(WOHA 건축사무소 협업)
크리스탈 메시는 5,000평방미터가 넘는
파사드 전면을 모자이크 식으로 뒤덮고
있는 3,000개의 다이 형식의 폴리카보네이트
모듈로 구성된다. 이는 1960~1970년대
환기를 위한 파사드의 디자인과
기능 그리고 20세기 엔터테인먼트 관련
지구들에서 이용된 전구들의 미학적
활용방식을 떠올리게 한다. 또 동시에 기존의
파사드 구조를 완전히 대체한 모니터로서의
'미래적' 콘셉트, 즉 디지털
매체로서의 파사드의 개념도 담고 있다.

→ 112   C3A
스페인, 코르도바 현대미술센터 미디어
파사드의 멀티 해상도 및 멀티 스케일 조명 작품,
2012/2016
(니에토 소베하노 건축사무소 협업)
본 작업의 건축적 모티프는 파사드에 특징적인
지형을 형성하고자 하는 것에서 시작되었다.
건물의 표면에는 다양한 크기와 깊이를
지니는 불규칙적 곡절들이 형성되어 있다.
건물 평면도의 지리적 해석에서 기인한 이 '홈'
들은 거대한 디스플레이 내에서 '픽셀'로
기능하도록 각각 점등된다. 이 프로젝트에서의
가장 큰 과제는 니에토 소베하노가
구상한 견고한 외형을 흐트러트리지 않으면서
파사드를 조명 및 미디어 디스플레이로
전환시키는 것이었다.

→ 113   2x5 (brothers)
키네틱 건축 현장 작품 설치, 브라운 대학교,
프로비덴스, 미국, 2012
'2x5'는 시간 기반의 작업으로 광고업계에서
흔히 활용되는 상업용 형식을 차용한다.
일련의 이미지들을 선보이는 대신 단색의
화면이 건물 입구의 두 패널을 차지한다.
하루 1~4번 변하는데, 변화가 잦지 않아 관객
들은 대부분 이를 정적인 것으로 인지한다.

→ 113   BIGGA
칼리파 공원 아트 수크 공모전,
아랍에미리트 아부다비, 2008
(덴마크 BIG 건축사무소 협업)
본 작업에서는 파사드에 삼각 튜브들이 회전
하며 3가지의 색상 또는 재료를 선보인다.
파사드 면적의 60%를 차지하며 마치
건물 전체 벽면이 무한히 변화하는 듯 보이도록
만든다. 이 느린 변화들은 극적인 효과를
만들어내는데, 넓은 면을 차지하는
색상과 질감이 나타났다 사라지기를 반복하며
지속적으로 변화하는 벽면과 근본적
특질을 건물에 부여한다.

see

Architecture of Autonomy

Architecture of Autonomy: Concept

33 triangular columns. Each one can be rotated. The text slogan "Change" always remains.

자율건축: 컨셉트

33개의 삼각기둥으로 구성된다. 각각의 기둥을 회전시킬 수 있으나 슬로건 'Change'는 늘 나타난다.

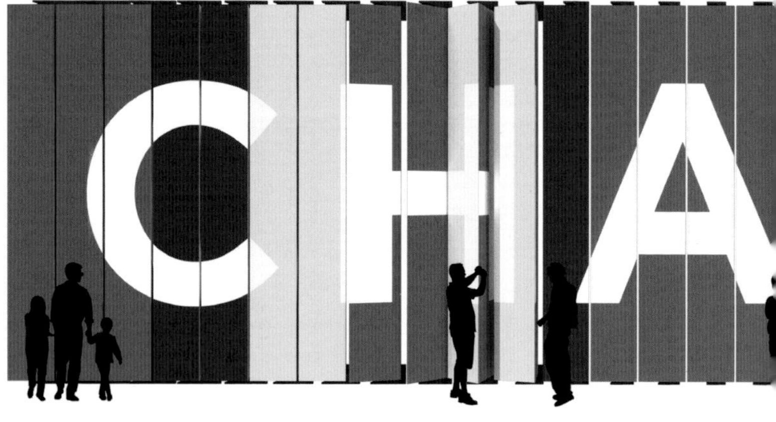

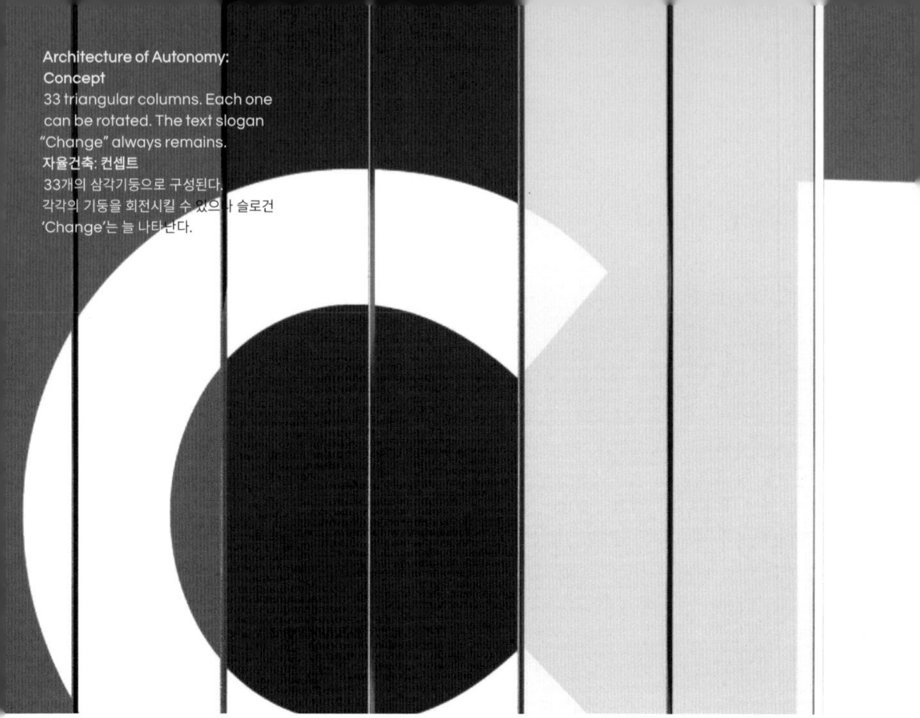

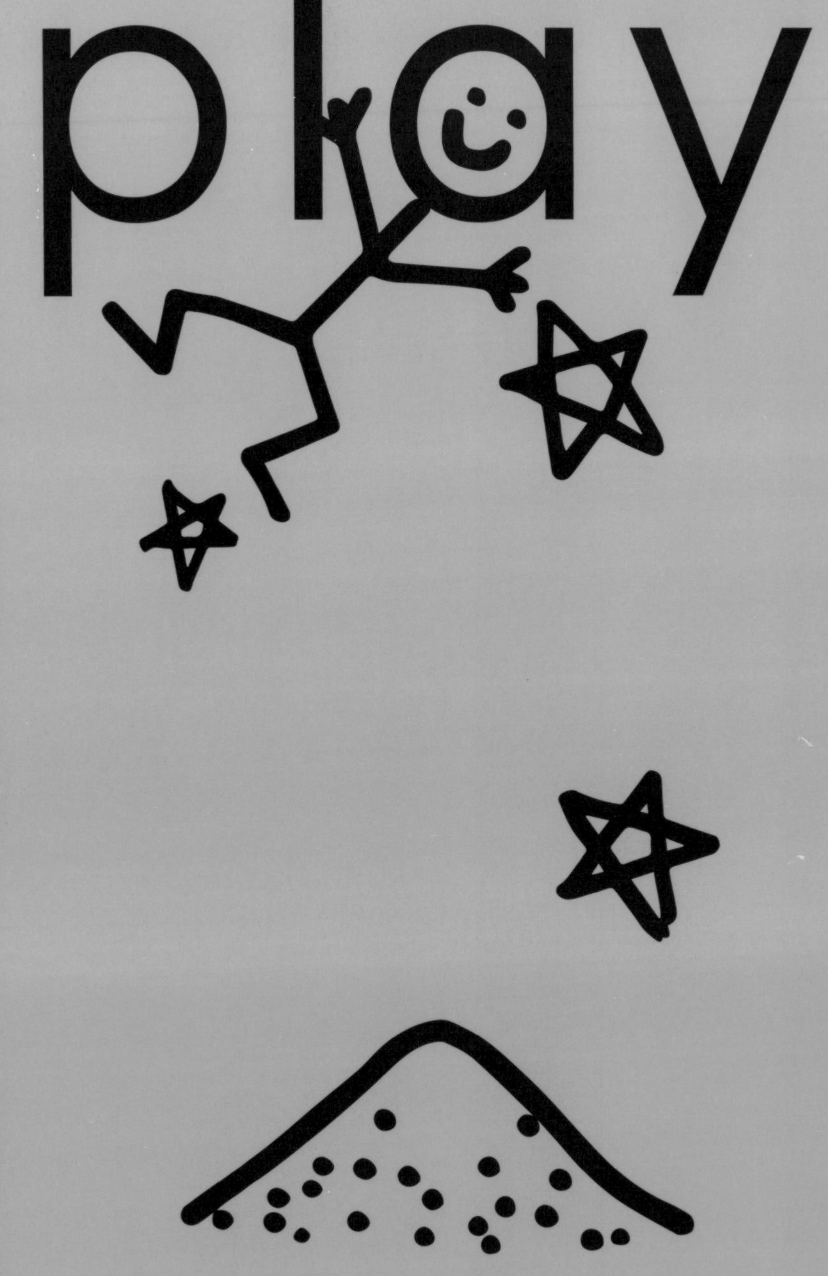
play

A collaborative project between **architecture and media**, the contest is based on an idea selected from a public open call which focused on the space in between urban buildings. When unmanaged spaces between buildings which are administratively private lands become public, they also become a site for communication.

Jin, Siyon added to the space, entertaining and vibrating elements through various interactive media.

Kim, Chanjoong's special door symbolises a new but unregistered address of the abandoned space. Just like train Platform Nine and Three-Quarters in the Harry Potter series, it inspires our imagination.

Moreover, this **moveable, reusable and adaptable Mini Folly**, which stimulates curiosity and encourages public engagement, acts as a space for diverse activities and events.

The implicit attributes of **playing**, namely that of reusing, moving and participating, are translated into different actions to provide **unexpected amusement**.

도심 건물 사이의 틈에 주목했던 시민공모전 당선작 아이디어를 발전시킨 **건축-미디어 콜라보레이션 프로젝트**이다. 관리되지 않은 건물 사이의 틈은 행정상 사유지이지만 이번 폴리를 통해 공공화되고 소통할 수 있는 공간이 된다.

진시영은 다양한 인터랙티브 미디어를 통해 공간의 재미와 활력을 주고 있다. **김찬중의 특별한 문**은 버려진 틈의 새로운, 하지만 **등록되지 않은**un-registered 주소를 상징한다. 이는 **해리포터의 9와 3/4 플랫폼**platform nine and three-quarters과 같은 상상력을 자극한다. 이에 더하여, 이동 가능하고 재사용되며 다양한 활용이 가능한 미니폴리는 호기심을 통해 시민의 참여를 이끌어내 다양한 행위와 이벤트의 공간이 된다. '**놀다**'라는 동사에 내재된 특질attributes–**재사용, 이동성, 참여**–을 다양한 작동으로 풀어내 일상 생활의 의외성, 유희를 제공한다.

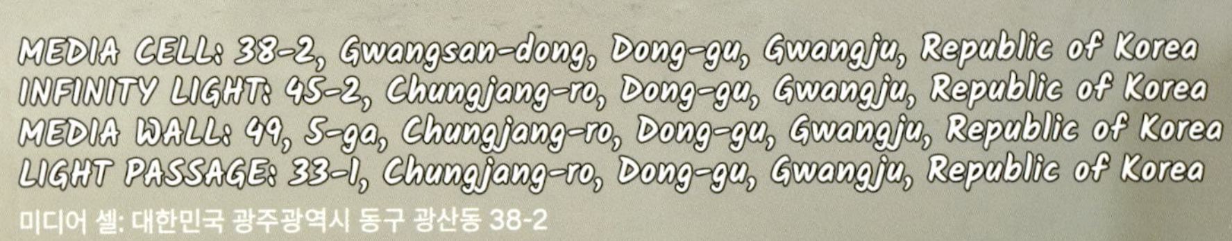

MEDIA CELL: 38-2, Gwangsan-dong, Dong-gu, Gwangju, Republic of Korea
INFINITY LIGHT: 45-2, Chungjang-ro, Dong-gu, Gwangju, Republic of Korea
MEDIA WALL: 49, 5-ga, Chungjang-ro, Dong-gu, Gwangju, Republic of Korea
LIGHT PASSAGE: 33-1, Chungjang-ro, Dong-gu, Gwangju, Republic of Korea
미디어 셀: 대한민국 광주광역시 동구 광산동 38-2
무한의 빛: 대한민국 광주광역시 동구 충장로 45-2
미디어 월: 대한민국 광주광역시 동구 충장로 5가 49
소통의 문: 대한민국 광주광역시 동구 충장로 33-1

Kim, Chanjoong + Jin, Siyon
LIGHT
SAGE
미디어 셀, 무한의 빛, 미디어 월, 소통의 문
김찬중 + 진시영

서울금방

라운헤어
민속촌
1989 민

방범용 CCTV 작동중
Infashion

9692S-9964
전산일
번호   지상변압기
시 228-3 2 246-3
LH   1 Ø 200KVA 2006.02
시공업체 삼원전력

인피니트 엘리먼츠
국형걸 + 신수경

Movable
이동식

광주비엔날레
GWANGJU BIENNALE

Kook, Hyoung-Gul + Syn, Sue Gyeong

Infinite
Elements

광주비엔날레
GWANGJU BIENNALE

SPECTRUM

스펙트럼
라이프 호그펠트 한센

Movable
이동식

Leif Høgfeldt Hansen

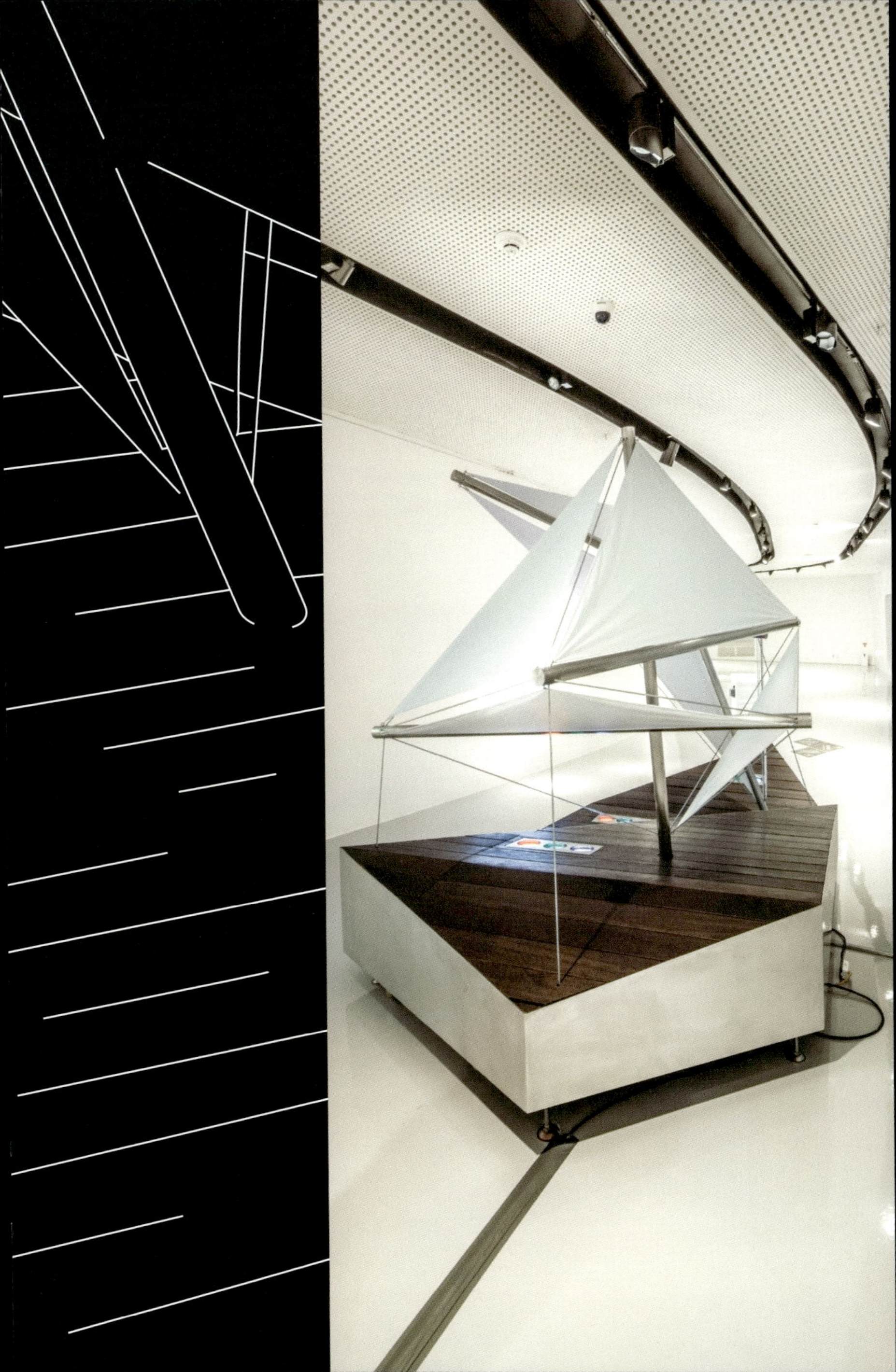

Project Name · 프로젝트 이름	SITE01_MEDIA CELL · 미디어 셀	SITE02_INFINITY LIGHT · 무한의 빛
	SITE03_MEDIA WALL · 미디어 월	SITE04_LIGHT PASSAGE · 소통의 문
Artist & Architect · 작가 & 건축가	Kim, Chanjoong + Jin, Siyon · 김찬중 + 진시영	
Location · 장소	SITE01_MEDIA CELL · 미디어 셀	
	38-2, Gwangsan-dong, Dong-gu, Gwangju, Republic of Korea	
	대한민국 광주광역시 동구 광산동 38-2	
	SITE02_INFINITY LIGHT · 무한의 빛	
	45-2, Chungjang-ro, Dong-gu, Gwangju, Republic of Korea	
	대한민국 광주광역시 동구 충장로 45-2	
	SITE03_MEDIA WALL · 미디어 월	
	49, 5-ga, Chungjang-ro, Dong-gu, Gwangju, Republic of Korea	
	대한민국 광주광역시 동구 충장로 5가 49	
	SITE04_LIGHT PASSAGE · 소통의 문	
	33-1, Chungjang-ro, Dong-gu, Gwangju, Republic of Korea	
	대한민국 광주광역시 동구 충장로 33-1	
Site Area · 부지 면적	SITE01(미디어 셀) + SITE02(무한의 빛) + SITE03(미디어 월)=0.7㎡	
	SITE04(소통의 문)=14.35㎡	
Materialisation · 작품 구현	Paint on Steel Plate and Reinforced Glass, FRP · 철판 위 도장 및 강화유리, FRP	
Design Period · 디자인 기간	6 months · 6개월	
Construction Period · 공사 기간	2 months · 2개월	

Short Description of the Concept	Just as it is read, FunPun Folly is a folly for joy and pleasure. Consisting of booths installed in 4 different sites, each embodies interactive contents with different themes. Occupying abandoned or unexpected spaces, they invite you to encounter a different world through a door. The FRP door not only function as a door but displays an organic design with a typical form that cannot be found in the old city centre. Additionally, the 4 media contents are not only there to be seen but can be manipulated and react to the movements of the visitors, making it a folly that anyone can enjoy and engage with. FunPun Folly will refresh the memories of Chungjang-ro 4-ga and 5-ga, attracting people and thereby contributing to the revitalisation of the old city centre.
컨셉에 대한 간략 설명	뻔뻔폴리는 제목 그대로 즐거움을 선사하는 폴리이다. 총 4개 사이트에 부스 형태로 구성된 폴리는 각각 서로 다른 주제의 인터랙티브 콘텐츠를 담고 있다. 폴리는 도시 안에 버려진 공간 혹은 예상하지 못했던 공간들에 자리 잡고 있으며 각각의 문을 통하여 새로운 차원의 세계로의 접근을 유도한다. 문으로서의 기능뿐만 아니라 유기적인 형태의 디자인을 갖고 있는 FRP 문은 구도심 안에서 볼 수 없는 비정형 형태를 띄고 있다. 또한 바라만 보는 폴리가 아닌 관람객이 직접 조작하거나 관람객의 움직임에 반응하는 4가지의 미디어 콘텐츠들을 제공하여 누구나 참여하고 즐길 수 있는 폴리가 될 것이다. 뻔뻔폴리로 인하여 잊혀져 가는 충장로 4가, 5가에 대한 기억을 되살릴 수 있으며 시민의 발길을 끌어 구도심의 활성화에 기여할 것이다.

Project Name · 프로젝트 이름	Infinite Elements 인피니트 엘리먼츠
Artist & Architect · 작가 & 건축가	Kook, Hyoung-Gul + Syn, Sue Gyeong · 국형걸 + 신수경
Location · 위치	Movable · 이동식
Site Area · 부지 면적	164㎡
Building Area · 빌딩 면적	69.4㎡
Materialisation · 작품 구현	Steel, Rope, LED · 스틸, 로프, LED
Design Technique · 디자인 테크닉	Digital Fabrication + Media Art · 디지털 패브리케이션 + 미디어 아트
Structure · 구조	Steel Structure · 스틸구조
Design Period · 디자인 기간	2016.03~05
Construction Period · 공사 기간	2016.06~08
Short Description of the Concept	Infinite Elements demonstrates a massive being that lives within a time that infinitely repeats the past, present and the future. The steel frame shaped as an infinite loop symbolises time, a physical and environmental infinite element and the LED helix of DNA, a biological infinite element. The art piece as a whole embodies a living creature that continues to evolve in the endless loop.
컨셉에 대한 간략 설명	인피니트 엘리먼즈는 과거, 현재, 미래로 무한반복하는 시간 안의 거대 생명체를 표현한 조형물이다. 무한궤도 형태의 철제 프레임은 물리적·환경적인 무한요소인 시간(Time)을 표현하며, 그 궤도 사이에 연결된 LED줄들은 생물학적·객체적 무한요소인 유전자(DNA)의 이중나선구조 형태로 완성되어 무한히 반복되는 환경 속에서 발전을 거듭하는 생물을 표현한다.

Project name · 프로젝트 이름	SPECTRUM 스펙트럼
Artist & Architect · 작가 & 건축가	Studio CONTEXT by Leif Høgfeldt Hansen · 라이프 호그펠트 한센의 스튜디오 컨텍스트
Project Team · 프로젝트 팀	Andrew Hogan, Anne Vingisar, Florence Mareen, Frederik Kromann Laursen Frederik Langhoff, Huang Qingsong, Karin Hauser, Lena Thomassen, Lisa-Marie Kolbinger, Mia Marker Marold Bøhnke, Miriam Eugenie Unsgaard, Paul Elliott 앤드류 호건, 앤 빙기사르, 플로랜스 마린, 프레드릭 크로만 로센, 프레드릭 랑호프, 후앙 칭송, 카린 하우저, 레나 토마센, 리사 마리 콜빙어, 미아 마커 마롤드 뵌케, 미리암 유지니 운스가르드, 폴 엘리엇
External Supervisors · 외부 감독	Cho, ByoungSoo Architect Associates · 조병수 건축연구소
Assistant · 어시스턴트	Jeong, Yunseok · 정윤석
Location · 위치	Movable · 이동식
Site Area · 장소	Gwangju, Republic of Korea · 대한민국 광주
Materialisation · 작품 구현	Steel with Wood and Fabric Cover - RGB Light Installed 스틸, 목재, 패브릭 커버와 RGB 조명 설치
Building Scale · 건물 규모	Urban Furniture · 도심 가구
Gross Floor Area · 연면적	17㎡
Design Technique · 디자인 기법	Tensegrity · 텐세그리티
Design Period · 디자인 기간	2016.02~03
Construction Period · 공사 기간	2016.04
Short Description of the Concept	SPECTRUM by Studio CONTEXT is a Mini Folly and has found inspiration in the aesthetic of the urban flux of the Asian city, where mobile elements such as stalls and street kitchens activate the life of the street both day and night. SPECTRUM is a flexible and mobile Mini Folly or street furniture, which can easily be moved to different locations in the cityscape according to the situation and assembled in various configurations adopting to the site conditions. It is constructed of a steel tensegrity structure with sails on a wooden base lit up at night by RGB lights. By stepping on the RGB light sources the colours will change and an interactive play of shades and colours occur. SPECTRUM is a small sculptural landmark and a platform for interactive activities in the pulse of the city.
컨셉에 대한 간략 설명	스튜디오 컨텍스트의 스펙트럼은 좌판이나 노점상과 같이 부유하는 요소들이 밤낮으로 거리에 생명을 불어넣는 아시아 도시들의 유동적 미학에서 영감을 받은 미니폴리다. 스펙트럼은 유연한 이동식 폴리 또는 거리의 가구로 상황에 따라 도심 곳곳으로 이동시키거나 장소에 따라 다양한 방식으로 조합할 수 있다. 철골 텐세그리티 구조를 지니며 목재 받침 위의 돛은 RGB 라이트로 밤에 빛을 내도록 제작되었다. RGB 광원에 올라서면 색이 바뀌면서 인터랙티브한 그림자와 색의 향연이 펼쳐진다. 소규모 랜드마크 조각인 스펙트럼은 도시의 맥을 따라 이동하면서 상호작용 활동의 장으로서 기능한다.

Work Description

Kim, Chanjoong + Jin, Siyon

작품설명서
김찬중 + 진시영

Asia Culture Centre~Chungjang-ro 4-ga, 5-ga

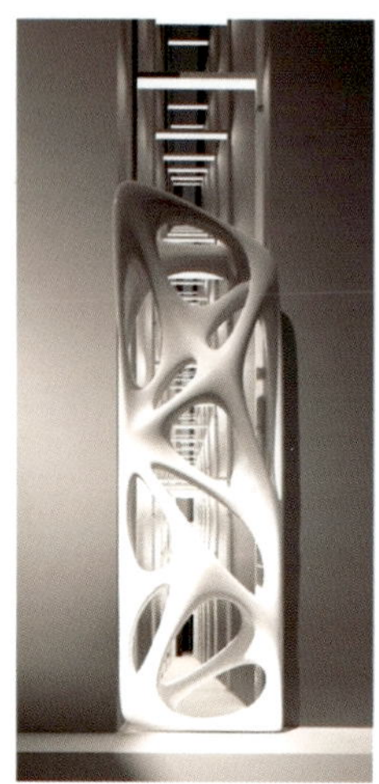

A Rendered Image of
LIGHT PASSAGE, FunPun Folly

Within a limited space, we plan to present a folly which en-
compasses the story of the light of Gwangju. Just like rays
of the world shining through a dark space, objects can only
become recognisable through light. The light of Gwangju
is equally the light of hope and humanity spread throughout
the world which has just pierced through a dark layer of
modern history.

The theme of FunPun Folly is the integration of Gwangju's spirit and the light of humanity,
which is reinterpreted and presented as a fun space. By
representing the spirit of Gwangju through the metaphor of
various light phenomenon, a series of booths will com-
municate with the public through their dynamically interactive
elements, signaling the peaceful yet powerful energy
of human sub-consciousness. That is the light of Gwangju.
The integration of dynamic new media art and existing
buildings takes places at four different sites with identically
shaped doors, but each space offers various events to
different kinds of audiences. As the name FunPun Folly suggests, the project literally creates fun activities and trans-

formations in the heart of a dry and vertical city through the use of familiar interactives.

The five human senses are categorised according to sense receptors. These are touch, hearing, sight, smell, and taste. Residents of Gwangju can interact with FunPun Folly through their five senses.

The booth, which was created by merging the Asia Culture Centre's *Public Room* with Francisco Sanin's Folly, marks its beginning as a tactioception booth, inviting passersby to encounter a unique light experience. Moreover, small booths created in between desolate areas of large buildings on Chungjang-ro 4-ga and 5-ga, which are reminiscent of old times, stimulate one's hearing and sight.

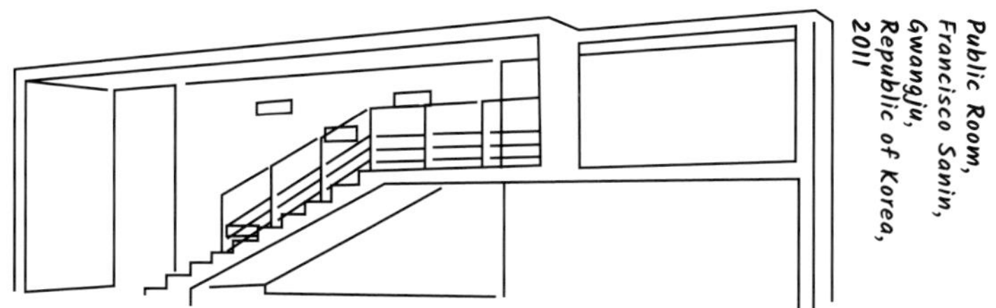

Public Room,
Francisco Sanin,
Gwangju,
Republic of Korea,
2011

After passing through all the booths of light mentioned above, viewers will encounter Line LED Interactive, which projects numerous rays of light in complete darkness, as a final destination. As technology is key to new media art, consistent maintenance is necessary. In order not to create a folly which only works in the beginning, we stayed very focused to achieve perfect installation and sustainability. Located in a straight line along the path lead-ing to Chungjang-ro 5-ga, these follies have been install-ed with a visitor's approachability in mind. After experiencing each booth and leaving the folly, visitors will be able to recall old memories.

Site 1 The folly situated in *Public Room* is the first booth, presenting a video which shows an unknowable space-time continuum when no one is touching,

 Work Description

and immediately stops as soon as someone opens the door. Curious visitors will then touch the screen again, at which time another image of an unknown space will appear.
As a folly which is activated only through touching, the work will appear as a new form of media art to the public.

A Rendered Image of
MEDIA CELL, FunPun Folly

The second folly visited by viewers will be the one located by Chungjang-ro 4-ga. Upon entering the space, an unexpected piece of cloth is placed on a person's body. Almost like a horoscope for the day, this interactive piece also relates to the history of Chungjang-ro as a silk street. By installing a local-specific and environment-specific folly on the declining street of Chungjang-ro, many people are expected to visit here.

A Rendered Image of
MEDIA CELL, FunPun Folly

Two other follies await viewers once they pass through Chungjang-ro 5-ga. Focusing on interactive audio/visual aspects, these follies project a composite drawing created by the movement of each viewer's hands on a large screen. By transferring the movement to an image on a screen, various sounds corresponding to the movement and speed of drawing will be played.
The large screen located outside of the booth will attract

play

passersby by showing this play on light. Through the stimulating wave of lights and sounds created from the interactive drawing, audiences can attempt to escape from the mundane sameness of everyday life.

The last folly in the series is created by densely connecting one side of the building to another with line LEDs almost like a silk thread. Numerous LEDs installed horizontally along the height of the walls will catch people's attention and invite them to enter into the space with its elaborate light work. Upon entering through the door, viewers will first encounter complete darkness, and only at a certain moment will they experience a sudden ray of interactive LED lights moving upwards. These strong rays of light flash on and off like drops of rain, creating a spatial experience of looking into a microscope. Light surpasses our ability to recognise colour, and in turn creates a highly unexpected and mathematical space. Standing inside the space created by the LED lines, one can reflect on the existence of human beings as a species.

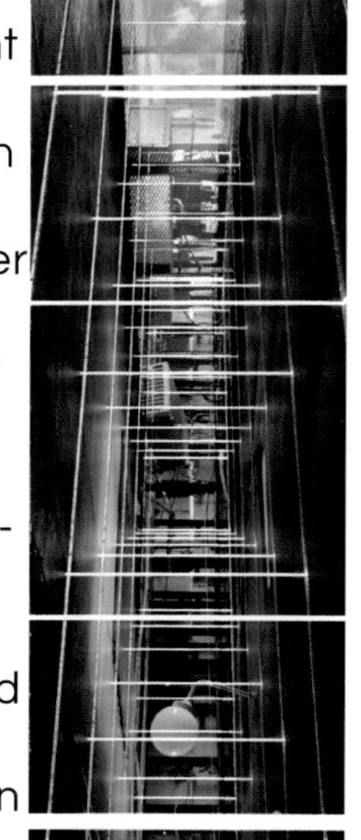

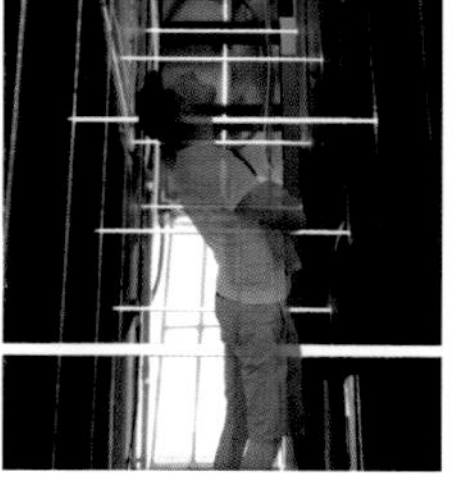

A Rendered Image of
LIGHT PASSAGE, FunPun Folly

 Work Description

작은 공간 속에서 광주의 빛 이야기를 담은 폴리를 선보이려 한다. 빛은 어두움 사이에 새어나간 세계의 줄기처럼, 매개체로 기능한다. 빛이 있어야만 어떠한 대상을 명확히 인지할 수 있다. 광주의 빛은 현대사의 어두운 막을 뚫고 세상에 펼쳐진 희망의 빛이며, 인권의 빛이다.

뻔뻔폴리의 테마는 광주정신과 인간의 빛이 융합되어 새롭게 해석된 유희적인 공간으로 재생한다. 광주정신을 다양한 '빛의 현상'으로 은유하며, 꼴이 같은 부스들은 빛을 통해 관객들에게 대화를 청하려 한다. 인간의 무의식처럼 고요하지만 강한 에너지, 즉 광주의 빛을 역동적인 인터랙티브를 통해 엿볼 수 있는 것이다. 역동적인 뉴 미디어 아트와 건축의 융복합으로 4가지의 장소에 설치된 같은 형태의 문을 통해 각기 다른 관객들의 소통을 이루고 이벤트를 선사하려 한다. 딱딱하고 수직적인 도시 한가운데에서 변화와 재미를 줄 수 있도록 친숙한 인터랙티브는 뻔뻔폴리라는 의미를 그대로 보여준다.

 사람의 신체에는 감각 수용기의 종류로 분류한 오감이 있다. 촉각, 청각, 시각, 후각, 미각. 시민들은 뻔뻔폴리를 만나는 과정에서 이 오감을 최대한 느끼게 된다.

국립아시아문화전당 광주사랑방 폴리와 병합하여 만든 부스는 촉각의 부스로 시작을 알리고, 우연히 길을 걷던 시민들에게 눈길을 사며 빛을 체험하도록 한다. 또한 충장로 4, 5가에 옛날 기억이 남아 있는 건물과 건물 사이의 죽은 공간을 되살리는 부스들은 청각과 시각을 자극한다.

위 모든 빛의 부스를 거치고 나면 마지막 거점인 라인 LED 인터랙티브가 기다리고 있다. 암흑 속 수십의 빛줄기가 찬란하게 관객들을 맞이한다. 광란하는 LED의 움직임 속에 잔잔한 기계음이 들리고 걸어가는 동안 빛줄기가 솟아오른다. 뉴미디어 아트는 테크놀로지를 사용하기 때문에 꾸준한 유지관리가 필요하다. 추후 멈춰버린 폴리가 되지 않도록 완벽한 설치와 지속성까지 고민하였다. 이 폴리는 국립아시아문화전당에서 충장로 5가까지 일직선상에 위치하여 관람객의 입장을 충분히 배려하도록 설치되었다. 관람객이 마지막 공간까지 체험을 마치고 돌아갈 때는 공간 하나하나에서 쌓은 기억의 조각들을 손에 담아 갈 수 있을 것이다.

가장 처음 위치한 광주사랑방 폴리의 사이트1은 시민들의 손이 닿지 않은 상태엔 알 수 없는 시공간에 흡수되는 듯한 영상이 보여지고, 문을 열고 들어오는 동시에 영상은 멈추게 된다. 궁금증이 생긴 시민들이 터치스크린에 손을 대게 되면 또 다시 미지의 공간이 나타난다. 촉각을 느껴야만 작동하는 폴리로, 시민들에게 새로운 미디어 아트로 다가갈 것이다.

 두 번째로 맞이하는 폴리는 충장로 4가에 위치한 부스이다. 부스의 문을 열고 들어가게 되면 예상치도 못한 옷이 방문한 이의 체형에 맞게 입혀진다. 마치 하루의 운세와도 같은 인터랙티브는 실크 거리로 유명한 충장로의 역사를 나타내기도 한다. 쇠퇴한 충장로 거리에 지역과 환경에 맞춤한 폴리를 설치함으로써 시민의 발길이 다시 이어질 것이 예상된다.

그다음 충장로 5가에서는 2개의 폴리가 기다린다. 시청각의 인터랙티브를 중점적으로 이용한 이 폴리들은 시민들의 손짓으로 그린 그림을 벽면 위에 옮겨놓는다. 죽어가는 빈 벽을 대형스크린으로 삼는 아이디어다. 그림이 옮겨지는 동시에 그린 속도나 크기에 따른 소리 역시 들려온다. 빛의 연주를 볼 수 있게 만들어진 대형스크린은 부스 밖의 시민들을 유혹한다. 이처럼 그림을 그릴 때마다 발생하는 멜로디와 일렁이는 빛들은 시각과 청각을 자극하며 시민들로 하여금 도심 속 일탈을 꾀하도록 만든다.

 마지막 폴리는 건물과 건물 사이에 명주실처럼 촘촘히 이어져 있는 라인 LED이다. 수평 상에 위치한 수십 개의 LED가 현란한 몸놀림을 표현하여 지나가는 시민들의 눈길을 사로잡아 문을 열고 들어오도록 구성되었다. 문을 통해 들어온 시민들은 암전 상태에서 길목을 지나가게 되는데, 갑작스럽게 거슬러 올라오는 인터랙티브 LED를 체험하게 된다. 어둠속에 길을 열어주는 빛이 강렬한 빗물처럼 쏟아지며 어릴 적 보았던 만화경 속으로 빨려 들어간 듯한 세계가 펼쳐진다. 빛은 우리가 인식할 수 있는 색의 한계를 넘어 우연적이면서도 수학적인 공간을 만들어낸다. LED가 만들어낸 공간 속에서 관객은 자기 자신이 얼마나 작은 존재인지 성찰할 수 있다.

Work Description

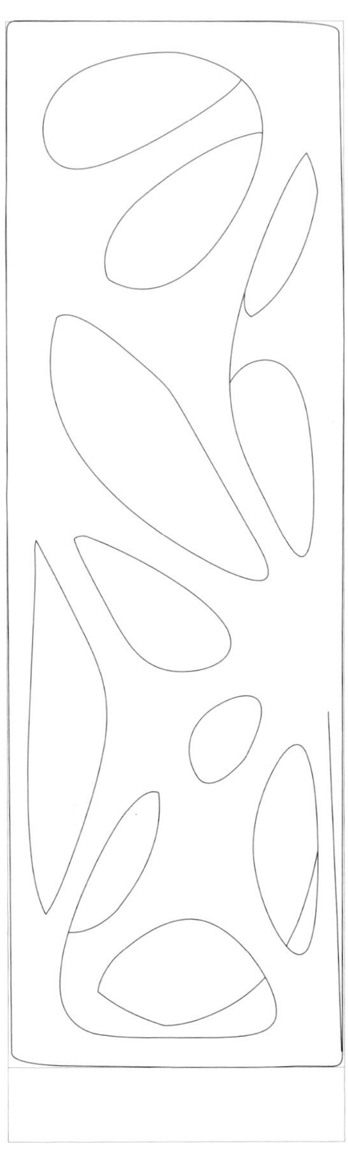

play

Work Description

play

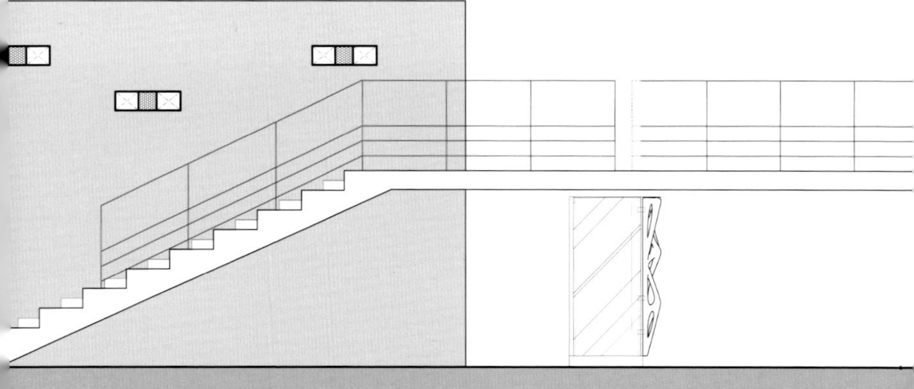

Work Description

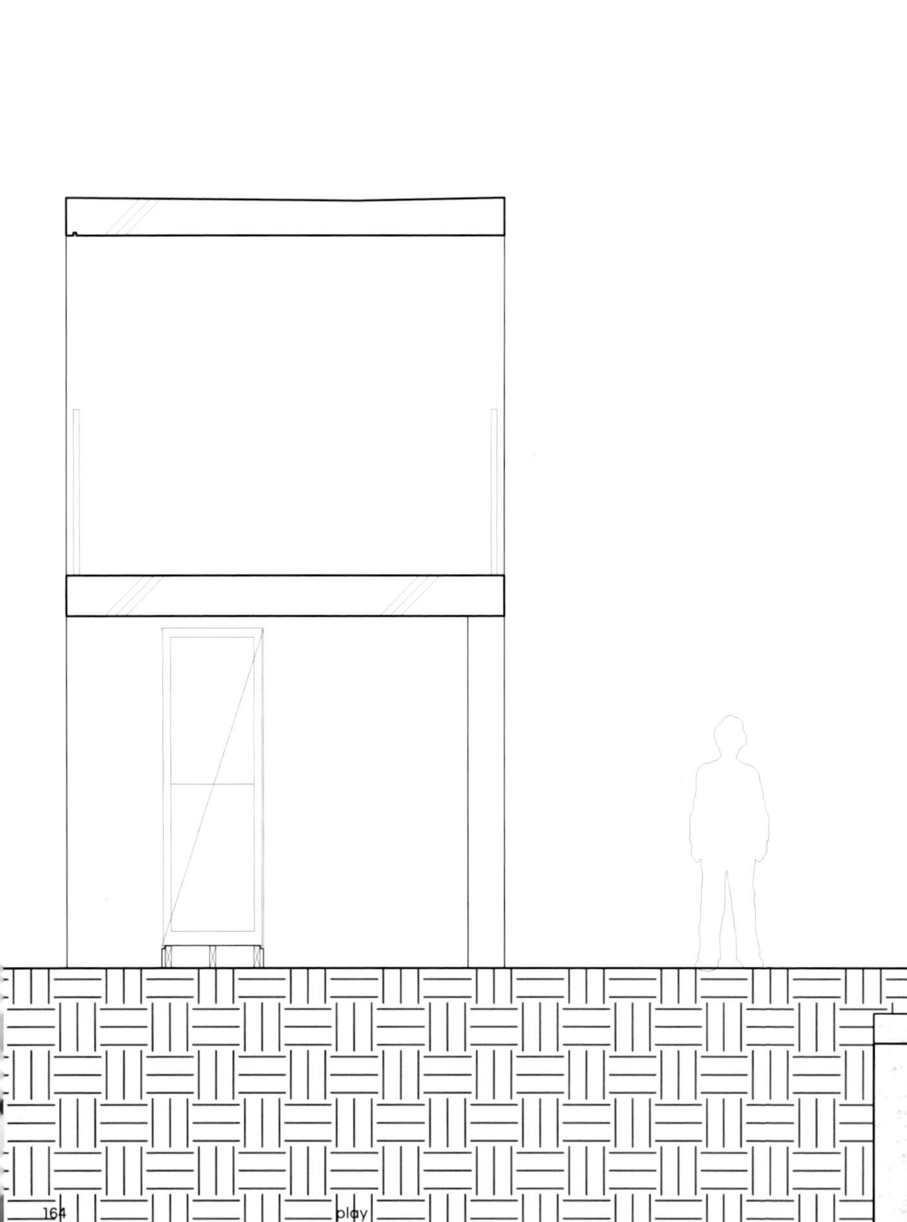

play

Infinite Elements

Kook, Hyoung-Gul + Syn, Sue Gyeong

인피니트 엘리먼츠

국형걸 + 신수경

Infinite Elements under the Universe, above the Earth: Time and DNA

We continuously carry out development initiatives
through constant reproduction within recurring time
— creatures of infinite repetition
living in an infinitely repeating environment

Key words
Time   physically, environmentally infinite elements
DNA   biologically, objectively infinite elements

The work Infinite Elements embodies a giant creature living
in a time that infinitely repeats the past and present all
the way to the future. The metal frame, which is in the form
of an unlimited orbit, symbolises time—the physically
and environmentally infinite element—whereas the LED strips
that connect in between resemble DNA's double helical
structure, the biologically and objectively infinite element that
represents a creature which continuously evolves.
The work that incorporates both an
architectural structure as its hardware and media art as its
software resembles life, and is only completed with the
body (hardware) and soul (software). Infinite Elements was
designed to show videos on the LED strips in an infinite orbit,
embodying a massive streamlined projection that breaks
from conventional forms that are flat and straight.
This Mini Folly suggests a new direc-
tion in combining architecture and media while mingling with
and speaking for the people in the city as one of the creatures residing in it.

About Architecture

1) Concept and Story Gwangju Biennale Square, fully open in all directions, acts like a lobby for visitors to the biennale and serves as a rest area for nearby residents. This project was designed to be a symbolic folly installation for visitors to the biennale, while to local residents it is an element that can liven up a space. In particular, it used as a platform at the top of an empty sewage disposal plant that is no longer being used, naturally inviting people to gather around and relax.

To embrace the surrounding area, it takes a geometric form (the trefoil knot) as its basis, and is not distinguished inside or outside, nor on its front or back. It shows a combination of three Möbius strips where each consecutive frame has triangular surfaces. Thus, wherever one is standing in the square, the form one sees changes accordingly, and the viewer encounters a strange, new and dynamic structure. The strips that connect and fill the inner part form a surface where the inside and outside are mixed, while delivering different stories as a medium at the same time.

Design Concept Drawing
View from
the Gwangju Biennale Hall
(Daytime/Nighttime)

Design Concept Drawing
View from
the Gwangju Biennale Square
(Daytime/Nighttime)

2) Technical Talk

In this project, the geometric form, the trefoil knot, is made into a Möbius strip composed of triangular surfaces. Such an ingenious approach was embodied through architectural design techniques that realise new forms as well as the most advanced digital fabrication technology of our time.

The pipe, which is twisted in a different breadth, forms three arcs that compose a three-dimensional module. Seven different modules are repeated three times to create a giant continuum.

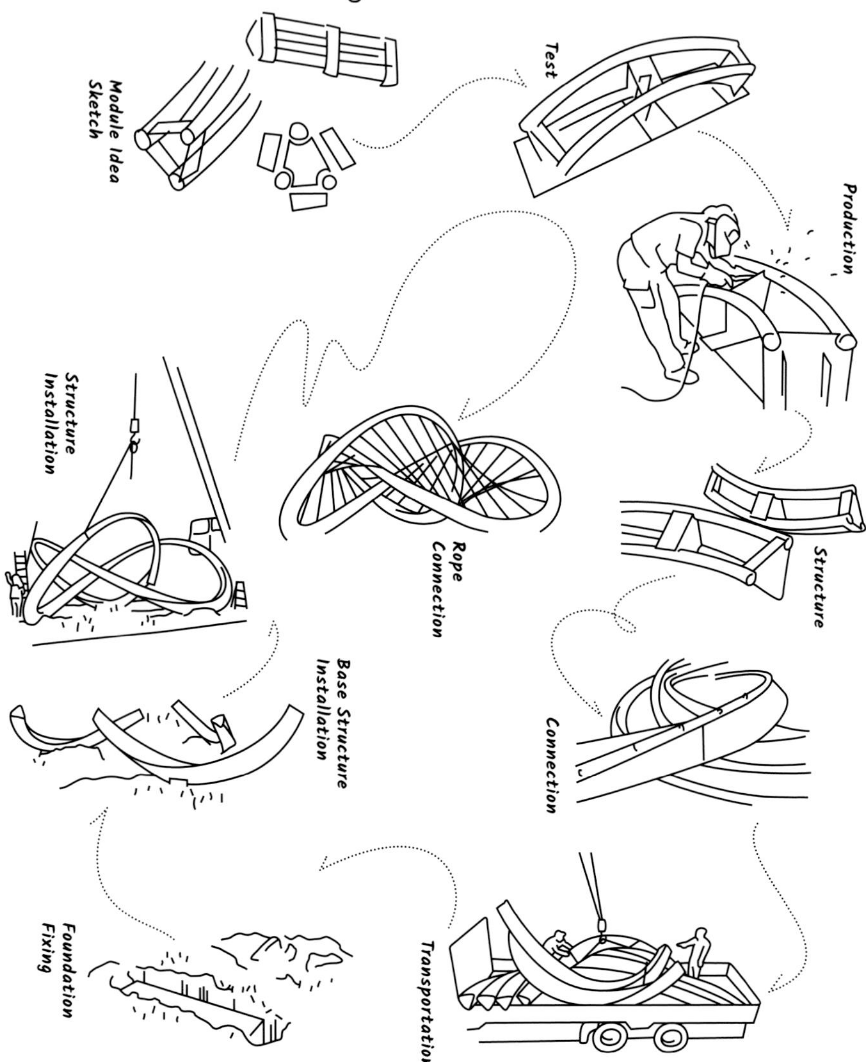

About the Media
1) Concept and Story

The idea was originally about a creature with a body made of architectural materials which form the hardware of the city and the sensitivity of human beings, the software of the city. Thus, it was to demonstrate the city, namely the incorporation of man and the man-made.

L. Concept Sketch 1
 ‹DNA Restructure›
R. Concept Sketch 2
 ‹Soul Installation›

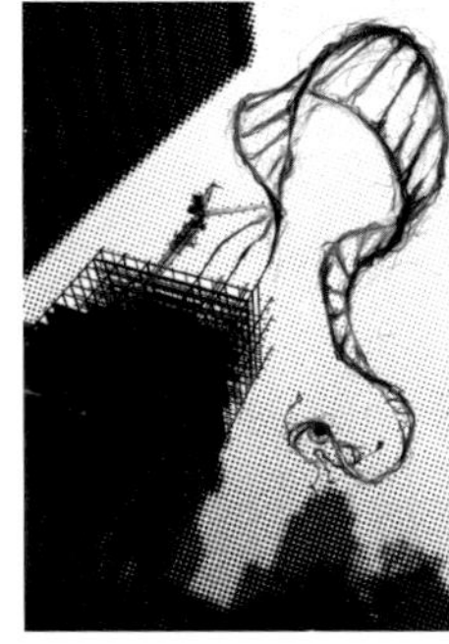

At the earlier stages of designing the media element, we first conceived of the character for the folly *Infinite Elements*, a character born and living in the city that also represents it and has the heart of a human. This step had a reason behind it. When urban architecture is made of architectural materials such as concrete or reinforced steel, it is necessarily categorised merely as an artifact or inanimate object, and deemed to have no soul. However, as an element of an urban space, it engages and grows together with people. Here, an identity that re-sembles people, it is surrounded by develops. In addition, its existence gradually gains meaning, just like living things. As the intention was to make *Infinite Elements* an instal-lation that embodies such a message, it was necessary to design it as a character with life.

   Infinite Elements

This living thing eventually found an opportunity to come into the world. On the opening of the Gwangju Biennale 2016, on September 1, the media show related to *Infinite Elements* was first presented to the public, describing the story about the birth of this creature.

L. Beginning
R. Fertilisation

L. Cell Growth
R. Cell Division

Proliferation

Birth

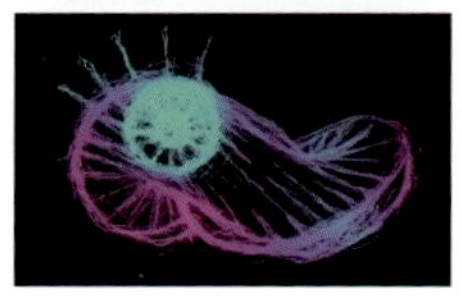

2) Technical Talk
Digital & Analog or Hardware & Software

Infinite Elements is a combination of digital media and a structure constructed with analog methods. The aim was to create a work where media is not merely adopted to make it look better, like a lighting element, for example, but where the structure becomes the body of the media and media becomes its soul. When the hardware and software become one, the sentiments and ideas of all the humanities can be demonstrated through both digital and analog.

Technology & Art We focused on creating a new case where media art technology different from ordinary modes, such as projections or video installations on a flat surface, is adopted as part of an architectural structure.

Conception, Design and Production
Instead of using something with only colours or lights, we conceived of a three-dimensional LED structure where we could project videos. Also, breaking out from the usually employed straight panel billboard LED structures, we realised a projection that was both large and three-dimensional.

If we were to unfold the twisted three-dimensionally curved surface in Infinite Elements, it would look like the following:

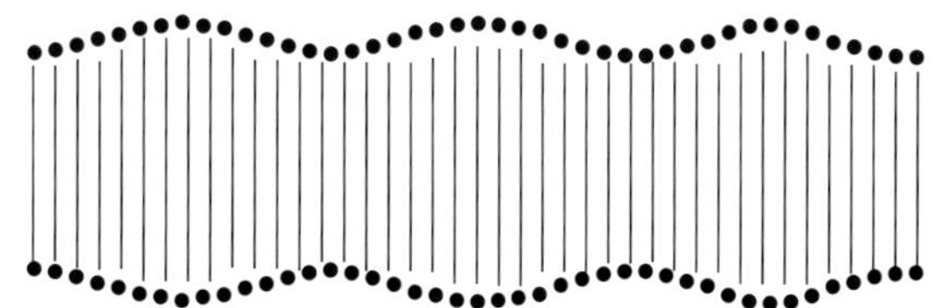

Unfolding a twisted
three-dimensionally curved surface
in Infinite Elements

It is made of RGB LED strips that can receive video signals which became like a huge LED monitor. The following depicts the large monitor screen twisted three-dimensionally along an infinite orbit:

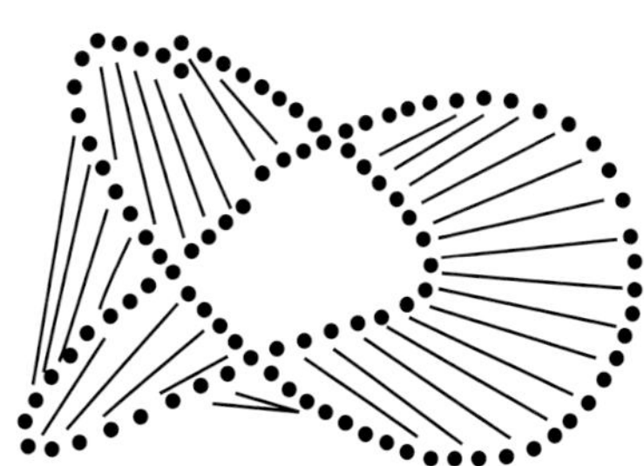

The Large Monitor Screen
twisted Three-dimensionally along
an Infinite orbit

Infinite Elements presents videos three-dimensionally, transforming itself into a giant three-dimensional projection surface. In addition, its system is connected to a computer and all the contents shown are made by programming the play code in real-time. Thus, the contents can be updated and changed anytime. Unlike standard architectural objects, where it is difficult to change the contents once something is constructed, *Infinite Elements* is alive, allowing flexible updates and advancements.

→ 165 <u>인피니트 엘리먼츠</u>

→ 166 우리,
       반복되는 시간 속에 복제를
       반복하며 발전을 거듭하는,
       - 무한반복 환경 속에 사는
       무한반복 생물 -

키워드
시간: 물리적, 환경적인 무한요소
유전자: 생물학적, 객체적인 무한요소

인피니트 엘리먼츠(Infinite Elements)는 과거, 현재, 미래로 무한 반복하는 시간 안의 거대 생명체를 표현한 조형물이다. 무한궤도 형태의 철제 프레임은 물리적·환경적 무한요소인 시간(Time)을 표현하며, 그 궤도 사이에 연결된 LED 줄들은 생물학적·객체적 무한요소인 유전자(DNA)의 이중나선구조 형태로 완성되어 무한반복 환경 속에서 발전을 거듭하는 생물을 표현한다.

하드웨어로서의 건축조형물과 소프트웨어로서의 미디어아트가 결합되어 완성된 이 작품은 몸(하드웨어)에 영혼(소프트웨어)이 깃들어 비로소 탄생하는 하나의 생명체와 같다. 인피니트 엘리먼츠는 무한 고리 형태의 궤도를 따라 둘러쳐진 LED 줄에 영상이 보여지도록 설계되어, 평면과 직선 형태를 탈피한 유선형의 거대 영상체로 구현되었다.

이 미니폴리는 건축물에 미디어가 결합된 새로운 형태의 발전 방향을 제시하며, 도심 속에 살아 있는 하나의 생명체로서 도시민들과 어우러지며 그들을 대변한다.

→ 167 건축
       ### 1) Concept and Story
       사방으로 트여 있는 광주비엔날레광장은 비엔날레 방문객들을 처음으로 맞이하는 비엔날레의 로비와 같은 공간이며, 지역의 주민들에게는 일상 속의 쉼터이다. 본 프로젝트는 방문객들에게는 광주비엔날레를 상징하는 하나의 상징적 폴리 조형물로, 지역 주민들에는 광장에 생생한 활기를 불어넣어주는 요소로 작용하도록 디자인 되었다. 특히, 노후해 사용되지 않는 오수처리장 상부를 작품의 플랫폼으로 활용하여, 작품 주변을 사람들이 자연스럽게 휴식하는 공간으로 활용하고자 하였다.

조형물은 사방으로 펼쳐진 광장 주변을 받아들이기 위해 안과 밖, 앞과 뒤 등 공간이 구분되지 않는 기하학적 형태를 기본 형태로, 모든 연속된 프레임이 삼각형 단면을 갖는 3개의 뫼비우스 띠의 조합으로 구현되었다. 즉, 광장의 모든 곳에서 볼 때마다 시선에 따라 다른 모습이 연출되고, 보는 이에게 항상 낯설고 신선함을 주는 역동적인 구조물이 된 것이다. 구조물의 내부를 연결하는 선들은 면을 이루며, 공간 안팎이 혼재하며 나타나도록 하여 이를 통한 미디어로 다양한 이야기를 전달할 수 있도록 하였다.

세 가닥의 구조적 파이프는 폭을 달리하며 역동적으로 트위스트 되나, 가장 안정적으로 세 저점에서 지면과 맞닿으며 고정적이라기보다는 언덕 위에 잠시 살짝 놓인 느낌을 준다. 파이프 안쪽의 등분점들에 붙어 고리에 연결된 로프는 면을 형성하며 적정한 높이와 폭으로 내·외부의 공간을 연속적으로 잇는다.

→ 167 ### 2) Technical Talk
세잎매듭(Trefoil Knot)이라는 기하학적 형태를 삼각형 단면의 뫼비우스 띠로 독창적으로 구현한 본 프로젝트는, 새로운 형태를 구현해내는 건축 디자인 기술과 동시대의 가장 진보적인 디지털 패브리케이션 기술을 통해 구현되었다.

세 가닥의 아크(Arc)로 이루어진 파이프는 폭을 달리하며 트위스트 되어 하나의 삼차원 모듈을 이룬다. 7개의 서로 다른 모듈은 3번 반복하여 하나의 거대한 연속적 구조물을 만들어낸다.

모든 제작의 과정은 정확한 계산과 계획을 통해 금속을 통한 디지털 제작기술과 공장형 가공으로 만들어졌고, 현장 작업과 설치과정은 최소화되었다. 이를 통해 경제성과 정확성이 확보되고 이동과 재설치가 용이해진다. 이는 하나의 조형적 프로토타입으로써, 다양한 장소와 공간, 다양한 목적에 따라 새롭게 응용이 가능한 구조체이다.

→ 167 **설계 개념도**
       광주비엔날레관에서 본 모습(낮/밤)

       설계 개념도
       광주비엔날레 광장에서 본 모습(낮/밤)

→ 169 미디어 아트
       ### 1) Concept and Story
       도시의 하드웨어인 건축 재료로 된 몸을 갖고, 도시의 소프트웨어인 인간들의 감성을 지닌 생명체를 만들고자 했다. 그리하여 도시, 즉 '인공물과 인간의 합체'를 표현했다.

미디어를 디자인하는 초반에 인피니트 엘리먼츠라는 폴리 작품에 주어질 캐릭터, 즉 '도시 안에서 태어나 도시에 사는, 그리고 도시를 대변하며 사람의 마음을 가진 캐릭터'를 먼저 디자인하게 되었다. 이러한 과정을 거친 이유는 다음과 같다. 도시의 건축물들은 콘크리트나 철근과 같은 건축 재료로 만들어 졌기에 그저 인공물 혹은 무생물로 분류되며 영혼을 갖지 않는다고 여겨진다. 그러나 인공물 또한 도시의 한 요소로 시민들과 함께 어울려 자라고 발전하여 인간을 닮은 아이덴티티를 갖게 되므로 점차 살아 있는 생명체와 마찬가지로 존재의 의의를 품게 된다. 인피니트 엘리먼츠를 그런 의미를 담은 도시의 설치물로 만들고 싶었기에 캐릭터를 가진 생명체답게 디자인하게 되었다.

그렇게 디자인된 생명체가 드디어 탄생할 기회를 얻었다.

2016년 9월 1일, 제11회 광주비엔날레 오프닝에 맞추어 인피니트 엘리먼츠를 처음 시동하여 미디어쇼를 하게 되었고, 그 쇼의 콘텐츠가 바로 이 생명체의 탄생을 그리는 스토리였다.

→ 169   L. 컨셉 스케치 1
      〈DNA 재구성〉
      R. 컨셉 스케치 2
      〈영혼 생성〉

→ 170   **2) Technical Talk**
      - 디지털 & 아날로그 혹은
      하드웨어 & 소프트웨어

인피니트 엘리먼츠는 디지털화된 미디어와 아날로그적 방식으로 시공된 건축물의 결합이다. 건축물을 돋보이게만 하는 조명과 같은 보조적 위치의 미디어를 넘어, 건축설치물이 미디어의 몸이 되고 미디어는 설치물의 영혼이 되는 작품을 목표로 하였다. 하드웨어와 소프트웨어가 완벽하게 하나가 되었을 때 의도했던 인문학적 감성과 철학을 디지털과 아날로그 양쪽 모두의 방식으로 보여줄 수 있었다.

→ 171   **기술 & 예술**

많이 쓰이는 미디어 설치 형식들, 즉 프로젝터로 투사하는 미디어나 평면구현 방식의 영상설치물 또는 단순한 조명을 이용한 형태를 탈피해 또 다른 미디어예술의 기술 형식을 고안하여 건축조형물에 적용한 사례를 만들고자 하였다.

→ 170   L. 시작
      R. 수태

      L. 세포성장
      R. 세포분열

      증식

      탄생

기획, 설계, 프로덕션

단순한 색상과 불빛으로 조명처럼 이용되는 것을 넘어, 영상물을 상영할 수 있는 LED 입체조형물을 기획하였다. 더불어 일반적인 평면과 직선의 패널형 전광판과 같은 LED 영상설치 형식에서 벗어나 유선형의 거대 입체 영상체를 구현하였다.

입체로 꼬여 있는 인피니트 엘리먼츠의 무한궤도 곡면을 풀어서 평면으로 펼쳐 놓으면 아래와 같다.

이것을 모두 영상시그널을 받을 수 있는 RGB LED 줄로 채워 길고 거대한 LED모니터처럼 만들었다.

→ 171   인피니트 엘리먼츠의 무한궤도
      곡면을 펼쳐놓은 형태

      인피니트 엘리먼츠의 무한궤도를
      따라 입체로 꼬아 놓은 모습

이 대형 모니터 화면을 인피니트 엘리먼츠의 무한궤도를 따라 입체로 꼬아 놓은 것이 아래 모습이다.

→ 172   인피니트 엘리먼츠는 영상물을 입체로 영사하여 스스로를 거대 입체영상체로 만든다. 더불어 이 영상체 시스템은 컴퓨터에 연결되어 있어, 현재 인피니트 엘리먼츠에 투사되고 있는 모든 콘텐츠들은 프로그래밍된 코드가 실시간으로 실행되어 보여지는 화면이라 할 수 있다. 따라서 언제든지 콘텐츠를 업데이트 하거나 콘텐츠에 변형을 가할 수 있다. 인피니트 엘리먼츠는 한 번 시공하여 설치되면 콘텐츠를 바꾸기 힘든 일반적인 건축 조형물들과는 달리, 지속적으로 업데이트되어 유연하게 발전하고 살아 있을 수 있는 폴리다.

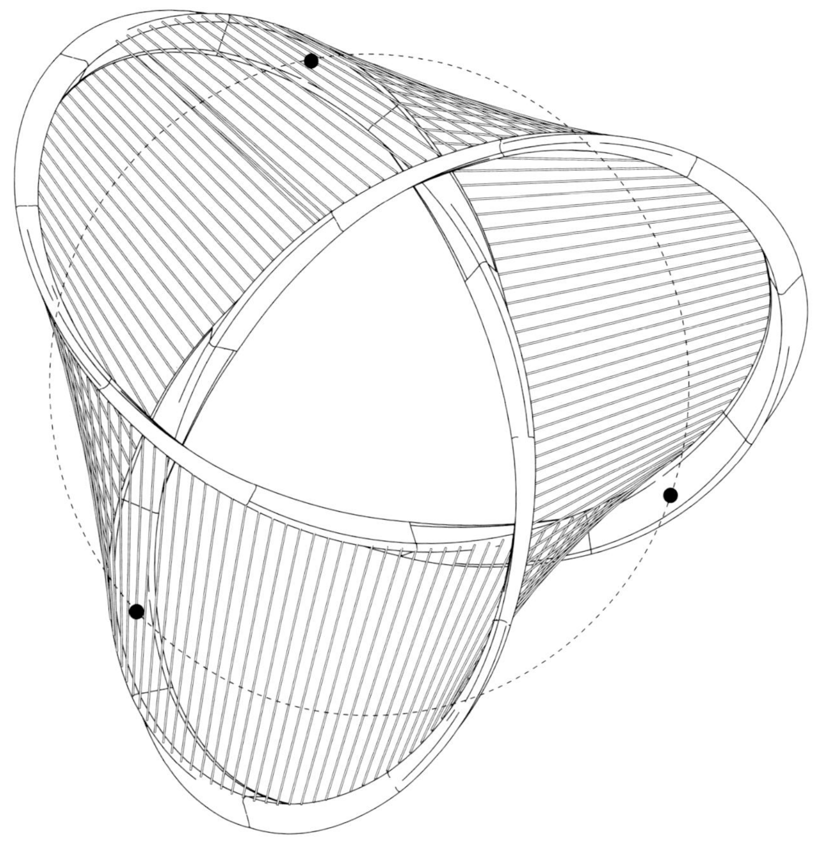

Infinite Elements

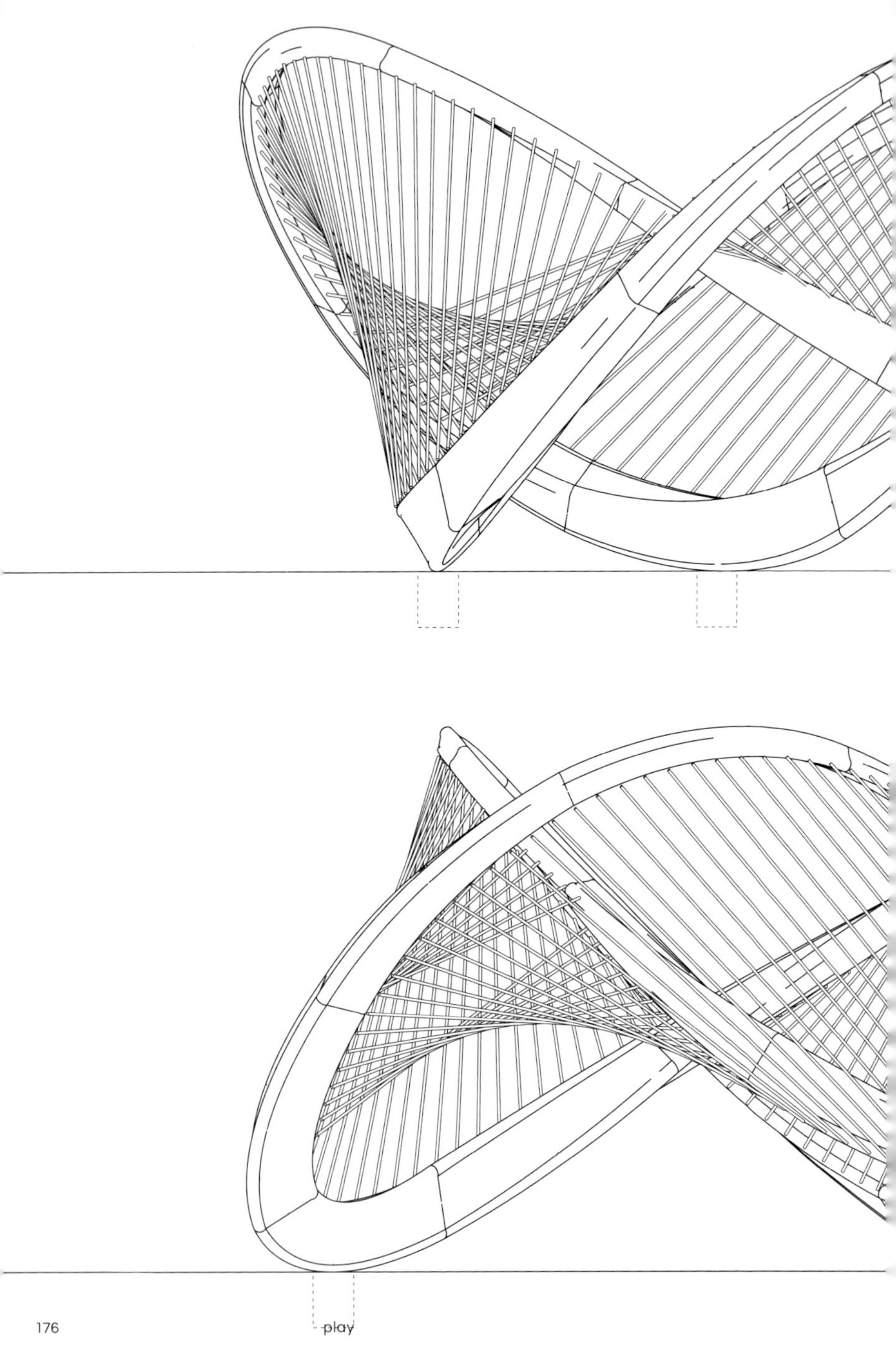
play

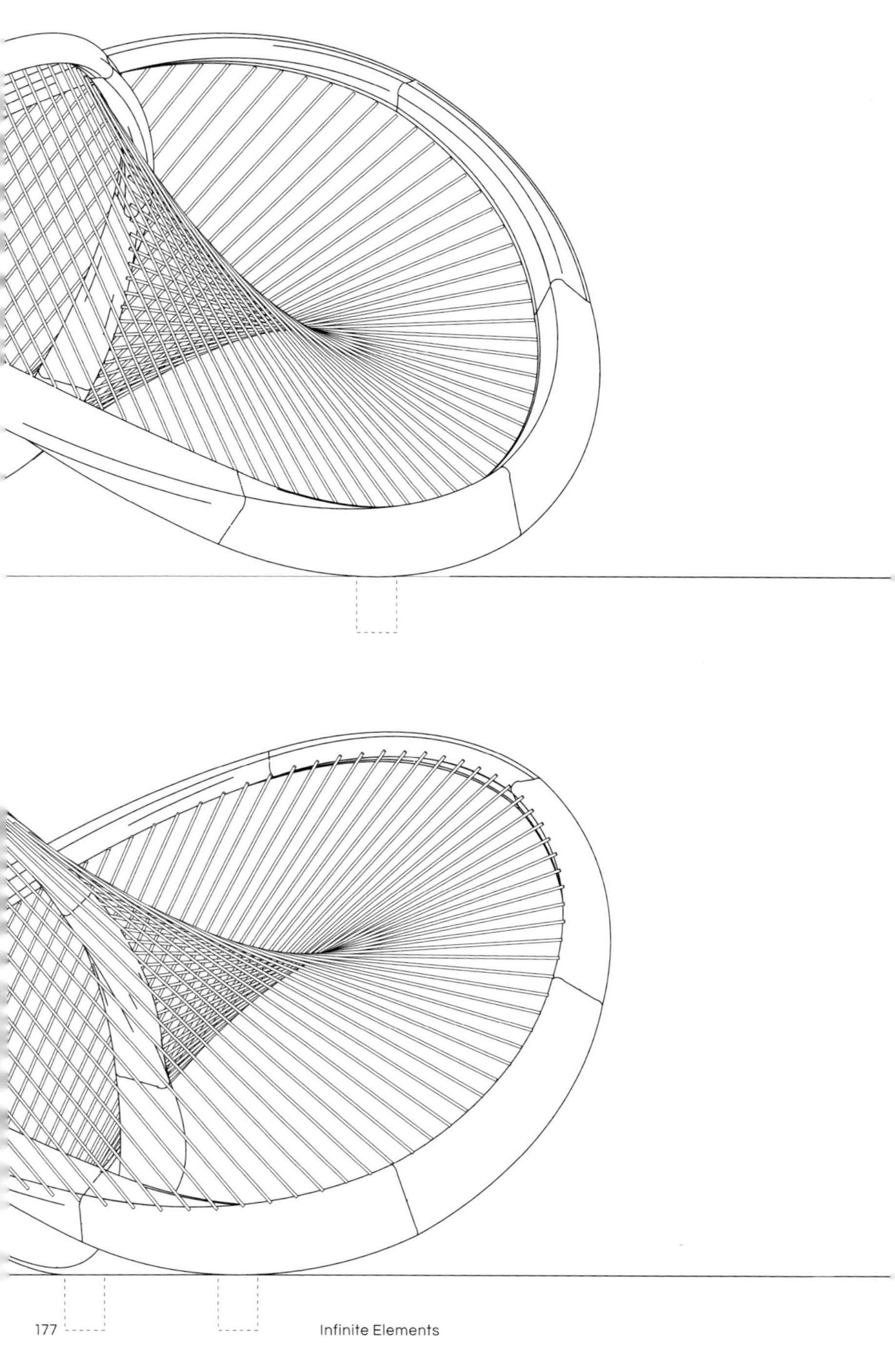

Infinite Elements

Mille
GWAN
play

The Search for the EXTRA Ordinary in Everyday Life

Studio CONTEXT by Leif Høgfeldt Hansen

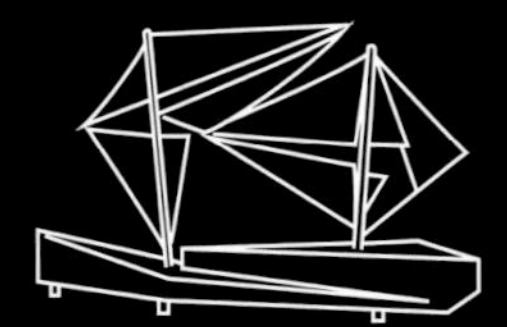

매일의 삶에서 번외의 일상에 대한 조사
라이프 호그펠트 한센의 스튜디오 컨텍스트

The EXTRA ordinary Inspirations for developing architecture can emerge from various sources and situations. Computers have taken over in an endless stream of parametric design, with shapes and spaces that radiate a feeling of "serious" precision where there seems to be an absence of relevant relation to the many aspects of the human body and mind.

On the other hand, it is possible in everyday life to experience situations on the street and in our immediate surroundings created by people—situations that strike us to be of an *EXTRA* ordinary kind—which trigger our memory and imagination to be active, and develop new and unseen solutions for architectural creations.

People who have spent time in India are often struck by the many methods by which Indian people transport things. It is especially fascinating to study the many ways bicycles can be used to carry heavy cargo, from wildly shaped bundles of baskets to carefully stacked bricks in a specifically arranged order. Situations like these both touch us aesthetically and make us laugh, revealing the very essence of life in our eyes.

Another major aesthetic aspect of the urban flux in Asian cities has to do with mobile elements such as stalls and street kitchens, which activate the life of the street both day and night. It often causes irritation for local governments to observe these uncontrolled elements in the street, creating an obsession for politicians to reduce these activities in an effort to clean up these areas and gain full control. On the contrary, for many ordinary people and daily users of the city's streets, these activities are the very essence of being part of the pulse of urban life, where unexpected meetings and incidents often occur.

In our streetscapes today there seems to be an endless amount of inspiration passing by in an active flow. This has great value for architects and is able to give a touch of the unexpected in the design phase, so the *EXTRA* ordinary can be realised.

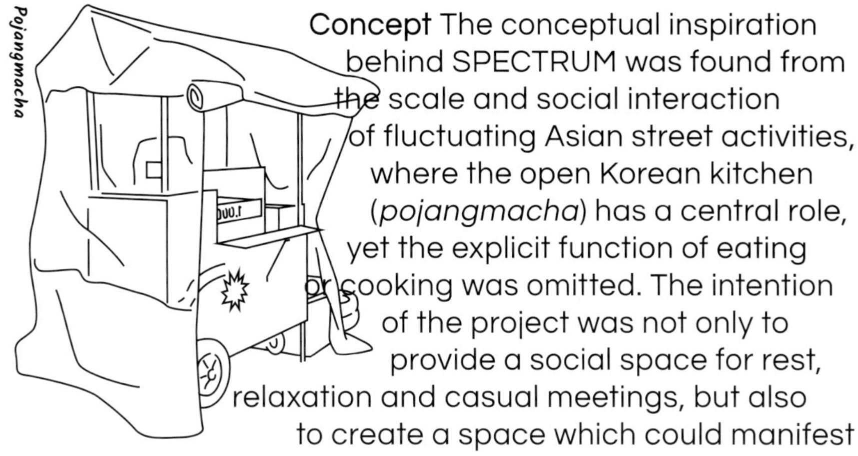

Concept The conceptual inspiration behind SPECTRUM was found from the scale and social interaction of fluctuating Asian street activities, where the open Korean kitchen (*pojangmacha*) has a central role, yet the explicit function of eating or cooking was omitted. The intention of the project was not only to provide a social space for rest, relaxation and casual meetings, but also to create a space which could manifest the same beauty as the street stalls, when people make casual movements with their bodies in front of the stall's night lights. This atmosphere of the night shadows was done by making a wooden base light up at night with RGB lights in three different colours. By stepping on the RGB light sources, the colours would change and an interactive play of shades and colours would occur on stretched fabrics.

The constructed elements of SPEC-TRUM have also found inspiration in the visual sight of the chaotic lines of electric cables mounted on tilted posts, which often can be seen when one's gaze is directed upward towards the sky inside the narrow streets of Asian cities. This inspiration was transformed to the wire and steel construction of SPECTRUM, which formed a tensegrity structure covered with sails on a wooden base.

The intention of SPECTRUM was to make a flexible and mobile Mini Folly, or street furniture like the *pojangmacha*, which could easily be moved to different locations throughout the city depending on the situation, and assembled in various configurations that adapt to the site conditions. In this way, SPECTRUM could become a small sculptural and interactive landmark.

Process Based on inspirations tied to Asian urban life, with chaotic bundles of electric cables on top of angled poles, movable city stalls with casual social gatherings, and the flux of urban night light, some abstract studies were conducted to find functional, formal and structural solutions to be developed later on. Many structural systems were considered, examining both their spatial and tectonic values, but at the end of much consideration, a tensegrity system placed on a raised platform became the focus for further study.

The inventor of this specific structural system was the well-known American architect, Buckminster Fuller, who coined the word "tensegrity" as a combination of the two words *tension and integrity*. Tensegrity works as a system of compressive parts and tensile parts, both of which are configured perfectly so that the opposing forces of each member is balanced into a stabilised structure. The system has been used largely by artists, and thus far nobody has been able to harness tensegrity into a built form which can define space. Furthermore, there is a distinct lack of design tools for tensegrity systems, which is one of the main reasons the system is largely unused. Inspiration was drawn from Buckminster Fuller and Kenneth Snelson both of whom wrote and solved their own complex mathematical equations to understand the dynamic forces in each tensegrity construction that would make their structures stable as well as formally controlled.

From the start, the tensegrity system presented many difficulties in the design process and took several stages of academic investigations and testing, which included digital simulations using Grasshopper, a visual programming language and environment, with a special plug-in for tensegrity structures to test the balance of the design to avoid a physical collapse of the built construction, as well as physical 1:1 model testing. The testing and learning from these processes made it possible to create a designed structure for SPECTRUM.

The base was intentionally designed so that it could be transported with a pallet jack or a forklift. The intention was to increase the longevity of the structures, and to allow, with relative ease, the transportation and final composition adjustments.

The assignment of Studio CONTEXT consisted of integrating the defined design approach, which could not just be a sculpture but also allow the public to interact with it, within a specific site in Gwangju, South Korea. An analysis stage of regional building processes and a field study on the site of a local community also took place. On the basis of these site experiences and the knowledge of the Korean *pojangmacha*, the program began to change into the design of a smaller project, with a focus on a transportable place-making object arrangement that could be located in different sites, immediately creating or defining new spaces.

The project was entitled SPECTRUM, and featured an interactive light display inspired by the flux of the urban night lights. From the surface of the platform, spotlights were directed so as to shine red-, green- and blue-led light onto stretched fabric sections across the tensegrity structure. As people interacted with the space, covering or uncovering the light sources, new colours and shadows would be created.

The base would be placed in a way which could be reconfigurable, making it adaptable to different sites and creating a number of unique formations. The base was intentionally designed so that it could be transported with a pallet jack or a forklift. The intention was to increase the longevity of the structures, and to allow, with relative ease, the transportation and final composition adjustments. The wooden decking was designed to be fitted in sections so that the base interior becomes accessible and alterations can be made to the tension wires and concrete blocks. Even sandbags can be added to form a heavier foundation. The final stage in composing the folly was the installation of the tailored fabric panels. The connections are designed for easy fitment and removal for the purposes of cleaning and maintaining the fabric.

Move One of the main ideas of SPECTRUM is to celebrate movement and the flux and actions of everyday life. By designing the folly as two parts, with three main ways of assembly, it is possible to move the objects around on a forklift across a city and have them adapted to different placements according to the situation. As such, the construction could be decentralised and form a series of small islands of form and light which can then connect a line of activities in a specific area of a city. At the same time, it can be assembled in a central formation in three different ways, depending on the function it has to serve, and placed as a focal point to act as a local stage and activity space for people.
The structure accommodates activities focusing on the movement of the body in a social context, be it sitting, standing, or laying down. It can also be

used as a setting for musical performances, speeches, and children's plays, or to create a "light play" by moving the body in front of the RGB light.

Play SPECTRUM is primarily an interactive creation which can be used for playing by children and adults. It is an abstract setting with a combination of sculpted platforms and angled steel poles projecting up with stretched fabric in between. This gives children some imaginative ideas of being on board a travelling vessel, like a ship or spaceship, where activities like playing catch, swinging on wires, or jumping from one surface to another can take place.

Children Playing at SPECTRUM

At night, this is all transformed into a play of forms and light by the two groups of RGB lights placed inside the wooden platforms, with RGB coloured light beams directed up towards the stretched-out fabric above. When the red/green/blue (RGB) light is mixed, it performs as white light. However, when one of the colours is stopped by an object, the remaining mix of coloured light will act as one colour. By stepping on the RGB light, or moving your body in front of the stretched-out fabric, a play of moving colours occurs and is a source of amusement for people.

RGB Light at Night

See SPECTRUM will function as a small visual landmark in the city for special social occasions. It will serve as a marker on the place it stands, and give it character during the period it is there. Its visual outlook inspired from

The Search for the EXTRA Ordinary in Everyday Life

electric cables on angled poles, movable city stalls, and
the flux of the urban night light, it will encourage spectators
to appreciate the extra ordinary visual beauty in everyday life.
Moreover, the angled composition
of the tensegrity construction imitates the dizziness often
experienced as a psychological phenomenon caused by
speed and volatility, which is part of people's contemporary
urban experience. The creation of a visual light play
across the creation by body movements in front of the RGB
lights makes a connection between the eye, as an observer,
and the body, as a participant. This makes SPECTRUM
a small sculptural landmark and a platform for interactive
activities in the pulse of the city.

→ 180　**번외의 일상**

성장하는 건축가에게 영감이란 다양한 자료와 상황에서 얻어지는 존재다. 컴퓨터는 '매우' 정확한 형태와 공간의 파라메트릭 디자인을 끊임없이 생산해낸다. 사실상 인간의 몸과 정신 등 여러 측면의 적절한 관계를 따져봤을 때, 인간에게는 이것이 없다고 볼 수 있다.

다른 한편으로 우리가 타인에게 받는 즉각적인 반응이나 거리에서 겪는 상황 등 일상의 경험은 우리에게 번외의 일상을 갑작스럽게 떠오르게 한다. 또한 이런 경험들은 우리의 기억이나 상상력을 활성화시키며 건축적 창의력을 위해 보이지 않는 해결책을 내놓기도 한다.

인도에서 머물렀던 경험이 있는 사람들은 인도인들이 물질을 변형시키는 수많은 방법을 종종 떠올릴 수 있을 것이다. 특히 자전거를 변형시키는 수많은 방법에 대한 연구가 매우 흥미로웠는데, 넓은 모양의 바구니 묶음에서부터 신중하게 쌓아올린 질서정연한 벽돌에 이르기까지 변형된 자전거는 무거운 짐을 나르는데 이용되었다. 동시에 이 같은 상황들은 우리의 미학적 감각과 기분을 건드리며, 삶의 궁극적 본질을 시각적으로 드러내기도 한다.

아시아 도시의 끊임없는 변화에 대한 또 다른 심미적 관점을 꼽아보자면 밤낮을 가리지 않고 거리를 활기차게 만들어주는 가판대나 노점식당 같은 것들이다. 이렇게 거리에서 허가 없이 운영되는 상점은 지방정부에게 종종 성가신 감시 의무를 유발하기도 하며, 정치인들은 깨끗한 거리풍경을 위해 노점들을 모조리 정리해야한다는 강박에 시달리기도 한다.

반면 서민들이나 도시의 거리를 매일 오가는 사람들에게 노점은 예상치 못한 만남이나 우연한 일을 만드는 등 도시생활의 활력으로 매우 중요한 기능을 한다.

오늘날 거리의 풍경에서 발견되는 디자인적 요소 중 '기대치 못한' 감동을 주며 건축가들이 가치 있다고 믿는 활동들은 끝없는 영감을 불러 일으킨다. 번외의 일상은 이런 이유로 탄생한다.

→ 181　**콘셉트**

스펙트럼의 개념적인 영감은 급변하는 아시아 거리활동의 규모와 사회적 상호작용에서 찾을 수 있다. 특히 한국의 오픈형 주방 혹은 '포장마차'라 불리는 것은 중심적인 역할을 한다. 그러나 본 스펙트럼에서 먹거나 요리를 하는 등 본래의 주요한 기능은 생략된다.

이 프로젝트의 의도는 사람들에게 쉬고, 긴장을 풀며, 캐주얼한 미팅 등을 진행할 수 있는 공간을 제공하는 것이다. 나아가 밤을 밝혀주는 가판대의 불빛 앞에서 사람들은 격식 없이 행동하게 되며, 가판은 이런 아름다움을 표현할 수 있는 공간이기도 하다. 특히 밤 거미의 분위기는 삼원색의 불빛으로 꾸며진 나무바닥이 완성시켜준다. 삼원색이 단계적으로 변화하면서 음영과 컬러가 서로 스치며 내뿜어지고, 좍 펼쳐진건물의 구조 안에서 그 빛을 발하게 된다.

스펙트럼의 고무적인 요소는 아시아 도시의 좁은 골목길에서 하늘을 바라보았을 때 보이는 기울어진 기둥과 뒤엉켜 있는 전선줄 등 시각적 요소에서 영감을 찾았다는 데 있다. 이러한 영감은 나무바닥 위에 돛으로 감싸인 텐세그리티 구조물 형태로 나타나게 되는데, 이는 곧 스펙트럼의 선과 철 구조물 형태로의 변형을 의미한다.

스펙트럼의 의도는 '포장마차'와 같은 거리의 가구나 유연하고 이동 가능한 미니폴리를 만들어내는 것에 있었다. 이런 특징은 각 장소의 조건에 맞는 다양한 형태로 배치가 가능하고, 상황에 따라 도시 안에서 이동하는 것을 쉽게 만든다. 즉, 스펙트럼이 작은 조각이면서도 상호작용이 가능한 랜드마크로서 기능하도록 하는 것이다.

→ 182　**과정**

기울어진 기둥에 뒤엉킨 전선줄, 격식 없이 만날 수 있는 거리의 이동 가판대, 도시의 화려한 밤 불빛 등 아시아 도시의 삶에서 얻은 영감을 기초로 하여, 몇몇 추상적인 연구에서 그 기능적이고 공식적이며 구조적인 해법을 개발하려 했다. 많은 구조적 시스템들은 공간과 구조상의 가치를 검토하여 고려되는데, 특히 그 끝에는 높은 플랫폼에 위치한 텐세그리티 구조가 상당히 유의미하게 여겨졌기에 추가적인 연구가 필요했다.

이 건축시스템의 개발자는 유명한 미국의 건축가인 벅민스터 풀러인데, 그는 텐션(긴장상태 tension)과 인테그리티(완전한 상태 integrity)라는 두 단어를 조합하여 텐세그리티(tensegrity) 라는 신조어를 탄생시킨 사람이기도 하다.

텐세그리티는 압축적인 파트와 인장의 파트가 완벽하게 구성된 시스템이다. 그럼으로써 각 요소들의 반작용은 안정적 구조를 '균형 잡히게' 만든다. 이 시스템은 주로 아티스트들이 사용하며, 따라서 그 누구도 공간을 규정하기 위한 건축적 형태에서 텐세그리티의 연결을 사용하기란 쉽지 않다. 사실상 이 시스템이 널리 사용되지 못하는 주된 이유 중 하나는 디자인 툴이 부족하다는 데 있다. 벅민스터 풀러와 케네스 스넬슨은 각각의 텐세그리티 건축의 구조 조절뿐 아니라 안정을 위해 동력학 등 복잡한 수학적 등식을 풀어냈는데, 이 과정에서 탄생한 텐세그리티 시스템은 앞서 언급한 이유 탓에 널리 쓰이지 못한다.

텐세그리티 시스템의 시작부터 디자인 과정까지 많은 어려움이 있었으며 조사구와 물리학적인 1:1 모델 테스트 등 몇몇 단계가 필요했다. 이 과정에서 시행한 테스트와 연구가 스펙트럼과 같은 구조물의 탄생을 가능하게 했다.

스튜디오 컨텍스트의 임무는 한국의 광주라는 특정한 지역에서 단순한 조각물을 넘은, 대중과 소통할 수 있는 명확한 디자인적 접근을 구현하는 것이었다. 지역의 건축 프로세스에 대한 분석과 지역 커뮤니티에 대한 배경적 연구도 동반되었다. 이 장소들의 경험적 배경과 한국의 '포장마차'에 대한 지식기반을 바탕으로 한 프로그램은 보다 작은 프로젝트를 제작하기 시작했다.

그 프로젝트는 각기 다른 장소들에서 즉각적으로 창조되거나 새로운 공간에 대한 정의가 가능한 곳에 위치하며, 변형 가능한 오브제를 배치하여 특정 장소에서 구현될 수 있도록 하는 데 집중되었다.

스펙트럼이라는 제목의 이 프로젝트는, 도시의 밤을 밝히는 불빛의 흐름으로서 인터랙티브 라이트 디스플레이를 시연한다. 플랫폼 스포트라이트의 표면에서부터 텐세그리티 구조로 가로지르는 건물의 기본 구조에 이르기까지 빨강, 초록, 파랑의 LED조명이 빛난다. 사람들은 이 공간 안에서 서로 소통하며, 새로운 색상과 그림자로 덮인, 혹은 덮이지 않은 빛의 향연을 창조해내게 된다.

이 프로젝트의 기초는 변동이 가능하며, 여러 독특한 포메이션을 탄생시키기 위한 방법으로 고안되었으며, 각기 다른 장소들에 알맞게 설치되도록 설계되었다. 기본적으로 디자인은 핸드잭이나 포트를 가지고도 변형 가능하도록 제작되었다. 이런 디자인은 구조물의 오랜 지속성을 위한 것이며 변형을 상대적으로 용이하게 할 뿐만 아니라, 나아가 최종적인 구성의 조정 역시 허용하는 것이다.

나무로 만들어진 바닥은 각 부분들에 부합하도록 디자인되었는데, 이로써 기본적인 인테리어가 잘 어울리게 되었다. 개조나 변형은 건축물의 선에 긴장을 불어넣어주기 위한 것이며, 콘크리트 블록이나 샌드백은 보다 중량감 있는 지반을 만들기 위해 추가되었다.

폴리를 구성하기 위한 마지막 단계는 잘 짜맞춰진 패브릭 패널의 설치이다. 이음새는 패브릭의 세탁 및 유지를 위해 쉽게 탈부착할 수 있도록 제작되었다.

→ 184 이동

스펙트럼의 주요한 정신 중 하나는 활동을 장려하는 것, 그리고 일상생활에서 변화와 액션을 취하는 것이다. 3가지 주요한 방식을 조합해 두 파트의 폴리를 제작함으로써 도시 안에서 포크리프트로 오브제를 이동하는 것, 상황에 따라 다른 장소에 오브제들을 설치하는 것 등이 가능해졌다. 이러한 방식으로 구조물이 분산될 수 있으며, 도시의 특정 구역에서 일어나는 활동들을 연결할 때 그 형태와 빛은 마치 작은 섬들이 모여 있는 것과 같이 보일 것이다. 사람들을 위한 지역 활동 공간에서 이 점이 작용한다는 것에 초점을 맞추어 보았을 때 그 기능에 따라 3가지 다른 방식으로 중심 포메이션을 이룰 수도 있다. 이 구조물은 앉거나, 서거나, 눕거나, 음악 공연을 세팅하거나, 연설을 하거나, 아이들과 놀이를 하거나, 혹은 삼원색의 불빛 앞에서 몸을 움직여 빛 놀이를 하는 등, 사회적 컨텍스트 안에서 몸의 움직임에 집중하는 활동을 가능케 한다.

→ 184 빨강, 초록, 파랑의 LED조명

→ 185 활동

스펙트럼에서는 아이와 어른 모두 놀이를 할 수 있으며 그 주된 기능은 상호작용이 가능한 구조물이라는 데 있다.

이 추상적인 설정은 조각된 플랫폼들과 펼쳐진 패브릭 사이로 쏘아올려진 비스듬한 철제기둥의 조합에서 온다. 이러한 설정은 아이들에게 마치 배나 우주선과 같은 여행용 선박에 탑승하고 있는 듯한 상상력을 불러일으키며, 잡기놀이, 그네타기, 혹은 다른 곳으로 점프하기 같은 활동들을 할 수 있다.

야간에는 이 구조물이 놀이 공간뿐 아니라 삼원색의 두 그룹으로 나뉜 불빛의 공간으로 변한다. 이 불빛은 원목 플랫폼 안에서 위쪽으로 펼쳐진 패브릭을 향해 직접적으로 쏘아올려진 삼원색의 라이트빔이다. 빨강/초록/파랑의 빛이 섞였을 때 그 조합은 흰 빛으로 보인다. 그러나 한 가지 색이라도 물체에 의해 막히는 경우엔 나머지 섞인 색상들이 또 다른 색상으로 나타나게 된다. 삼원색 위에서 걸어보거나, 혹은 변화하는 색상들이 투영된 패브릭 앞에서 몸을 움직이는 행동 등은 사람들에게 흥미로울 것이다.

스펙트럼은 특별한 사회적 기능을 위한 작은 시각적 랜드마크가 될 수 있다. 또한 어떤 장소를 표시하기도 하며, 스펙트럼이 그곳에 설치된 동안에는 특징적인 의미를 지니기도 한다. 기울어진 기둥의 전선들, 도시의 움직이는 가판대들, 그리고 밤을 밝히는 불빛의 화려함 등으로부터 영향을 받은 관점이 보는 이들로 하여금 시각적 아름다움을 누리는 번외의 일상을 선물한다.

텐세그리티 구조물의 기울어진 구성은 현대 도시의 경험 중 일부인 속도와 변동으로 인하여 야기되는 정신적 현상, 즉 아찔함을 모방한다. 구조물을 가로지르는 삼원색 앞에서 몸을 움직이며 만들어내는 빛의 향연은 관찰자로서의 눈, 그리고 참여자로서의 몸 사이에서 연결고리를 만들어낸다. 이 2가지 요소가 스펙트럼이라는 작은 조각 랜드마크, 그리고 도시의 활기 속에 상호활동을 하는 플랫폼을 만들어낸다.

→ 185 스펙트럼에서 놀고 있는 아이들

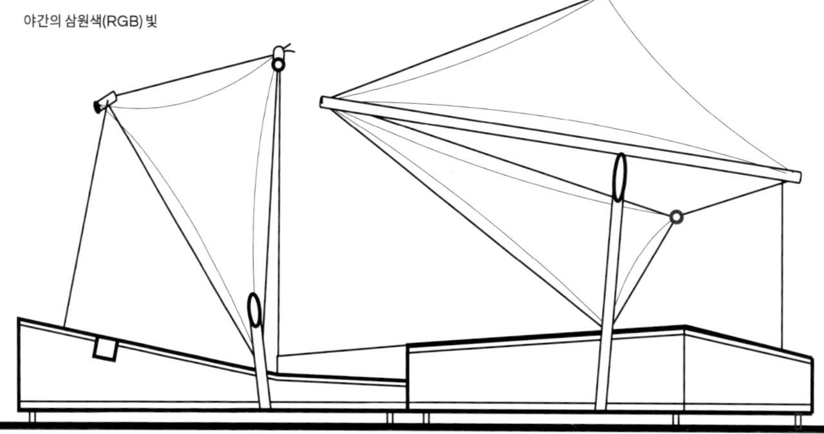

The Search for the EXTRA Ordinary in Everyday Life

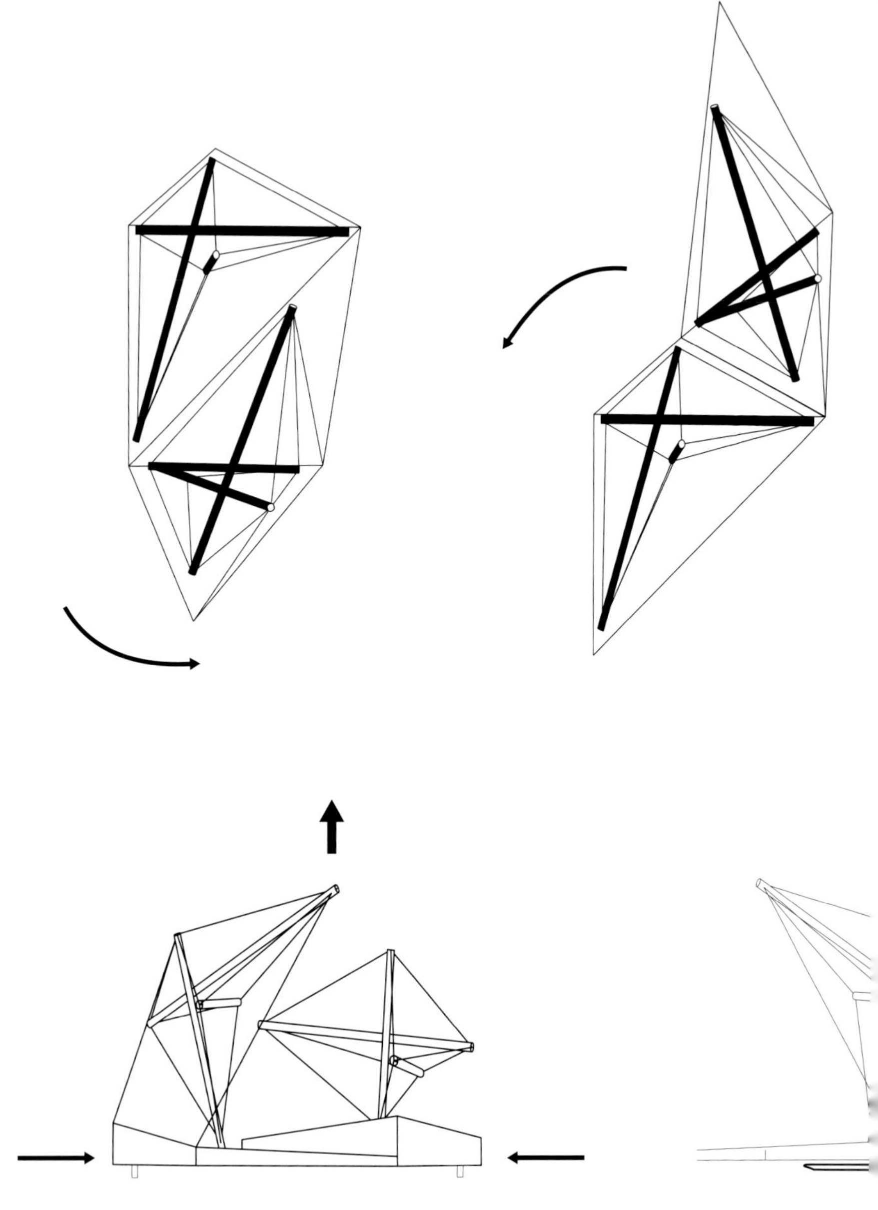

play

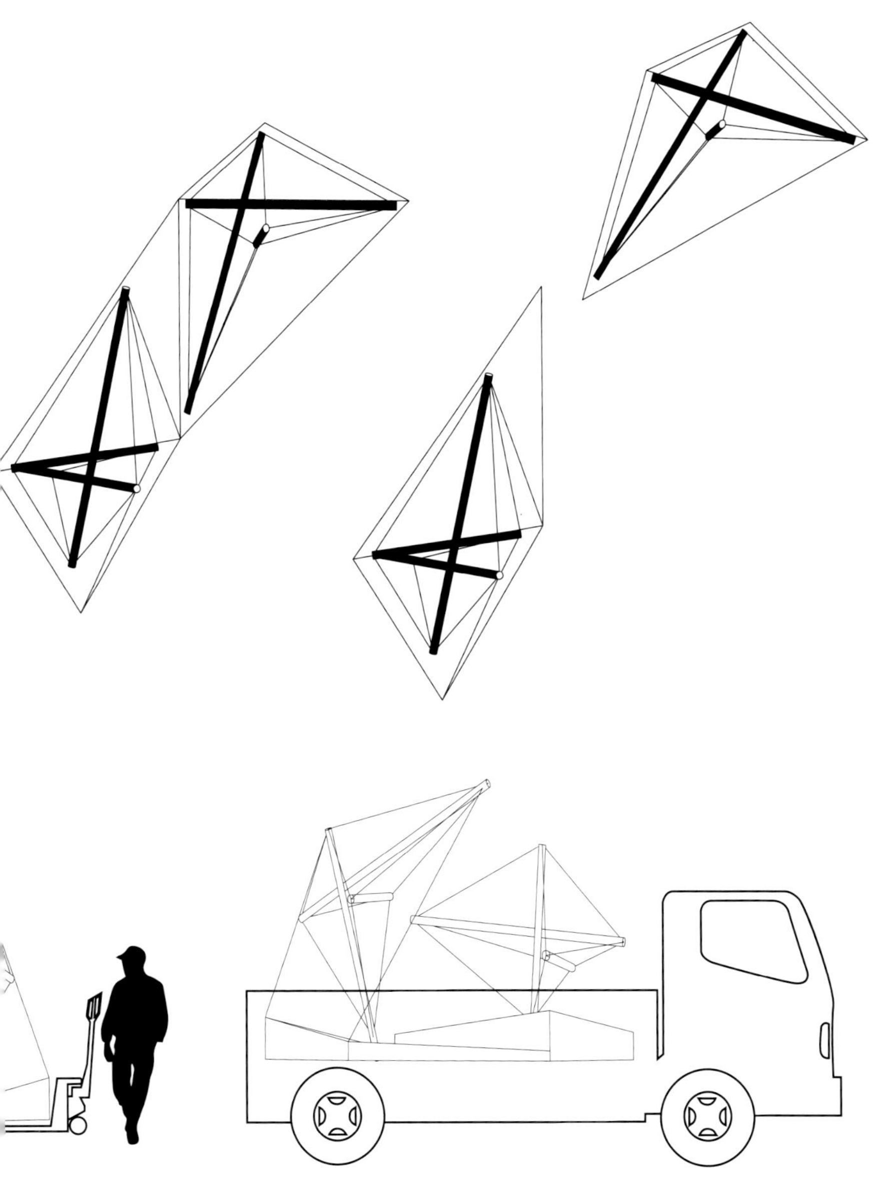

The Search for the EXTRA Ordinary in Everyday Life

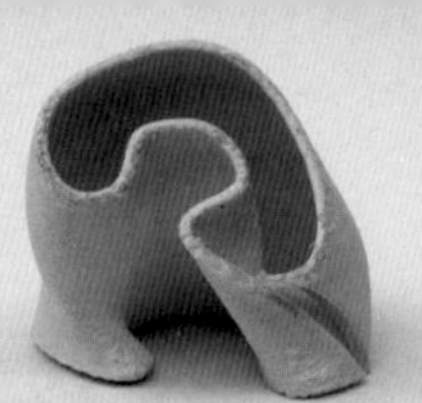

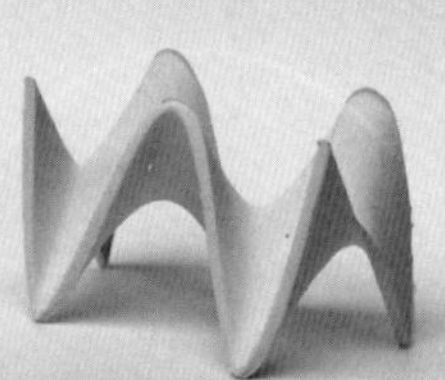

play

eat

Gwangju is a city in the southern part of Korea which is famous for its **food**. **Chang, Jinwoo** is a young F&B entrepreneur who created the brand **Chang, Jinwoo Street** follow-ing his success with a small restaurant on Gyeongridan-gil Road. Notably, Chang is running a platform to sublate real estate speculation, criticise the side effects of the injection of existing capital, such as gentrification or leasing and franchising, and nurture young start-ups.

Through this Folly, Chang **helped** carry out the selection and education of those **preparing to start their own businesses based in Gwangju,** which culminated in Café **Congzib** and a restaurant called **Chungmijang.**

Operative action is when **eating** becomes a spatial content that socio-culturally liquefies real estate as well as an imperative operative element for **urban regeneration.**

광주는 음식으로
유명한 대한민국 남쪽의 도시이다.

장진우는 서울의 낙후된 거리인
경리단길에 조그마한
식당들을 성공시키면서
'장진우길'이라는 브랜드를 만든
젊은 F&B 사업가이다.
특히 부동산 투기를 지양하고,
임대를 통해 프랜차이즈화와
젠트리피케이션과 같은
자본투입으로 인한 기존의
부작용을 비판하며,
젊은 창업자를 육성하는 플랫폼을
운영하고 있다. 장진우는
이번 폴리를 통해
광주지역 출신 예비 창업자
들을 선발하고 교육했다.
청년들의 공동 창업을 돕는
동시에 카페 콩집 및
식당 청미장을 탄생시킨 것이다.

'작동행위―먹다'는 부동산을
사회·문화적으로 유동화liquefy
하는 공간의 콘텐츠이자
도시재생을 위한 중요한 작동
요소가 된다.

콩집
장진우
Congzib
Chang, Jinwoo
16-15, Donggye-ro, Dong-gu, Gwangju, Republic of Korea
대한민국 광주광역시 동구 동계로

BY JANGILUNG

COOK HOUX

16-19, Donggye-ro, Dong-gu, Gwangju, Republic of Korea
대한민국 광주광역시 동구 동계로 16-19
Chang, Jinwoo
Chungmi-jang
청미장
장진우

청 미 장

Project Name · 프로젝트 이름	Congzib 콩집
Artist & Architect · 작가 & 건축가	Chang, Jinwoo Formative Architects (Koh, Youngsung, Lee, SeongBum, Kim, JeongEun) Seoro Architects.Co.Ltd (Jung, Gwangmin) 장진우, 콩집 디자인 및 설계-포머티브 건축사(고영성, 이성범, 김정은), 서로건축사사무소(정광민)
Location · 위치	16-19, Donggye-ro, Dong-gu, Gwangju, Repulic of Korea 대한민국 광주광역시 동구 동계로 16-19
Site Area · 부지 면적	198m²
Building Area · 빌딩 면적	72.25m²
Gross Floor Area · 총 바닥 면적	72.25m²
Building Scale · 건물 규모	1 Story Building · 지상 1층
Materialisation · 작품 구현	Aluminum Frame · 알루미늄 프레임
Construction · 시공사	SEA-Design & Construction · 시-디자인 & 컨스트럭션
Structure · 구조	Steel Frame Structure · 철골구조
Design Period · 디자인 기간	2016.07~09
Construction Period · 공사 기간	2016.10~12

Project Name · 프로젝트 이름	Chungmijang 청미장
Artist & Architect · 작가 & 건축가	Chang, Jinwoo · 장진우
Location · 위치	16-15, Donggye-ro, Dong-gu, Gwangju, Repulic of Korea 대한민국 광주광역시 동구 동계로 16-15
Site Area · 부지 면적	136m²
Building Area · 빌딩 면적	63.07m²
Gross Floor Area · 총 바닥 면적	63.07m²
Building Scale · 건물 규모	1 Story Building · 지상 1층
Materialisation · 작품 구현	THK 12 Tempered Glass, THK16 Pair Glass, Hanok Wood THK 12 강화유리, THK16 복층유리, 한옥목재
Construction · 시공사	Handeul Co., Ltd. · ㈜한들
Structure · 구조	Post Beam Structure · 중목구조
Design period · 디자인 기간	2016.07~09
Construction period · 공사 기간	2016.10~12

Short Description of the Concept	The main concept of Cook Folly is to have the new space transplanted in the city keep traces of the past while aptly assimilating with the surroundings. Moreover, we hope it could become a space that benefits all, influencing and being influenced by the others. It might be worth asking, wouldn't assimiliation and win-win be the true urban regeneration?
컨셉에 대한 간략 설명	쿡폴리의 주요 개념은 새롭게 도시에 이식되는 장소가 기존의 시간을 일부분 간직하고 주변과 적절히 동화되는 것에 목적을 가지고 있다. 더불어 쿡폴리라는 장소 그 속에서 일어나는 모든 행위들이 주변에 영향을 주고 받는 상생의 공간이 되었으면 한다. 동화되고 상생하는것 그것이 진정 문화적 도시 재생이 아닐까? 반문해 본다.

Untitled

Chang, Jinwoo

무제
장진우

Eating is an activity that is intimately related to human beings. It is a prerequisite for survival that also offers sensual pleasure and emotional happiness. Eating is beyond a matter of survival; it involves complex implications. It is not difficult to find relevant examples immediately around us, as in phrases like "humans live by the energy of rice" or "a dish of rice embodies the universe." Food, or the act of eating, embraced in the word "rice" has more than just a literal meaning; it entails a unique philosophy.

The Korean word *sik* (식, from the Chinese 食), which refers to *rice*, *food* and *eating*, exists somewhere in between conflicting words. Eating together shows a relationship, but eating alone means isolation. The process of food being served is dynamic, while the act of eating is static. Though the word *sik* has its own uniqueness, its meaning varies depending on the circumstances. Cook Folly is also positioned in between contrasts. The project that combines *folly*, which refers to architecture, and cook is located among unemployment and start-ups, old towns and regeneration, and regional imbalance and balance, claiming to act as an organic link that integrates them.

Cook Folly pursues a virtuous circle. It considers the end of one project as a new beginning. For this, Cook Folly operates within the frame of a restaurant. Congzib and Chungmijang, which have both just revealed themselves to the world, not only aim at resolving unemployment issues among young people, urban regeneration, and balanced development, but also at founding a tourism infrastructure and branding a city. This occurs within the

 eat

larger cycle of education-development-achievement.
Young people interested in the restaurant business accum-
ulate practical experience at Congzib and Chungmijang,
developing self-reliance skills in the process. Based on this,
they can start their own business or expand their practice.
In addition, 20 percent of all revenue is donated to the
Gwangju Biennale to support young people with their start-
ups, and complete the virtuous cycle model that can also
contribute to solving social problems. Such a cycle can
also facilitate the incubation of young entrepreneurs. Furthermore, by attracting young people from all over the country,
it can establish new tourism infrastructure. Solving the
problem of youth unemployment can stimulate the old city
centre of Gwangju, too. By locating Cook Folly in the relatively run-down area, it seeks balanced development in the
region. Taking the names from Congzib and Chungmijang—
the first standing bar in town and a restaurant that enjoyed
huge popularity—demonstrates what Cook Folly is looking
to achieve. Located in the central area of Jeollanamdo,
this is somewhere you can experience all the tastes of the
province. Such variety can be also found in the fine details
of Cook Folly. Chungmijang adopts the form of "select dining,"
reflecting such variety by offering the very best cuisine
from Jeollanamdo province, and aims at establishing a solid
brand power that corresponds to global trends.

    After the project has been completed
by combining *sik* and architecture, this will mark the true
beginning, or the present Cook Folly. Although Cook Folly is
currently located in Gwangju, the spirit of realising organic
development and symbiosis is alive everywhere. There
are infinite ways of utilising the theme of food, as it opens a
horizon of various possibilities. Just as *sik* keeps its uniqueness while continuously changing, it is also imperative for
Cook Folly to remain firmly rooted in the belief of a virtuous
cycle to achieve its goals.

 Untitled

→ 210 식(먹다, eat, 食)이라는 행위는 인간과 밀접한 행위이다. 이는 인간 생존을 위한 필수조건인 동시에 감각적 쾌락과 감정적 행복을 제공한다. 먹는다는 것은 생존의 범주에만 국한되는 것이 아니며, 그 이상의 힘을 내포한 복합적인 의미를 지닌다. 이러한 예는 우리 주변에서도 찾을 수 있다. '사람은 밥심으로 산다', '밥 한 그릇에 우주가 담겨 있다'라는 말에서 알 수 있듯 '밥'이라는 단어에 응축된 음식 또는 먹는다는 행위에 우리 민족은 사물의 기본적인 의미를 넘어 고유한 철학을 담아낸다.

'밥' 혹은 '음식' 혹은 '먹다'로 일컬을 수 있는 식(食)의 의미는 서로 상반된 단어 사이, 그 어딘가에 자리한다. 함께 먹는 음식은 관계를 나타내지만, 혼자 먹는 음식은 단절을 의미한다. 음식이 상에 오르기까지의 과정은 동적이지만, 앉아 식사를 하는 행위는 정적이다. 식(食)이라는 단어에는 스스로의 고유함이 있지만, 이를 포함하는 범주에 따라 그 의미가 다양하게 변화한다. 쿡폴리 역시 식(食)과 같이 상반된 단어들 사이에 위치한다. 건축을 뜻하는 폴리(Folly)와 요리를 뜻하는 쿡(Cook)이 합쳐진 이 프로젝트는 실업과 창업, 구도심과 재생, 지역불균형과 균형이라는 단어 사이에서 이를 통합하는 유기적 연결고리 역할을 하고자 한다.

쿡폴리는 선-순환적 구조를 지향한다. 곧 한 프로젝트의 마침점을 새로운 시작으로 생각한다. 이를 위해 쿡폴리는 식당이라는 범주에서 운영된다. 이 프로젝트를 통하여 새로이 세상에 모습을 드러낸 '콩집'과 '청미장'은, 앞서 이야기한 청년 실업문제 해결, 도심재생, 지역균형 발전은 물론 관광인프라 구축, 지역 브랜드화까지 목표로 한다. 이는 '교육-발전-성취'라는 큰 구조 안에서 이루어진다. 요식업에 뜻이 있는 청년들이 '콩집'과 '청미장'에서 실제적 경험을 축적하여 스스로 자립할 수 있는 힘을 키우며 성장할 것이다. 이를 바탕으로 청년들은 창업을 하거나, 보다 넓은 단계로 나아갈 수 있다. 더욱이 매출의 20%를 다시금 광주비엔날레에 기부함으로써, 청년들이 다른 이들의 창업을 지원해주며 사회적 문제를 해결하는 선-순환 모델을 완성한다. 이와 같은 선-순환으로 다양한 방면의 청년 사업가 배출이 예상되고, 이러한 사례가 쌓이며 전국에서 수많은 청년들이 몰리면 새로운 관광인프라의 구축도 기대할 수 있다. 청년 세대의 실업문제 해결은 광주 구도심에 활력을 불어넣는다. 상대적으로 낙후된 광주 구도심에 쿡폴리를 건축함으로써 지역균형발전을 도모하는 것이다.

광주 최초의 스탠드바와 옛날 엄청난 인기를 누렸던 식당이었던 '청미장'과 '콩집'의 이름을 딴 것은 쿡폴리가 지향하는 바를 단적으로 드러낸다. 광주는 지역적으로 전라남도의 중부에 위치해 있어, 전남의 모든 맛을 맛볼 수 있는 지역이다. 이와 같은 다양성을 발전시켜 광주가 전라남도 모든 도시의 통합체임을 부각시켜야 한다. 이러한 다양성은 쿡폴리의 구체적인 부분에도 녹아들어 있다. 식당 '청미장'은 전남의 대표 음식을 모아놓은 '셀렉다이닝' 형태로 다양성을 드러내는 동시에, 전 세계적 트렌드에 발맞추어 브랜드 파워의 입지를 다지고자 한다.

→ 211 식(食)과 건축이 어우러진 쿡폴리는 프로젝트가 마무리된 지금 이 시점부터 다시 시작된다. 현재 쿡폴리는 광주라는 한 지역에 자리하지만, 유기적인 발전과 공생을 위한 정신은 끊임없이 살아 움직인다. 음식이라는 범주를 활용하는 방법은 무궁무진하며, 이는 다양한 가능성의 지평을 열어준다. 식(食)이라는 것이 변화무쌍한 모습을 보여주면서도 자신의 고유성을 지켜내듯, 쿡폴리 역시 다양한 방법 안에서 선-순환적 신념과 철학을 지켜야만 이 프로젝트의 궁극적 목표를 이룩할 수 있을 것이다.

Urban Daily Lives

Formative

도시의 일상성
포머티브

How We See Urban Daily Life

Daily lives in an urban space refer to the usual, everyday phenomena that stem from the combination of architecture, which is its hardware, and the daily programs of those who reside in it. Taste & Beauty at the Gwangju Biennale are elements that cannot be missed in those usual daily phenomena, and Cook Folly will only become more meaningful when it fulfills them both. Thus, the agents at Cook Folly create, organise and operate the programs, leading the immaterial folly, while the architectural folly that relates with the city closely connects with the outer domain, allowing the program inside to blend. Here, we focused on the architectural method to make the folly assimilate into the city and its surrounding landscape, how it would work, and how it can coexist and fit into the surrounding environment and its residents.

The Context of Sansu-dong in Cook Folly

Before modernisation, the city used to have a form of organisation that spontaneously developed. After industrialisation, however, it saw gradual changes, with larger scale developments taking place based on urban planning. As the volume of development changed, existing urban structures that developed spontaneously were torn down and dismissed. Sansu-dong, Dong-gu, Gwangju also contained empty houses which shed light on the necessity of urban regeneration. The significance of Cook Folly lies in the fact that, even if it is a government-led program, it aims at coexistence, seeking cultural regeneration that focuses on transforming and harmonising existing programs instead of employing typical Korean urban restoration methods, which usually involve redevelopment.

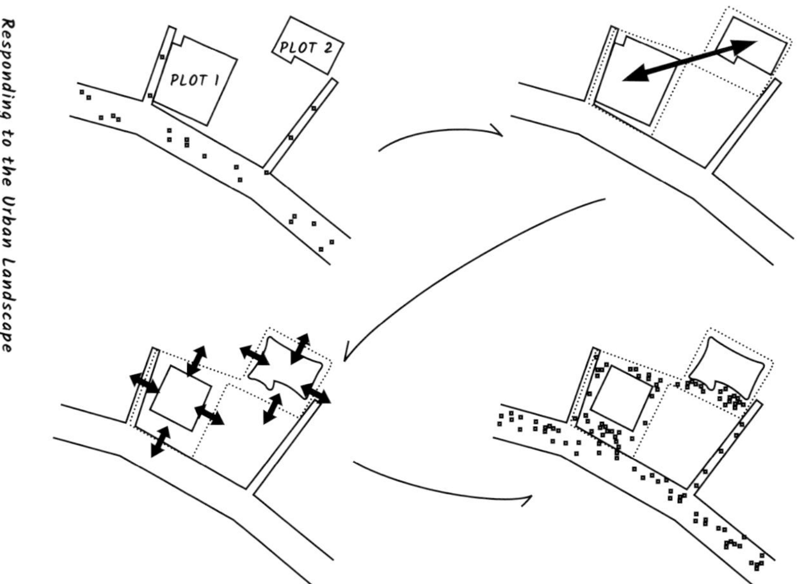

Responding to the Urban Landscape

In terms of architecture, the way Cook Folly responds to the city is through two key terms: materials and preservation of time.

First, glass materials blur the boundary between the inside and outside, projecting the context of the existing city. This was not an artificial intervention to decorate the interior and make it trendy. Rather, it was meant to allow people to experience the local context of Sansu-dong inside the Folly as well. In other words, it was an architectural measure to adopt the view as the interior and incorporate the changes outdoors within Cook Folly itself, thus blending it with the surroundings.

Second, the preservation of time refers to our suggestion of a way to harmonise the temporal gap with the surroundings when a new structure is transplanted within the urban "tissue." Outside Congzib, for example, there are remains of previous buildings, while the pillar inside is also preserved.

This was conceived to have the people in Sansu-dong recognise Cook Folly not as an exclusive space but more as
a part of a close-knit neighbourhood. The steps at the
briquette storage, walls that were torn down to the height
of a chair, and the newly built bench were all designed
in response to the low benches and chairs in alleys throughout the area.

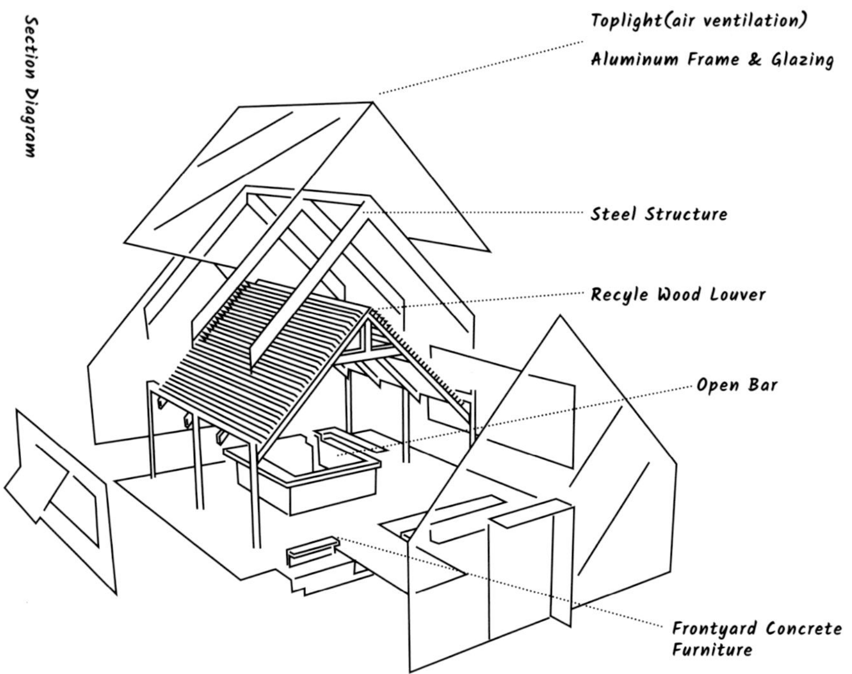

Chungmijang, which is a renovated
hanok (traditional Korean houses), maintains traditional wood-
en furniture while adjusting the opening and interior walls.
We tried to keep the original form as much as we could
because hanok are valuable pieces of architecture and keep
traces within them that are not only important elements
in sustaining people's daily lives in urban circumstances, but
also crucial in that they document the city's history when
it comes to city regeneration.

                    eat

Folly and Alleys

Congzib acts as a pavilion, symbolically showing the beginning of the Folly at the entry of an alley in Sansu-dong. The front yard of the Folly is an expanded alley where the community of the neighbourhood can freely come and go. The pathway that runs outdoors smoothly connects through the hanok Folly Chungmijang, which is located deeper in the neighbourhood. Upon leaving the narrow alley, one encounters another Gwangju Folly. This is what the Cook Folly wanted to realise through the alleys—both a place and road that people want to visit, which of course is part of cultural urban regeneration.

A Rendered Image of Congzib

→ 214　도시의 일상성을 바라보는 우리의 시각

도시의 일상성은 도시의 하드웨어인 건축, 그리고 그 안에서 살아가는 이들의 일상인 프로그램의 결합에서 오는 보편적인 생활 현상을 의미한다. 광주비엔날레에서 말하는 맛과 멋은 그 보편적인 생활 현상 속에서 결코 빼놓을 수 없는 것이며, 쿡폴리 역시 이 두 가지를 모두 충족시킬 때 의미가 있을 것이다. 그러므로 쿡폴리의 내부적 주체는 그 속에서 프로그램을 만들고 조직화하며 그것을 운영해나가는 역할로 비물질적 폴리를 이끌어나가고, 도시와 관계하는 건축적 폴리는 그것을 외부영역들과 긴밀히 연결시켜주어 자연스럽게 내부 프로그램과 섞일 수 있게 하는 역할을 한다. 우리는 도시 속 마을 풍경에 동화될 수 있는 폴리의 건축적 방법과 그 속에서 작동하는 모든 것, 즉 인간과 주변 환경 등이 기존의 것과 어떠한 방식으로 공존하고 버무려질지 초점을 맞추고 고민하였다.

쿡폴리 - 산수동의 위치적 맥락

근대 산업화 이전의 도시는 점적인 조직 형태의 자연발생적 도시개발 형식을 보이다 산업화 이후 점차 도시계획 위주의 대규모 개발 형식으로 바뀌게 되었다. 그렇게 개발 규모가 변하면서 자연스럽게 생겨난 도시의 기존 조직들은 파괴되고 도태되었다. 이미 곳곳에 빈집들이 생겨나기 시작한 광주 동구 산수동 역시 도시재생 사업의 필요성이 대두되었다.

쿡폴리가 들어설 산수동은 한국형 도심재생의 표본인 전면적 재개발 방식이 아닌, 관이 주도하면서도 기존 도심 프로그램의 변형과 공존을 통해 문화적 도심재생을 이루는 상생의 계획이라는 점에서 큰 의미를 갖는다.

→215　도시풍경에 대한 대응

건축적인 면에서 쿡폴리가 도시에 대응하는 방식은, 재료의 구성과 시간의 보존이라는 2가지 키워드로 접근할 수 있다.

첫 번째, 재료의 구성에 있어 유리라는 투명한 물질을 통해 기존 도심의 컨텍스트를 투영시키며 내·외부의 경계를 모호하게 한다.

이는 인위적인 연출로 쿡폴리의 내부를 트렌디하게 꾸미는 것이 아닌 산수동이라는 지역적 맥락을 내부에서도 그대로 느낄 수 있게 하는 건축적 장치를 마련하고자 한 것이다. 마을의 풍광이 인테리어가 되고 외부 환경의 변화 자체가 쿡폴리의 일부가 되어, 폴리가 주변과 자연스럽게 어우러지게 하려는 의도가 담겨 있다.

두 번째, 새로운 건물이 도시 조직에 이식될 때 생기는 갭이 적절히 융화될 수 있도록 시간의 보존이라는 방법을 제시한 것이다. 여기서의 갭이란 기존 주변 환경의 모습과 폴리 사이에 발생하는 시대적 괴리를 말한다. 콩집 외부 공간에는 대지에 있던 기존 건물의 흔적을 그대로 두었으며, 내부에는 옛 기둥도 유지되어 있다.

이는 산수동 주민에게 쿡폴리라는 공간이 배타적이지 않도록 기존 마을의 일부로 인식, 인지되도록 계획된 것이다. 외부에 남겨진 연탄 창고 계단과 의자 높이까지만 철거된 담벼락 그리고 새롭게 구성된 벤치 역시 기존 마을 골목의 평상과 의자 등과 함께 작동할 여지를 두고 계획되었다.

그리고 한옥을 리노베이션한 청미장의 경우 한국 전통 목가구조 방식을 그대로 살리고 개구부와 내부 벽체만 조정하였다. 기존의 흔적을 남기고 보존하는 것은 도시의 일상성을 유지하는 아주 중요한 요소일 뿐만 아니라 더 나아가 도시재생의 방식에 있어 도시의 역사를 그대로 기록하고 남기는 매우 중요한 일이라 생각했기에 보존 가치가 있는 전통한옥의 원형을 최대한 보존하고자 했다.

→ 216　섹션다이어그램 이미지

폴리와 골목길

→ 217　콩집은 하나의 파빌리온 역할로, 산수동 골목길 초입에서 폴리의 시작을 상징적으로 알린다. 폴리 앞마당은 확장된 골목길로 마을의 커뮤니티 장소가 된다. 골목 내부에 깊숙이 위치한 한옥 폴리 청미장까지 자연스럽게 외부공간을 통해 동선이 이어지며, 산수동 안쪽까지 자연스럽게 사람의 발길이 이어진다. 좁은 골목길을 빠져나가면 또 다른 광주 폴리와 만나게 된다. 이것이 쿡폴리가 골목길을 통해 이뤄내고자 하는 '사람이 찾는 거리'이며 이는 곧 문화적 도심재생이다.

→ 217　콩집 렌더링 이미지

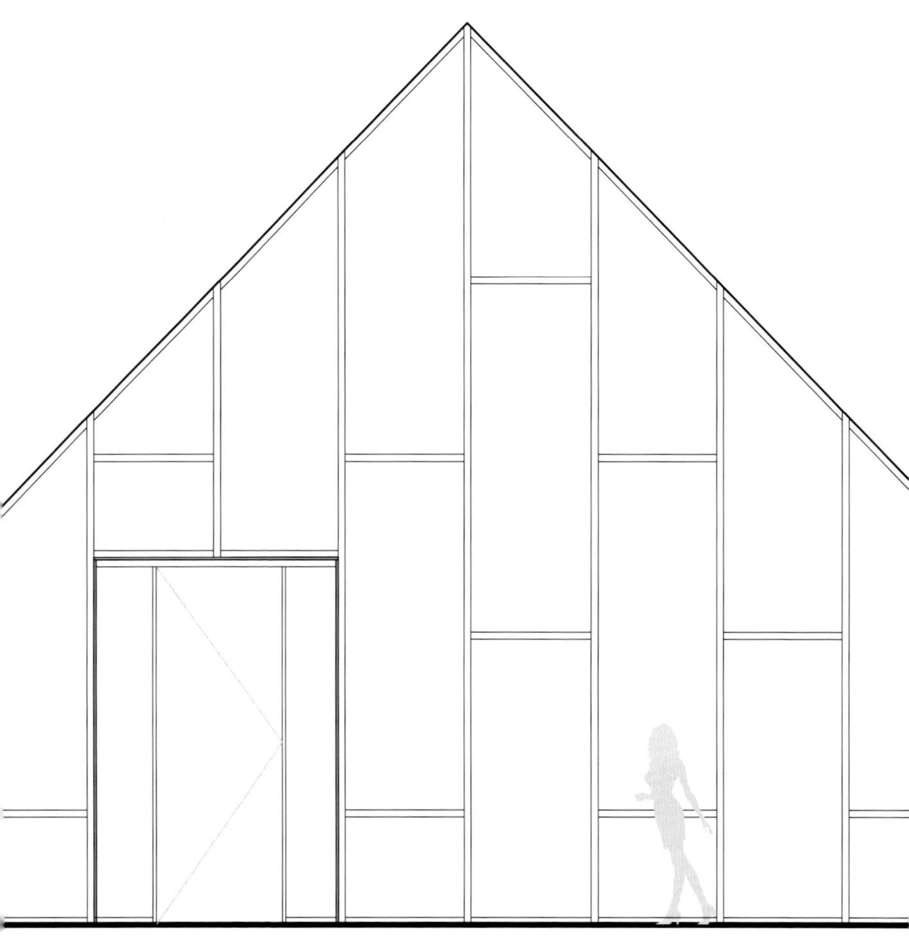

Urban Daily Lives

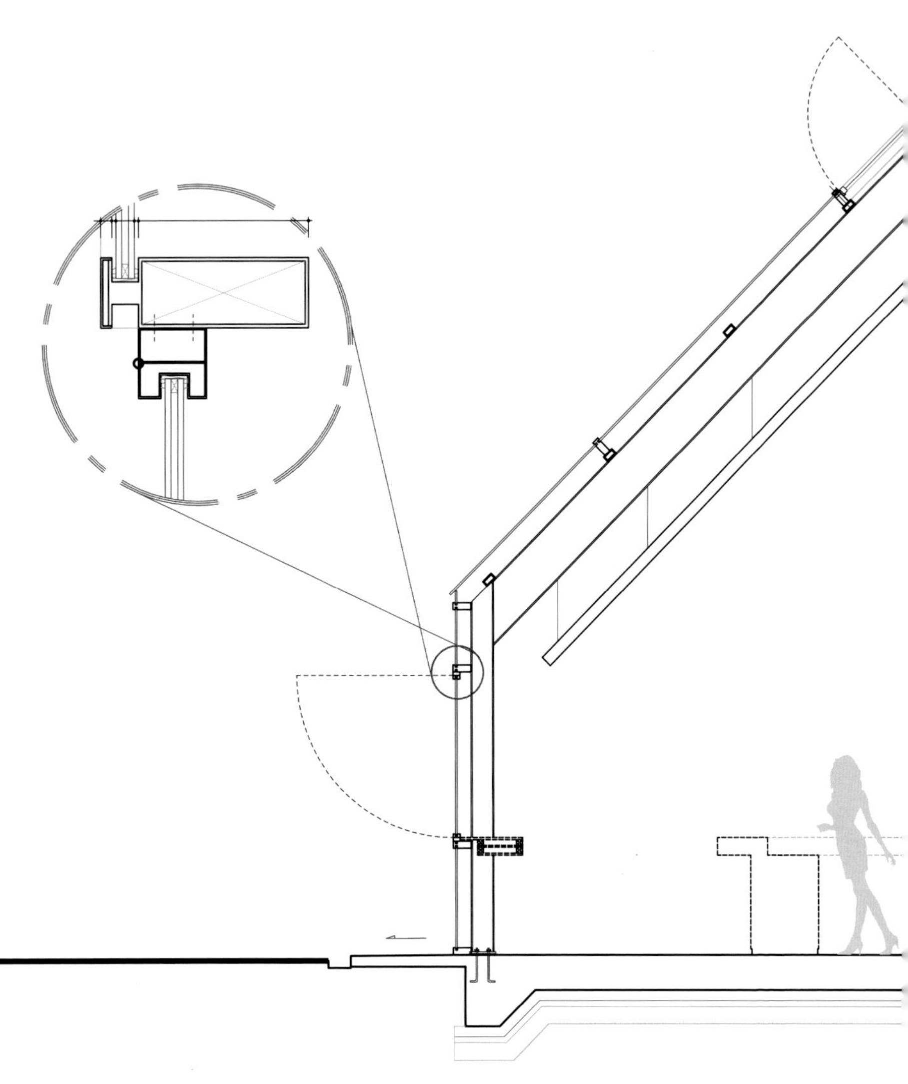

eat

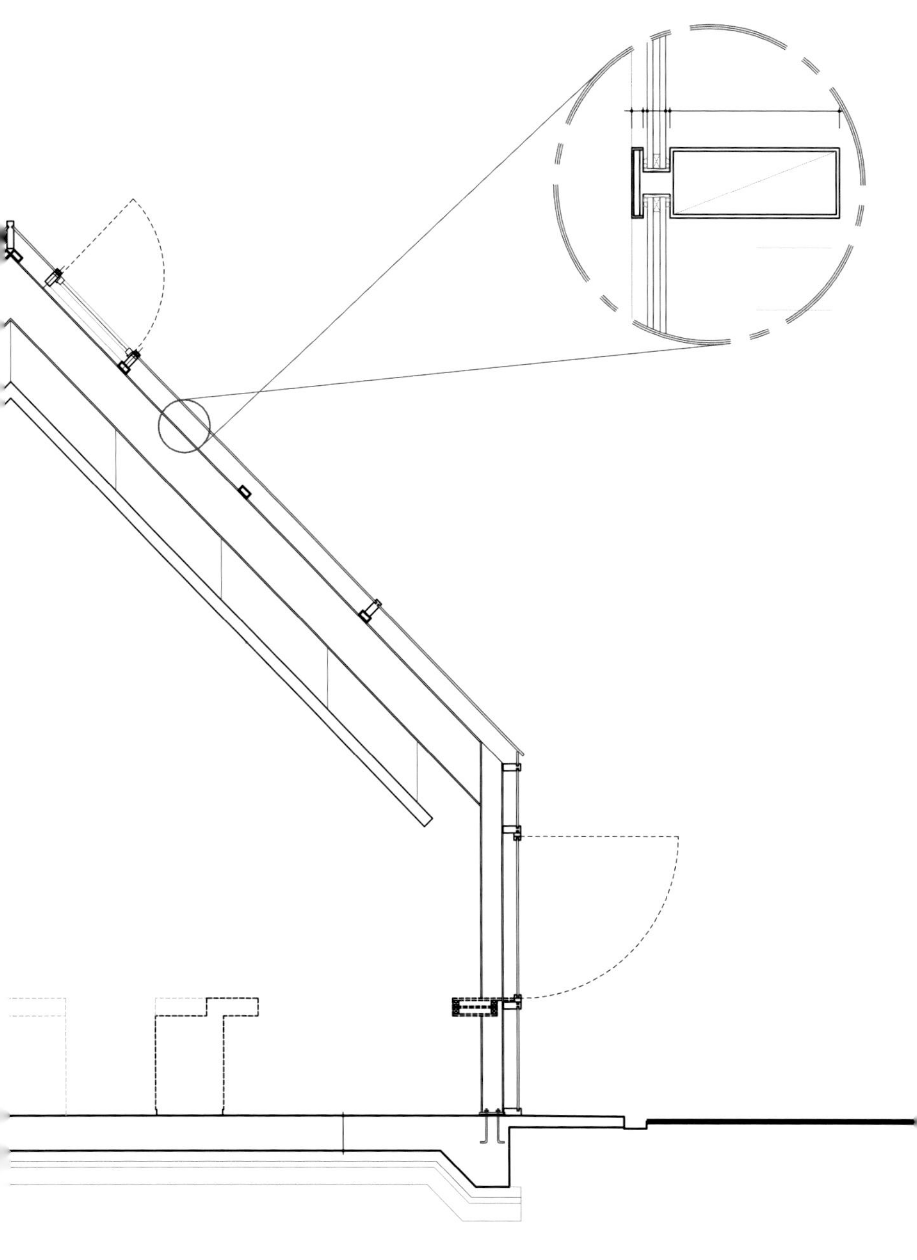

Urban Daily Lives

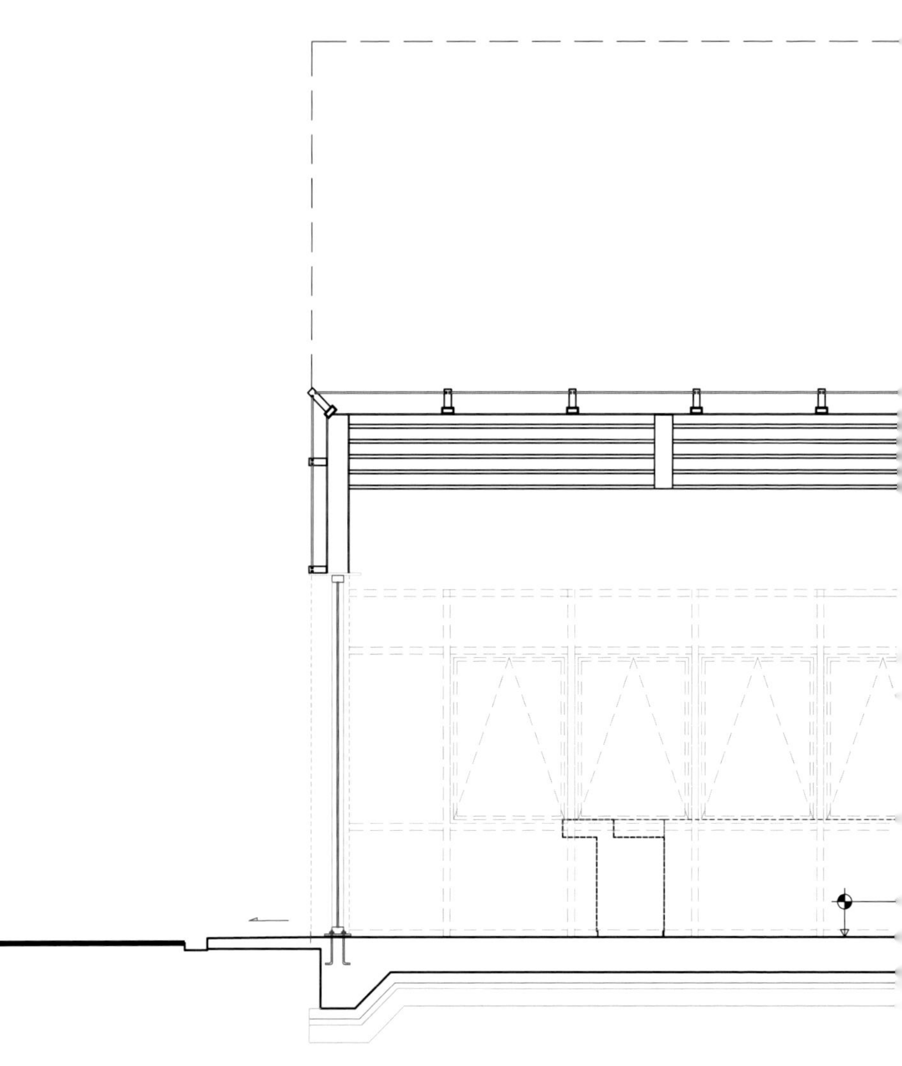

eat

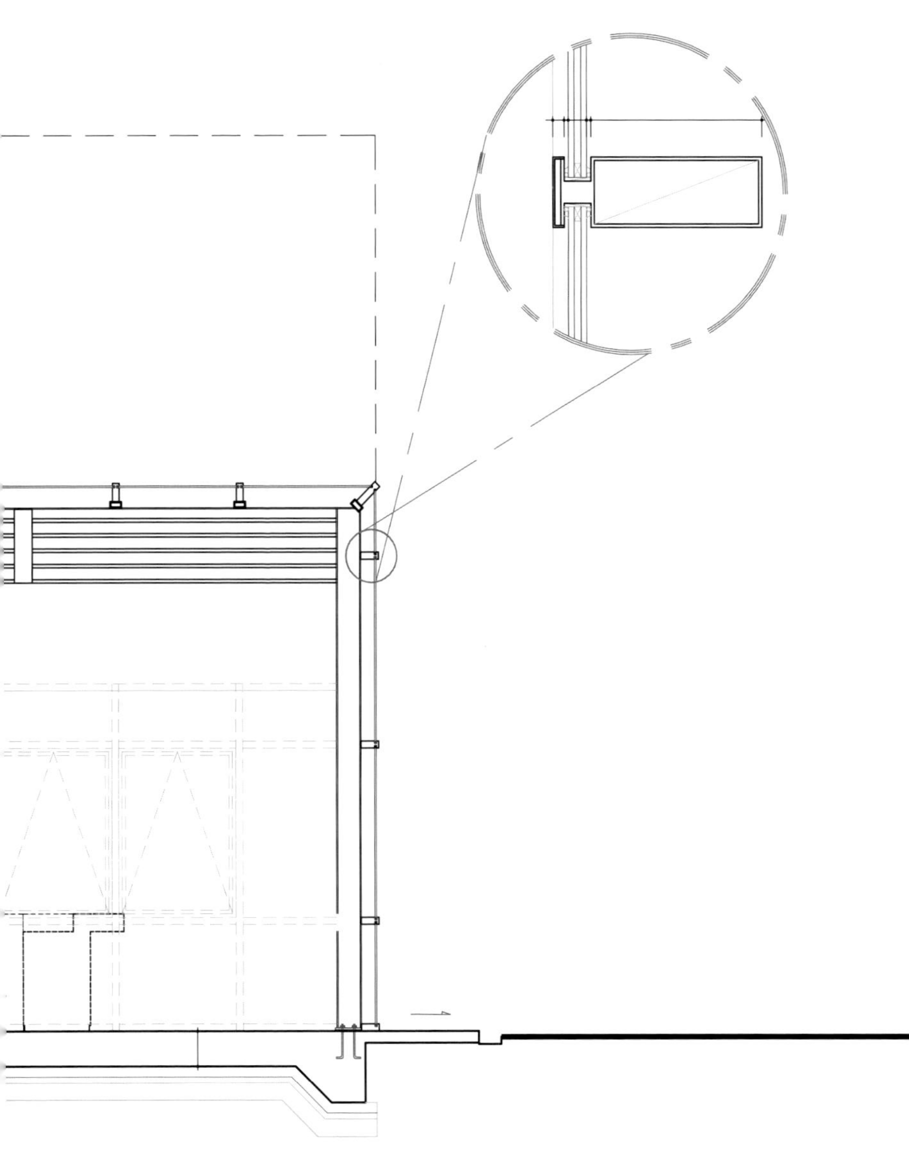

Urban Daily Lives

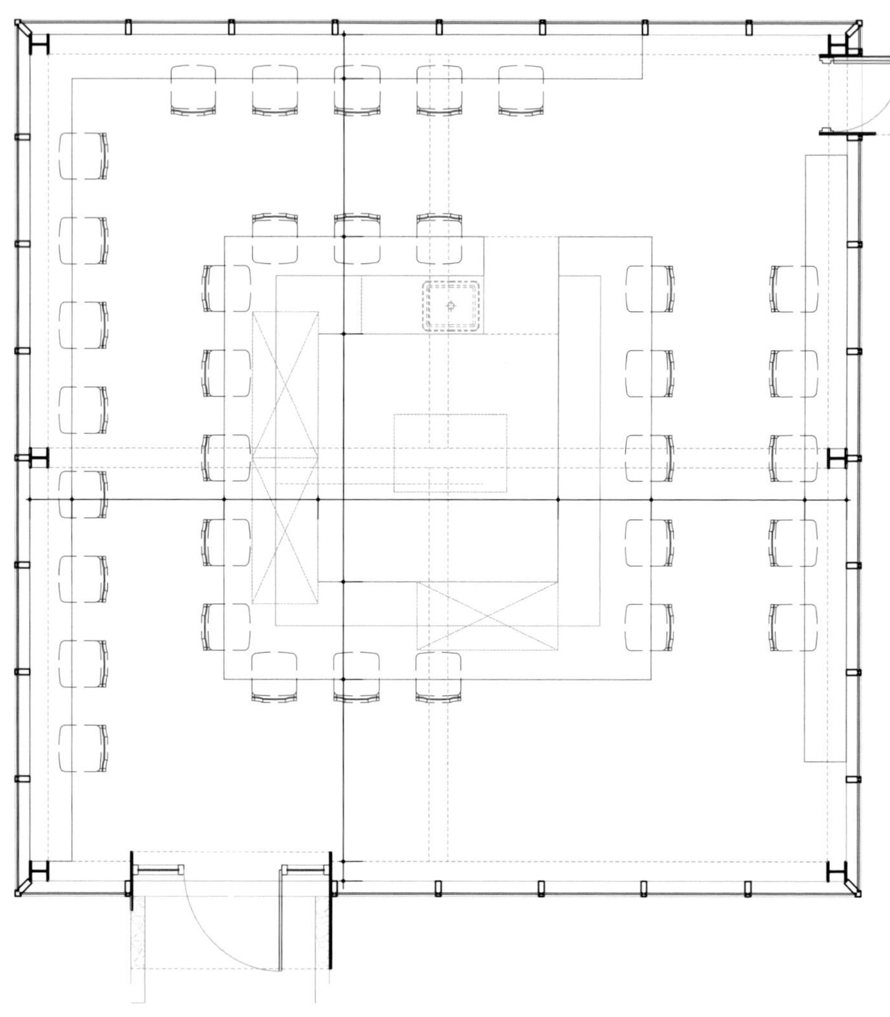

eat

walk

Walking is a crucial keyword in the city. Just because it was administratively a driveway, the pedestrian road that had been there for more than a hundred years was about to be reconstructed into a driveway for a large car park.

This Folly is a "**citizen Folly**" that fought for and resecured **the right to walk together with civic society**.

Through the process of communicating with civic groups for the specific site and bringing up and securing the issue of the right to walk, it demonstrates that Follies are not just a tangible device but a progressive one, too.

Winy Maas rematerialised the pedestrian zone in front of an primary school to provide children and local residents with a pedestrian park, while **Cho, ByoungSoo** designed a special space that allows people to rest there "**poetically.**"

걷는다는 행위는 도시에서
중요한 키워드이다.

100년 넘은 초등학교 앞 보행로가
행정상 도로라는 이유로
대규모 주차장의 통행로가 되는
공사를 앞두고 있는 상황이었다.
이 '시민폴리'는 시민사회와
함께 싸워 이곳의 보행권을 다시
확보해냈다. 특정한 사업지
획득을 위해 시민단체와 함께
소통, 보행권리 확보 등의 이슈를
제기하고, 보행권을 확보해가는
과정을 통해 폴리가 유형적
디바이스에서 과정의 디바이스가
될 수 있음을 보여 주고자 한다.

위니 마스는 초등학교 앞 보행
공간을 재물성화rematerialize
하여 시민들과 아이들에게 즐거운
보행-공원을 제공하고, 조병수는
공원에 시적 휴식을 제공하는
특별한 공간을 디자인하였다.

THE I LOV
Winy Maas, MVRDV

E STREET

Seoseok Primary School, 26, Jebong-ro 82beon-gil, Dong-gu, Gwangju, Republic of Korea

대한민국 광주광역시 동구 제봉로 82번길 26 서석초등학교

23, Dongmyeong-ro 67beon-gil, Dong-gu,
Gwangju, Republic of Korea
대한민국 광주광역시 동구 동명로 67번길 23
Dre

꿈 집
조병수
Cho, ByoungSoo
am House

Project Name · 프로젝트 이름	THE I LOVE STREET 아이 러브 스트리트
Artist & Architect · 작가 & 건축가	Winy Maas, MVRDV · 위니 마스, MVRDV
Project Team · 프로젝트 팀	Winy Maas, Jacob van Rijs and Nathalie de Vries with Wenchian Shi, Lee, Kyosuk Lee, Dongmin, Bowen Zhu, Sen Yang 위니 마스, 야콥 판레이스와 나탈리 드 프리스, 웬치안 슐, 이교석, 이동민, 보원 주, 센 양
Location · 장소	Seoseok Primary School, 26, Jebong-ro 82beon-gil, Dong-gu, Gwangju, Republic of Korea 대한민국 광주광역시 동구 제봉로 82번길 26 서석초등학교
Site Area · 부지 면적	959,07㎡
Materialisation · 작품 구현	Concrete, Wood Plank, Grass, Gravel, Urethane Chip, Trampoline Rubber Net, Soil, Steel 콘크리트, 목판, 자갈, 우레탄 칩, 트램폴린 고무 네트, 흙, 철근
Construction · 시공사	Gongjeong Construction Co. · ㈜공정건설
Design Period · 디자인 기간	2016.02~2017.08, 18 months · 18개월
Construction Period · 공사 기간	2017.08, 1 month · 1개월
Short Description of the Concept	THE I LOVE STREET The Jebong-ro, 82beon-gil closed for traffic. In a strong collaboration with the Seoseok Primary School, a series of their wishes have been explored. That has led to a series of different pavements that can be used for sitting, painting, jumping on trampolines, playing in sand. By shaping these pavements in a series of letters, a true text appears, that indicate the love for many things: I LOVE… A neutral square space at the end of the text is kept for everyone's personal addition that can be painted and adapted: the canvas. I LOVE can thus become I LOVE KOREA, I LOVE KIM, I LOVE WALKING, I LOVE THE MAYOR, I LOVE GWANGJU, I LOVE YOU. This text can be seen from a special tribune at the beginning of the street. This tribune gives access to a platform at 5 meters high, with a bench and a table. From here the school gardens can be overviewed. And a selfie can be taken…
컨셉에 대한 간략 설명	아이 러브 스트리트 작품 설치로 제봉로 82번길은 교통이 통제되었다. 작가들은 서석초등학교와 긴밀히 협력하여 구성원이 소망하는 바가 무엇인지 분석했다. 그 결과 학교 앞 도로는 앉거나, 그리거나, 트램폴린처럼 그 위를 뛰거나, 모래밭에서 노는 등 다양한 용도로 이용될 수 있도록 구현되었다. 편지를 통해 보도를 만드는 과정에서 사랑하는 여러 가지 대상을 표현하는 진실한 문장을 발견할 수 있었다. 나는 …를 사랑한다. 각자가 개인적인 문구를 그리거나 활용할 수 있도록 문장의 끝에 중의적인 사각 공간, 즉 캔버스를 만들었다. 따라서 '사랑해요'는 '한국을 사랑해요', '민수를 사랑해요', '걷기를 사랑해요', '시장님을 사랑해요', '광주를 사랑해요', '당신을 사랑해요'가 될 수 있다. 이는 길 초입에 마련된 특별한 연단에서 만나볼 수 있다. 연단을 거쳐 벤치와 테이블이 있는 5미터 높이의 플랫폼에 오르면, 학교 정원을 감상하거나 셀카를 촬영할 수도 있다.

Project Name · 프로젝트 이름	Dream House 꿈 집
Artist & Architect · 작가 & 건축가	Cho, ByoungSoo · 조병수
Project Team · 프로젝트 팀	Cho, ByoungSoo, BCHO Architects Associates · 조병수, 조병수 건축연구소
Location · 장소	23, Dongmyeong-ro, 67beon-gil, Dong-gu, Gwangju, Republic of Korea 대한민국 광주광역시 동구 동명로 67번길 23
Site Area · 부지 면적	1,200㎡
Building Area · 빌딩 면적	22㎡
Materialisation · 작품 구현	Coloured Titanium, Brass Plate with Steel Pipe Structure · 색 티타늄, 놋판, 철골 구조물
Construction · 시공사	CNO
Gross Floor Area · 총 바닥 면적	22㎡
Structure · 구조	Steel Pipe Structure · 철골구조
Design Period · 디자인 기간	2016.02~11
Construction Period · 공사 기간	2016.11~2017.01
Short Description of the Concept	Dream House is made of 850 brass plates and 680 coloured titanium plates. This allows for a beautiful natural colour spectrum caused by the interference of light on the surface. Shape of Dream House, on the other hand, looks like a somewhat tilted and distorted traditional gable house from the countryside. Dream House provides a resting place for local residents and features a special sense of space.
컨셉에 대한 간략 설명	'꿈 집'은 850개의 놋판과 680개의 색 티타늄판으로 제작되었다. 표면에 작용하는 빛으로 인해 아름다운 천연 스펙트럼을 감상할 수 있다. '꿈 집'은 기울어지고 왜곡된 형태의 지역의 박공 주택을 닮아 있다. 특별한 공간감을 지니는 휴식처를 제공하기도 한다.

Gwangju Folly Town

Small Things Do Help!

Winy Maas, MVRDV

폴리타운 광주, 작은 것들도 도시를 바꾼다!
위니 마스, MVRDV

THE CITY OF THE FUTURE When
people fantasise about the future of cities, they often specu-
late about the large-scale changes that are necessary:
"We want more nature and an absence of cars to make cities
cleaner and friendlier"; "We want more space for bikes
and pedestrians, as well as, better transportation so we
don't have to commute for so long to work"; "We want to live
in the city again instead of some non-descript suburb";
"We want more green spaces to let our children play within
the city, cool breezes blowing through when we take time
to meet friends in pleasant areas"; "We want access to
more clean water so that our cities become less dependent
on sources far away, and more energy resources so that
our cities become more resilient."

TIME The realisation of most of these
dreams takes much time and much conviction. Laws have
to be changed to make it possible. Discussions have to
be undertaken to come to mutual and collective agreements.
More funding needs to be found to make it possible.
A lot of work has to be done. Most of these fantasies and
dreams need a serious amount of time to be realised.

SMALLNESS Sometimes smaller and
even temporary interventions can help in this process.
As they can be carried out in a short period, these types of
interventions can be accomplished within the political
terms of politicians and governments. They can also be
done within a relatively small surrounding, with direct communication among a limited number of stakeholders.
This can help to accelerate the decision-making process,
to develop collective enthusiasm, and to realise and
show the full idea behind the intervention.

FOLLIES: SENSE AND NONSENSE

Follies can be used for those purposes. They are, essentially, small interventions in our urban spaces. Although
they are considered to be art pieces, somehow they are also
seen as frivolous, temporary, and therefore innocent
and unserious. They are there for our pleasure, some say.
They are made by artists and architects, mostly on the basis
of their own fantasies. They are elements that aim to make
'no sense'. Some go so far as to say they can even be
'nonsense'. But is that completely true? As they can help to
point the observer in another and surprising direction, they
can help to visualise current problems. They can make us
laugh and think, too. They allow for direct criticism, and can
thus allow us to pay more attention to broader dreams.
At the same time, they can bring about smaller examples of
grander dreams. Prototypes sometimes. And because
they can be tested at small locations, they can be real drivers
of policy changes in a city.

GWANGJU 1 Not many people outside
of Korea have heard of Gwangju. That seems strange, as
the city has some very special and remarkable traits. It has
a booming car industry, for example. It is also situated
between beautiful surrounding hills featuring cherry blos-
som trees, a place many people like to go in the spring
when they're blossoming. It is also where Korean democracy
has been tested like no other city in the country, home to
the May 18 Democratic Movement that took place in 1980.
Today, it has a beautiful museum that celebrates and
teaches about all this.

GWANGJU 2 However, this is a city where cars dominate the streets, a place where it is hard to walk or bike. In addition, it is a city where the majority of the buildings are relatively modest and do not feature many outstanding architectural qualities. Furthermore, it is a city that has not treated its rivers and riverfronts very well, and does not have a lot of green space. As an outsider, I can easily imagine a shopping list of wishes to help make this a better, more beautiful city.

KOREAN CITIES Gwangju is basically like many other Korean cities. As it turns out, many Korean cities look quite the same. They are all situated on relatively flat grounds. Most are surrounded by hills and low mountains. They are composed of a non-descript road network dominated by cars. They are constructed with houses that all look the same, and by housing that is repetitive and essentially the same. How, then, can we help to make Gwangju more noticeable? How can we make it stand out so that more people want to go there?

GWANGJU FOLLY TOWN The decision a while ago to make a series of follies in Gwangju was a courageous first step. Some have become highly successful, like the lifted band designed by Juan Herreros that helped to raise attention about a neglected part of the city, turning it into a highly used area afterwards. There are also the stairs to the city's Green Corridor, designed by Seung, H-Sang, which functions as a small culture centre. The follies are a phenomenon that no other city has developed. Thus, they are able to make the city of Gwangju sexier, more attractive, and more widely known. This now starts to come down to one thing other cities don't have: a Folly Town.

The Green Way Culture Centre Ruined Steps & May, Seung H-Sang, Gwangju, Republic of Korea, 2011

Communication Hut, Juan Herreros, Gwangju, Republic of Korea, 2011

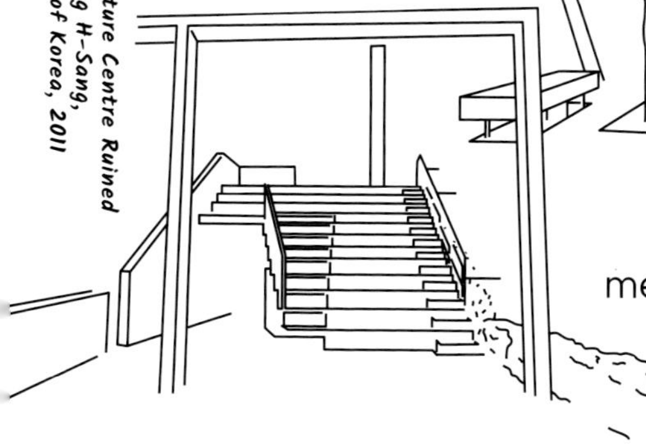

Ultimately, it is a phenomenon that no other city has. It thus is able to make the city of Gwangju sexier, more attractive, and more widely known. This now comes down to one thing other cities dont have: a Folly Town.

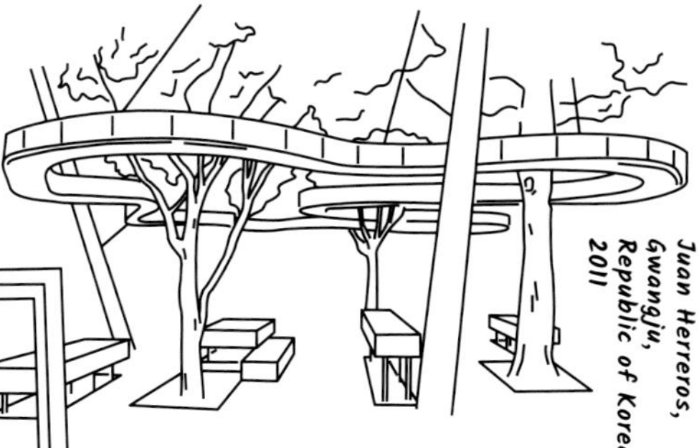

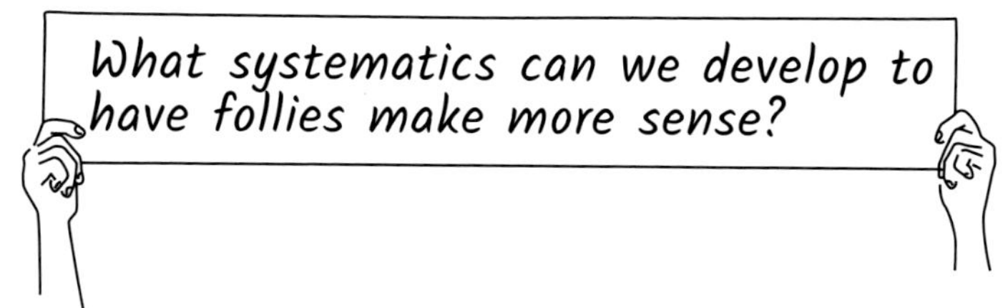

DO FOLLIES MAKE SENSE?

It would seem that some residents of Gwangju doubt if the follies make much sense. Some people seem to wonder if public budgets should be allocated to them, in fact. They also question if the city should continue with this folly initiative. Can this be answered by showing how these nonsensical elements can create sense? In order to examine the potential of future follies, exploratory research has been conducted. This includes asking the following question: What systematics can we develop to have follies make more sense?

FOLLY RESEARCH Concentrating on
the old city of Gwangju, a series of research initiatives
has been undertaken. By comparing Gwangju to other cities
in Korea and around the world, its strengths and weak-
nesses have been evaluated. Gwangju, for instance, seems
less walkable than other cities, and has insufficient public
transportation. It is less bikeable, less attractive for tourists,
has fewer green spaces, and is less cool in the summer
than other cities. In addition, it is less energy independent
and features fewer libraries, exhibitions, theatres, sports
venues, playgrounds, and urban events than many cities.

THE PEDESTRIAN FOLLIES

Walking ratio in 2013 (%)	
Seoul	55.9
Daejeon	50.3
Incheon	48.9
Busan	42.8
Daegu	42.1
Gwangju	38.4
Ulsan	41.9

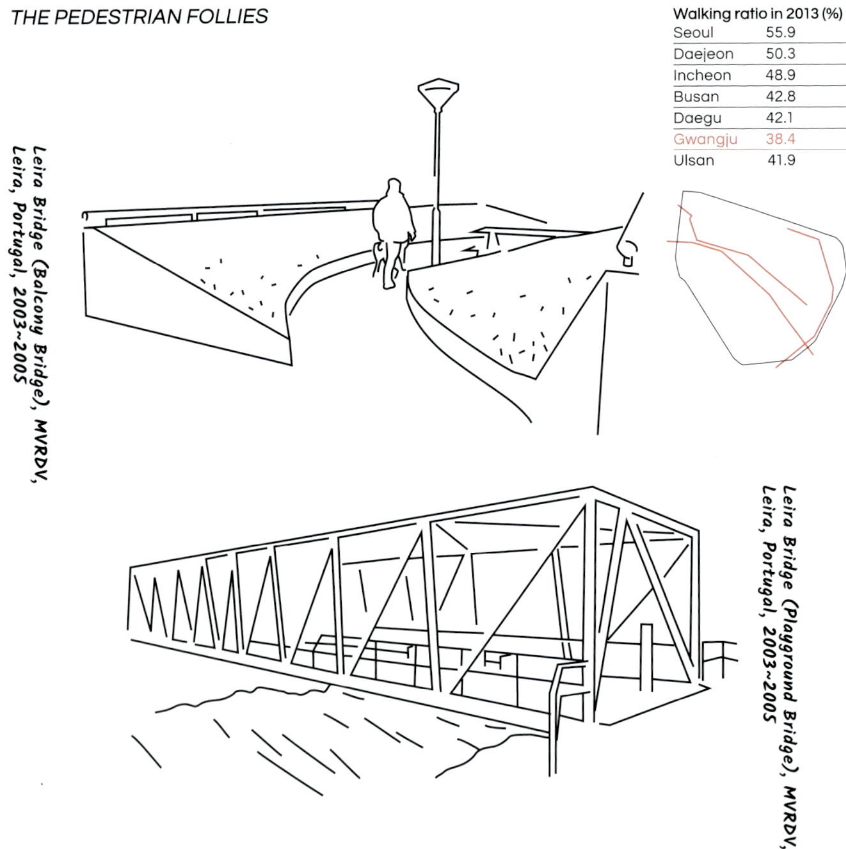

*Leira Bridge (Balcony Bridge), MVRDV,
Leira, Portugal, 2003~2005*

*Leira Bridge (Playground Bridge), MVRDV,
Leira, Portugal, 2003~2005*

THE PUBLIC TRANSPORTATION FOLLIES

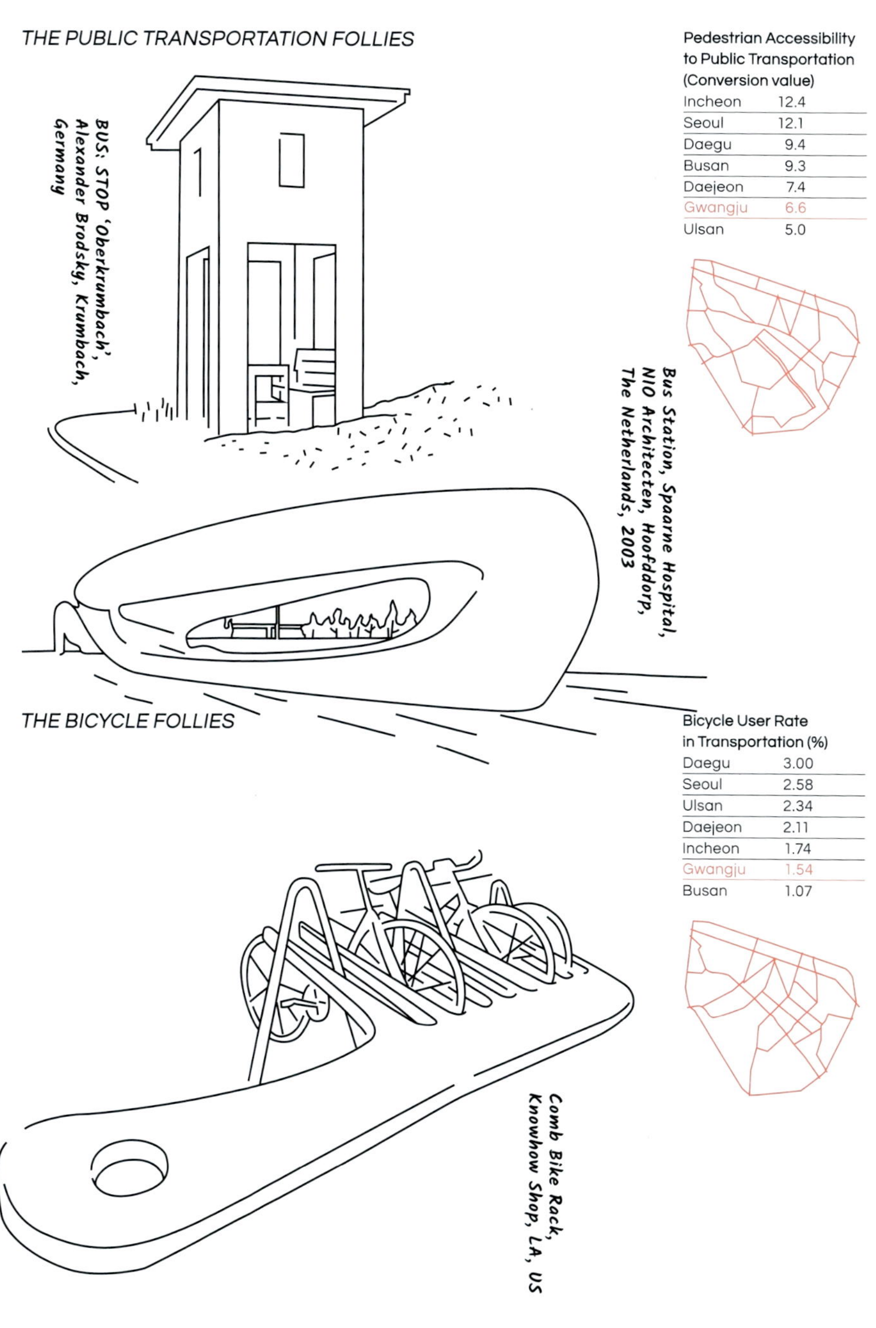

Pedestrian Accessibility
to Public Transportation
(Conversion value)

Incheon	12.4
Seoul	12.1
Daegu	9.4
Busan	9.3
Daejeon	7.4
Gwangju	6.6
Ulsan	5.0

Bicycle User Rate
in Transportation (%)

Daegu	3.00
Seoul	2.58
Ulsan	2.34
Daejeon	2.11
Incheon	1.74
Gwangju	1.54
Busan	1.07

THE HERITAGE FOLLIES

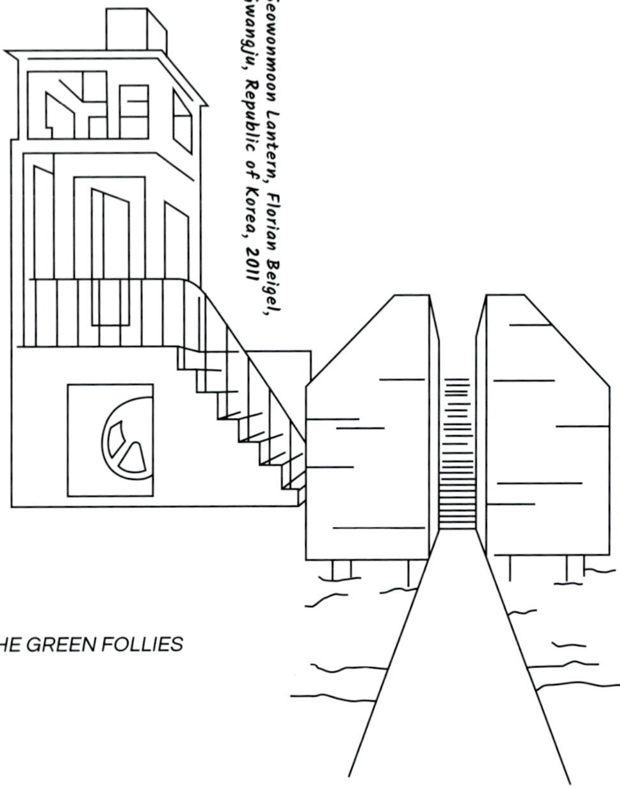

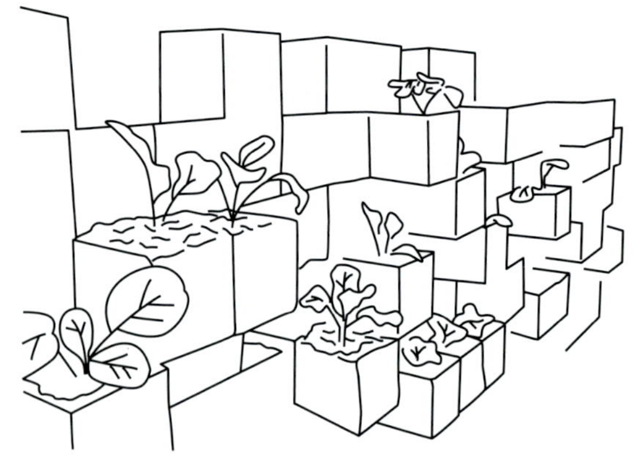

Seowonmoon Lantern, Florian Beigel, Gwangju, Republic of Korea, 2011

Bunker 599, RAAAF and Atelier Lyon, The Netherlands, 2010

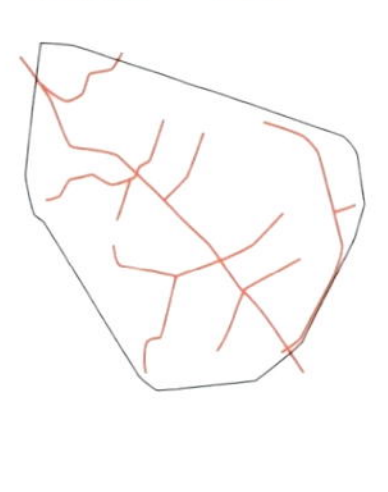

Visitor Number per capita (2010)	
Busan	16.3
Daegu	13.59
Ulsan	13.63
Daejeon	11.03
Gwangju	9.01
Incheon	4.28
Seoul	N/A

THE GREEN FOLLIES

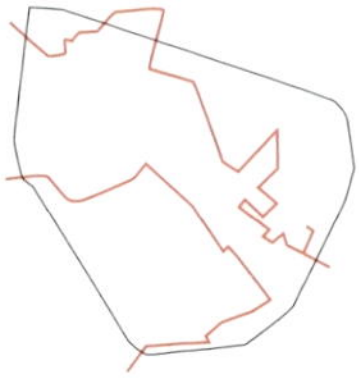

Urban Park Area per capita (m^2)	
Ulsan	39.84
Daejeon	34.88
Daegu	34.21
Incheon	32.46
Seoul	23.14
Busan	16.13
Gwangju	13.22

Cinderblock Wall Vegetable Garden

THE COOLING FOLLIES

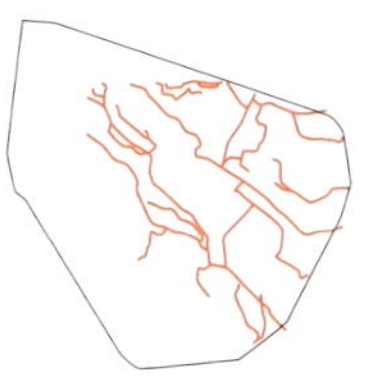

*Ice Pavilion, Olafur Eliasson,
Reykjavik Art Museum,
Kjarvalsstadir, 1998*

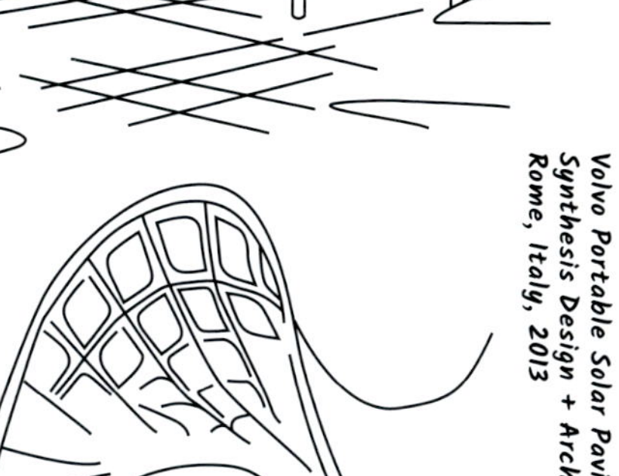

*Volvo Portable Solar Pavilion,
Synthesis Design + Architecture,
Rome, Italy, 2013*

THE ENERGY FOLLIES

*Endesa Pavilion,
Institute for Advanced
Architecture of Catalonia (IAAC),
Rodrigo Rubio and Miguel Guerrero,
Barcelona, Spain, 2011*

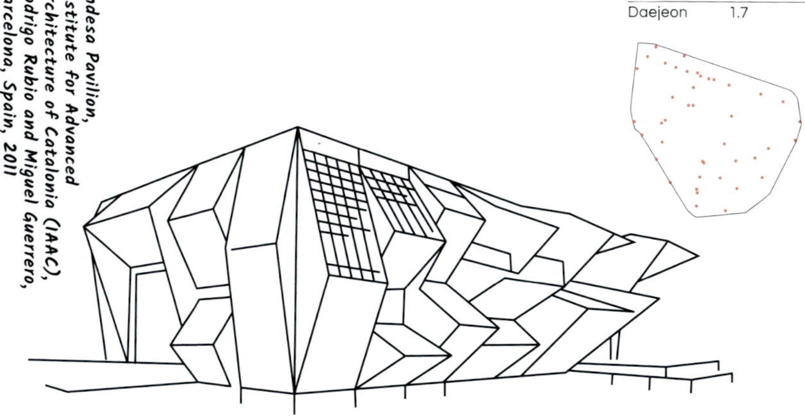

Gwangju River Reading Room,
David Adjaye & Taiye Selasi,
Gwangju, Republic of Korea, 2013

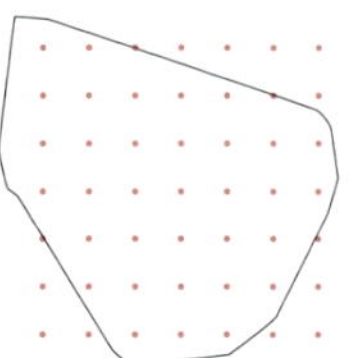

Monthly Use Frequency of Public Library

Seoul	1.1
Incheon	0.9
Gwangju	0.6
Busan	0.6
Daegu	0.6
Ulsan	0.6
Daejeon	0.5

Public Outdoor Library,
New York, US

THE EXHIBITION FOLLIES

Annual Exhibition Number (2014)

Seoul	7533
Busan	880
Daegu	497
Gwangju	279
Daejeon	241
Ulsan	217
Incheon	176

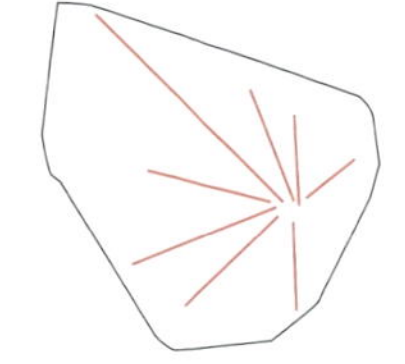

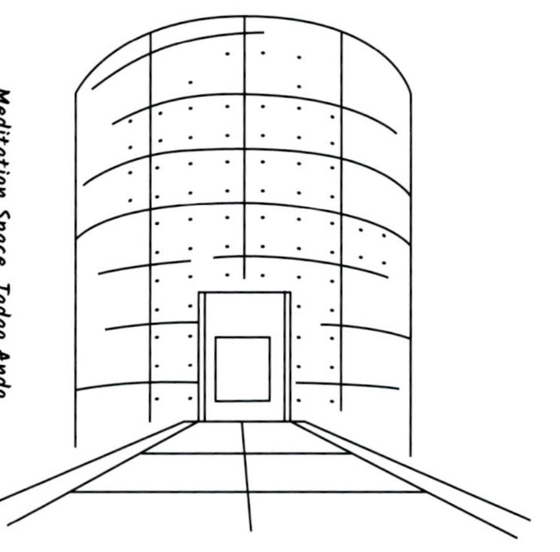

Meditation Space, Tadao Ando,
Paris, France, 1995

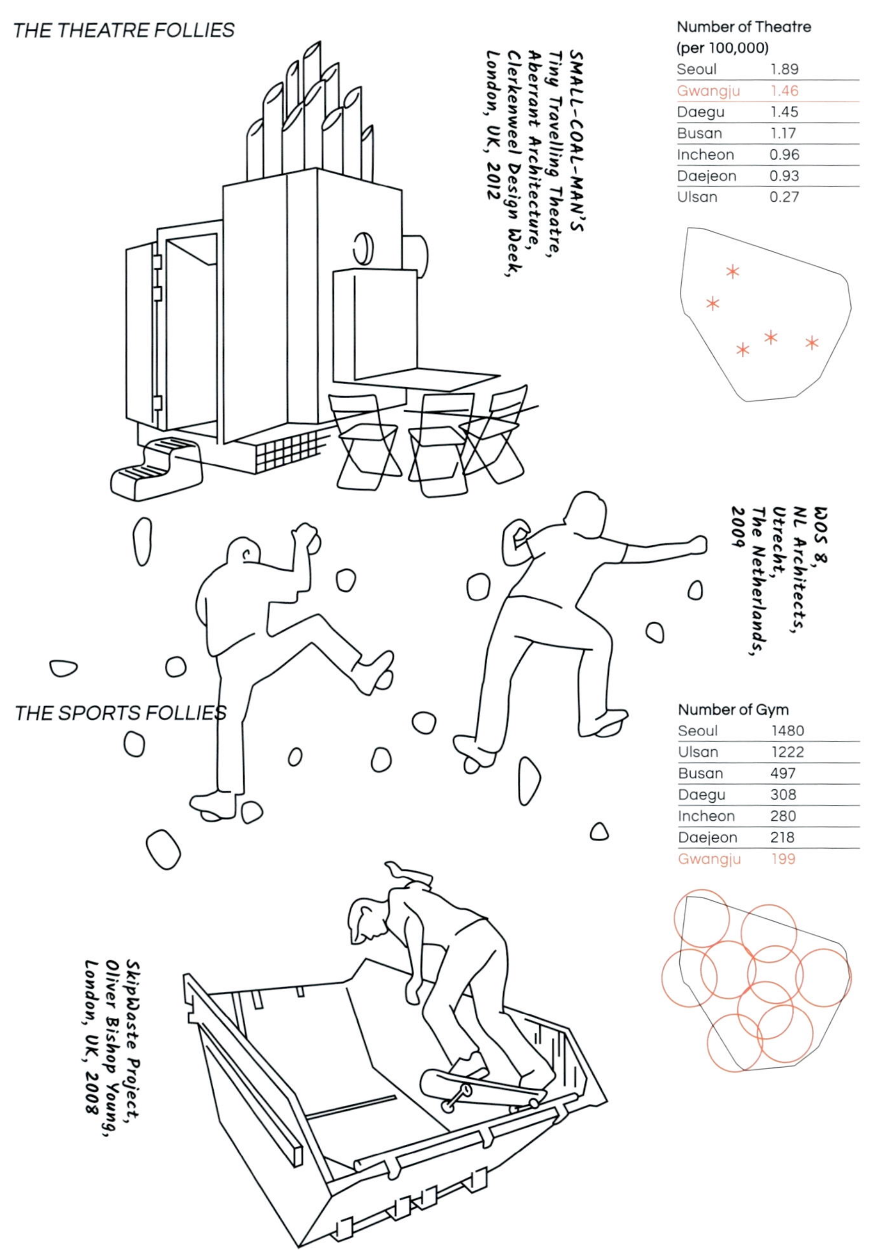

Number of Theatre
(per 100,000)

Seoul	1.89
Gwangju	1.46
Daegu	1.45
Busan	1.17
Incheon	0.96
Daejeon	0.93
Ulsan	0.27

Number of Gym

Seoul	1480
Ulsan	1222
Busan	497
Daegu	308
Incheon	280
Daejeon	218
Gwangju	199

THE PLAYGROUND FOLLIES

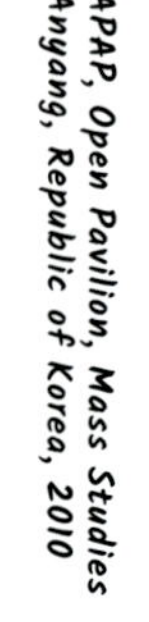

APAP, Open Pavilion, Mass Studies
Anyang, Republic of Korea, 2010

Flower Pavilion,
A2C (ATELIER ZÜNDEL CRISTEA),
Berlin, Germany, 2014~

THE EVENT FOLLIES

Degree of Children's Happiness (rank)

Daejeon	1st
Seoul	2nd
Busan	3rd
Incheon	4th
Ulsan	5th
Daegu	6th
Gwangju	7th

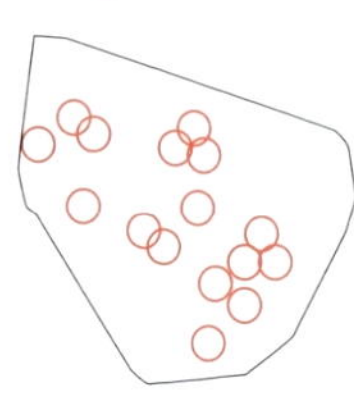

Number of Festival in 2012

Seoul	113
Busan	39
Incheon	31
Daegu	29
Gwangju	14
Daejeon	14
Ulsan	11

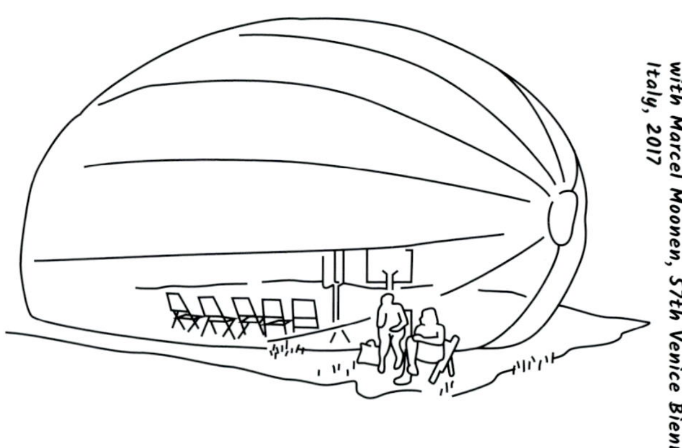

Giardini Pavilions, RAAAF
(Rietveld Architecture-Art-Affordances)
with Marcel Moonen, 57th Venice Biennale,
Italy, 2017

THE PEDESTRIAN FOLLIES
THE PUBLIC TRANSPORTATION FOLLIES
THE BICYCLE FOLLIES
THE HERITAGE FOLLIES
THE GREEN FOLLIES
THE COOLING FOLLIES
THE ENERGY FOLLIES
THE LIBRARY FOLLIES
THE EXHIBITION FOLLIES
THE THEATRE FOLLIES
THE SPORTS FOLLIES
THE PLAYGROUND FOLLIES
THE EVENT FOLLIES

POSSIBLE RESPONSES What can be done about these observations? What can small interventions do about these characteristics and tendencies? Where should they then be taken to make them most effective? Can new follies be used to test these directions at one spot? At which one, then? What would be the best place?

THE CATALOGUE This has led to a catalogue of illustrative folly dreams that indicate and demonstrate these interventions: from the pedestrian follies, via the public transportation follies, the bicycle follies, the heritage follies, the green follies, the cooling follies, the energy follies, the library follies, the exhibition follies, the theatre follies, the sports follies, and the playground follies all the way to the event follies themselves.

THE NEXT STEPS Some of these interventions have been developed in more detail. Strategically located in Gwangju, each intervention activates the public space of the area. They are all situated close to the other follies. They can also reinforce the pedestrian connections between two major green spaces of the area, Sajik Park and Greenway Park. Some examples including the following:

L. THE CLOSED STREET FOLLY
R. THE UNDERGROUND CITY FOLLY

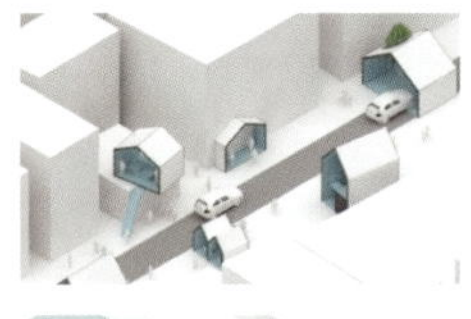

L. THE ACTIVITY BRIDGE FOLLY
R. THE TRAFFIC ISLAND FOLLY

THE EMERGING VILLAGE FOLLY

walk

THE CLOSED STREET FOLLY

Pedestrians in the centre of Gwangju are being threatened by cars. Put simply, one cannot walk. At MunHwa JeonDang 23rd Street (Munhwajeondang-ro 23beon-gil, Dong-gu, Gwangju), various small-scale shelters have been erected to define a more pedestrian-oriented lane and to slow down vehicle traffic. These efforts will bring life back to the street and re-activate the city centre.

THE UNDERGROUND CITY FOLLY

An old military bunker from the Japanese ruling era (1910-1945) is situated under a hill at Sajik Park, and it has been proposed that it be re-opened for holding exhibitions. A mirror floor could be added to dramatise the inherent beauty there, making it a true round tunnel. Media projections on the floor could amplify the anti-gravity experience for visitors and attract more people.

THE ACTIVITY BRIDGE FOLLY

Despite of it strategic location within the pedestrian network of the city, Keum Bridge, which is located on the Gwangju River, has been mainly used for motor vehicle traffic. By reducing car lanes and adding a wider sidewalk/lane for pedestrians & bikes, as well as creating some kind of public-oriented program, the bridge could function as a public 'living room', with fantastic views over the river. That would help turn it into a destination and not just a transit space.

THE TRAFFIC ISLAND FOLLY

Ironically, traffic islands in Gwangju could be what oases are for a desert. By adding zebra paths, and trees, and a mirrored wall, people could experience infinite nature within islands like this one at an intersection in front of Dong-gu Office (intersection of 1, Seonam-ro, Dong-gu, Gwangju).

THE EMERGING VILLAGE FOLLY

Dongmyeong-ro, No. 67 Rd. used to be a part of an urban village. In 2013, a series of houses began to be torn down to provide more space for cars. How could anyone see this as a good idea? Is there any way to repair the damage already done? By changing the current pavement, cars can be blocked and space can be provided for playing. By tearing up the pavements here and there, the former village can reappear, commemorating the former houses, as if resurrected from below the pavement.
A love song (duet) is added by artist Jeroen Kooijmans that tells the (love) story of former residents.

THE "I LOVE" STREET FOLLY

Jebong-ro 82 (Seoseok Primary School, 26, Jebong-ro 82beon-gil, Dong-gu, Gwangju) closed for traffic. In collaboration with Seoseok Primary School, a series of their requests has been explored. That has led to multiple different pavements that can be used for sitting, painting, jumping on trampolines, and playing in the sand.

Children Playing in the Sand at
THE I LOVE STREET

By shaping these pavements in a series of letters, a true text appears, indicating people's love for many things through 'I LOVE'. At the same time, a neutral square space at the end of the text is maintained for everyone's personal use, and it can even be painted and adapted like a canvas. I LOVE can thus become I LOVE KOREA, I LOVE KIM, I LOVE WALKING, I LOVE THE MAYOR, I LOVE GWANGJU, or I LOVE YOU, for example. This text can be seen from a special tribune spot at the beginning of the street. This tribune also provides access to a platform that is five meters high, with a bench and a table. From here, the gardens can be viewed and a selfie can be taken. The chalkboard space is transformed into a dance floor every evening with special lights, while love songs from Jeroen Kooijmans will be played to get people dancing – I LOVE DANCING!

Selfie at Yellow Tribune,
THE I LOVE STREET

Drawings by Seoseok Primary
School Students

WHAT'S NEXT? Within the current time frame and budget, the I LOVE folly and street has been realised. But why not follow through with the rest, and even more? If we can do that then we will all be able to walk around the emerging city and soak in, with its observations on the future. Folly Town.

Winy Maas
November 17, 2017

Urban Sketchbook Event with
Seoseok Primary School
Students at GD Folly (Sep. 18, 2017)

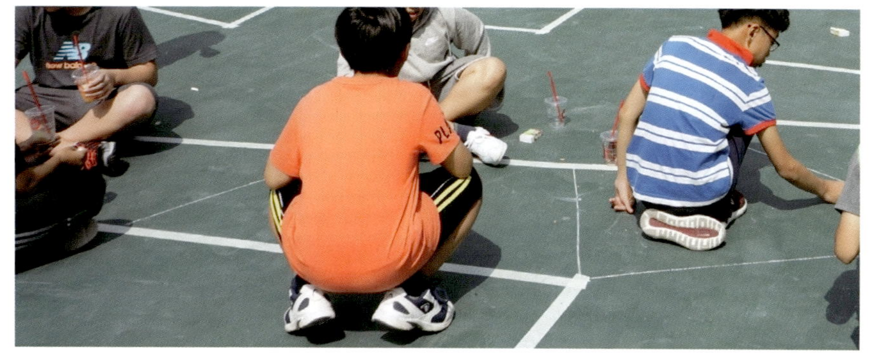

 Gwangju Folly Town, Small Things Do Help!

Urban Sketctchbook Event with
Seoseok Primary School
Students at GD Folly (Sep. 18, 2017)

walk

→ 258 **미래의 도시**

우리는 미래를 상상할 때 우리에게 필요한 크고 급격한 변화들을 그려보곤 한다. '우리를 채워줄 더 넓고 풍부한 자연', '오염을 줄이고 도시를 더 친화적으로 만들기 위한 차량 금지 조치', '자전거와 보행자를 위한 보다 넓은 공간', '더 나은 교통수단 덕에 더 이상 직장까지 멀리 통근할 필요가 없게 되는 것', '무색무취의 어느 변두리 지역이 아니라 우리가 도시에 다시 살 수 있게 되는 것', '우리 아이들이 뛰어놀 수 있도록 녹지를 늘리고, 시원한 바람이 부는 쾌적한 도시에서 친구들을 만나는 것', '풍부한 수자원을 바탕으로 도시의 의존도를 낮추고, 도시의 회복력을 위해 에너지의 원천은 늘리는 것'.

시간

이 모든 꿈을 실현시키려면 아주 긴 시간과 굳은 신념이 필요할 것이다. 현실화를 위해 법도 개정해야만 할 것이다. 상호적, 집단적 합의를 위해 무수한 토론이 벌어질 것이며. 이를 실현하기 위해서 더 많은 예산이 요구되고 일도 많아질 것이다. 이러한 환상과 꿈을 이루기 위해서는 상당한 시간이 소요된다.

작음

때로는 작은 개입이 도시의 변화를 이끌 수 있다. 단기간에 달성할 수 있기 때문에 정치인들이나 정부의 정치적 역량 안에서 가능하다. 상대적으로 덜 복잡한 주변 환경 속에서, 한정된 이해당사자들과의 직접적인 소통을 통해 실현될 수 있다. 이는 의사결정 과정을 가속화하고 대중적 열광을 고취시켜 실현 과정에 기여하게 만들 수 있다.

→ 259 **폴리:**
     터무니 있음과 없음의 차이

폴리는 터무니 있음으로, 동시에 터무니 없음으로 여겨진다. 도심 공간 안에서의 작은 개입이다. 간혹 예술 작품의 일부로도 취급되지만 왠지 경박하고 임시적이며 무해하고 만만하게 여겨진다. 혹자는 폴리가 우리의 유희를 위해 존재한다고도 이야기한다. 보통 작가나 건축가들이 그들의 환상에 기반해 만들어낸다. 폴리는 본디 말이 되지 않는 요소들이다. 심지어 터무니없기도 하다. 그런데, 이것이 정말 모두 진실일까? 폴리는 관찰자들로 하여금 놀라운 시각을 갖게 할 수 있기 때문에 기존의 문제를 시각화 하는데 도움을 줄 수 있다. 폴리는 사람들을 웃게도 하고 고민하도록 하기도 하는데 비판을 가능하게 하여 더 넓은 꿈을 볼 수 있도록 하는 것이다. 동시에 커다란 꿈을 조그마한 사례들로 실현 가능케 하며, 때로는 프로토타입처럼 도시의 아주 작은 장소에서 테스트할 수 있기 때문에 도시 정책 변화에 실제로 적용될 수 있다.

광주1

대한민국 광주라는 도시는 외국인들에게 잘 알려져 있는 곳은 아니다. 하지만 몇몇 놀라운 특징들을 가지고 있다. 자동차 산업이 매우 발전했고, 모든 이들이 봄에 걷고 싶어 할 벚꽃 흐드러진 능선들 사이에 자리하고 있다. 대한민국의 민주주의가 시험대에 올랐던 장소이기도 한다. 이를 기리는 아름다운 문화시설(국립아시아문화전당)이 있는 곳이기도 하다.

→ 260 **광주2**

그러나 자동차가 점령한 거리들로 인해 걷거나 자전거를 타기엔 힘든 도시이기도 하다. 대부분의 건축물들이 평범하고 눈에 띄는 건축적 특징들을 지니고 있지는 않은 도시이다. 강이나 강가가 세심하게 관리받지 못하기도 하다. 도시 내에 녹지 또한 많지 않다. 도시에 활력을 줄 수 있을만한 개선점들을 나열하는 것은 외지인인 나에게 전혀 어렵지 않은 일이다.

한국의 도시

어떻게 보면, 이는 광주만의 특징은 아니다. 솔직히 말해 한국의 도시들은 모두 비슷한 모습이다. 상대적으로 평평한 지대에 자리하며, 산으로 둘러싸여 있다. 차들이 점령한 무색무취의 도로들이 지나간다. 모두 똑같아 보이는, 반복적이고 유사한 형태의 주택들로 구성되어 있다. 우리는 어떻게 광주가 드러나 보이도록 할 수 있을까? 어떻게 차이를 만들어낼 수 있을까? 어떻게 하면 호기심과 감탄, 그리고 광주의 멋을 끌어올릴 수 있을까? 그래서 사람들이 더 오고 싶어 하도록 만들 수는 없을까?

폴리타운 광주

수년에 걸쳐 광주 내 일련의 폴리를 구축하기로 한 몇 해 전의 그 결정은 과감한 발걸음이었다. 그 중 몇몇은 아주 성공적이었다. 후안 헤레로스가 설계한 공중에 부양하는 띠의 형상은 도심에 버려진 한 모퉁이의 존재를 환기시키며 다수가 사용하는 팝업 지대로 변모시켰다. 푸른 길로 이어지는 승효상의 층계들은 작지만 효과적인 문화공간으로 기능하고 있다. 이들은 어떠한 도시들에서도 나타나지 않은 현상을 만들어낸 것이다. 이렇게 그들은 광주를 더 흥미롭고 매력적으로 만들 수 있다. 다른 도시에는 없는 단 한 가지 그것이 바로 광주의 폴리타운이다.

→ 261 ### 광주폴리 사업은 타당한 것인가?

하지만 일부 시민들은 광주폴리 사업이 타당한 것인가에 대해 의구심을 갖고 있는 듯하다. 그들은 예산이 광주폴리 사업에 배당되는 것이 과연 옳은 것인지, 도시가 지속적으로 광주폴리 프로젝트를 추진할 것인지에 대해 확신이 없는 것 같다. 터무니없는 듯한 이 폴리들이 실제로 터무니가 있는지 없는지, 어떻게 그러한지에 대한 이야기가 혹시 이러한 질문들의 답이 될 수 있을까? 광주폴리의 미래가 가지고 있는 잠재성에 대한 탐구는 이미 진행되고 있다. 우리는 어떠한 방법을 통해 앞으로의 광주폴리가 더 '말이 되는 것'으로 만들 수 있을까?

→ 262 ### 광주폴리 리서치

광주의 구도심을 중심으로 여러 차례의 도시 리서치를 진행했다. 광주와 한국, 다른 나라에 있는 여러 도시들을 비교하면서 광주가 가지고 있는 강점과 약점을 정리할 수 있었다. 예를 들자면, 광주의 경우 다른 도시보다 걷기가 쉽지 않고 대중교통 시설이 부족할 뿐만 아니라 자전거전용도로, 관광지, 녹지 비율, 혹서기 기온, 에너지 자립도, 공공도서관, 전시, 공연장, 체육시설, 놀이터와 도시이벤트 등 많은 부분들이 타 도시들에 비해 상대적으로 부족하거나 낮았다.

→ 262 **보행로 폴리**

2013 걷기 실천률(%)

서울	55.9
대전	50.3
인천	48.9
부산	42.8
대구	42.1
광주	38.4
울산	41.9

위. 레이라 육교(발코니 육교),
MVRDV, 레이라,
포르투갈, 2003-2005
아래. 레이라 육교
(놀이터 육교),
MVRDV, 레이라,
포르투갈, 2003-2005

→ 263 **대중교통 폴리**

여객시설주변 접근로
보행환경(환산값)

인천	12.4
서울	12.1
대구	9.4
부산	9.3
대전	7.4
광주	6.6
울산	5.0

자전거폴리

보행환경(환산값)

대구	3.00
서울	2.58
울산	2.34
대전	2.11
인천	1.74
광주	1.54
부산	1.07

위. 크룸바흐 버스정류장,
알렉산더 브로드스키,
크룸바흐, 독일
중간. 버스정류장,
스파른 병원, NIO 건축사,
호프도로 네덜란드, 2003
아래. 빗 모양 자전거 거치대,
노하우 샵, 미국

→ 264 **문화유산 폴리**

자전거 교통수단 분담률(%)

부산	16.3
대구	13.59
울산	13.63
대전	11.03
광주	9.01
부산	1.07
서울	N/A

녹지 폴리

1인당 도시공원 면적(m^2)

울산	39.84
대전	34.88
대구	34.21
인천	32.46
서울	23.14
부산	16.13
광주	13.22

위. 서원문 제등, 플로리안
베이겔, 광주, 대한민국
중간. 599벙커, RAAAF와
아틀리에 라이온, 네덜란드
아래. 신더블록 벽돌을
이용한 채소 정원

→ 265 **쿨링 폴리**

1인당 도시공원 면적(m^2)

대구	21.17
광주	16.43
울산	13.67
대전	10.83
서울	6.57
인천	3.4
부산	2.1

에너지 폴리

폭염일수(일)

인천	325.2
부산	187.3
대구	34.2
울산	33.1
광주	4.9
서울	1.8
대전	1.7

위. 아이스 파빌리온,
올라퍼 엘라아슨,
레이카비크 아트 뮤지움,
레이캬비크, 1998
중간. 볼보의 휴대용 솔라
파빌리온, SDA
(Synthesis Design +
Architecture)
아래. 엔데사 파빌리온,
IAAC 건축연구소,
로드리고 루비오,
미구엘 게레로, 바르셀로나,
스페인, 2011

→ 266 **도서관 폴리**

공공도서관 월 평균 이용 빈도

서울	1.1
인천	0.9
광주	0.6
부산	0.6
대구	0.6
울산	0.6
대전	0.5

전시 폴리

연간 전시 횟수(2014)

서울	7533
부산	880
대구	497
광주	279
대전	241
울산	217
인천	176

위. 광주천 독서실,
타이에 셀라시, 데이비드
아자예. 광주, 대한민국
중간. 공공 야외 도서관,
뉴욕, 미국
아래. 명상공간, 안도 타다오,
파리, 프랑스, 1995

→ 267 **공연장 폴리**

10만명 당 공연장 수

서울	1.89
광주	1.46
대구	1.45
부산	1.17
인천	0.96
대전	0.93
울산	0.27

스포츠 폴리

체력단련장 수

서울	1480
울산	1222
부산	497
대구	308
인천	280
대전	218
광주	99

위. 작은 석탄 배달부의
조그만 순회 극장, 애버랜트
아키텍쳐, 클러큰월 디자인 위크,
런던, 영국, 2012
중간. 스킵웨이스트 프로젝트,
올리버 비숍 영,
런던, 영국, 2008
아래. WOS 8, NL아키텍츠,
위트레흐트, 네덜란드, 2009

→ 268 **놀이터 폴리**

어린이 행복감 순위

대전	1
서울	2
부산	3
인천	4
울산	5
대구	6
광주	7

이벤트 폴리

2012 축제 총괄표(개)

서울	113
부산	39
인천	31
대구	29
광주	14
대전	14
울산	11

위. APAP 오픈 파빌리온,
마스 스터디즈, 안양공공예술
프로젝트, 안양, 대한민국, 2010
중간. 꽃 파빌리온,
AZC(ATELIER ZÜNDEL
CRISTEA), 베를린, 독일, 2014
아래. 지아디니 파빌리온,
RAAAF와 마르셀 무넨,
57회 베니스 비엔날레,
이탈리아, 2017

→ 269 **오버랩**

보행로 폴리
대중교통 폴리
자전거폴리
문화유산 폴리
녹지 폴리
쿨링 폴리
에너지 폴리
도서관 폴리
전시 폴리
공연장 폴리
스포츠 폴리
놀이터 폴리
이벤트 폴리

→ 270 **가능한 제안**

이러한 조사 결과에 대해 우리는 무엇을 할 수 있을까? 작은 개입들이 광주가 가지고 있는 이러한 특징과 성향에 어떤 작용을 할 수 있을까? 이러한 개입들이 어느 장소에서 이루어져야 가장 효과적일까? 한곳에서 다양한 방향들을 시험에 볼 수 있는 매개체로 새로운 폴리를 사용할 수는 없을까? 만약 그렇다면 어디에? 어느 곳이 최적의 장소일까?

도록

이러한 연구의 결과는 도시에 개입한 시도들을 표시하고 보여주는 이미지들로 구성된 도록으로 완성되었다. 보행자 폴리를 시작으로, 대중교통 폴리, 자전거 폴리, 문화유산 폴리, 그린 폴리, 쿨링 폴리, 에너지 폴리, 도서관 폴리, 전시 폴리, 극장 폴리, 스포츠 폴리와 놀이터 폴리, 이벤트 폴리에 이르기까지…

다음 단계

이들 중 몇몇의 개입들은 보다 구체적으로 발전되었다. 광주라는 전략적 맥락 안에서 각각의 개입들은 공공장소를 활동적인 공간으로 변모시킨다. 다른 폴리들과 근접한 곳에 자리하며 광주의 대표적 녹지 공간인 사직공원과 푸른길공원을 잇는 보행자 공간을 강화하는 역할을 한다.

→ 270 L. 보행자 전용 폴리
R. 뒹굴뒹굴 폴리

L. 금교 폴리
R. 교통섬 폴리

부활하는 마을 폴리

→ 271 **보행자 전용 폴리**

광주 도심의 보행자들은 자동차로부터 위협받고 있다. 걷기가 불가능할 정도다… 문화전당 23번길에는 소규모의 상점들이 세워져 보행자 도로를 구분 짓고 승용차 속도를 제한하는 역할을 한다. 이들은 도로 위의 삶과 도심의 새로운 활력을 가져다줄 것이다.

뒹굴동굴 폴리

사직공원 지하에는 일제강점기(1910-1945) 시절에 지어진 옛 군사 벙커가 자리하고 있는데, 현재는 전시공간으로 재사용되고 있다. 이곳 바닥에 거울을 설치해 공간의 아름다움을 보다 극적으로 드러낼 수 있을 것 같다. 이렇게 비로소 완벽한 원형의 형태를 갖춘 터널이 되기 때문이다. 지면을 향해 투사하는 미디어 프로젝션 작업은 무중력 상태의 경험을 선사해 시민들의 관심을 사로잡을 것이다.

금교 폴리

도시의 보행네트워크에서의 전략적 위치에도 불구하고, 광주천 금교는 대체로 차량의 통행을 위해서만 사용되어 왔다. 보행자와 자전거를 위해 차선을 줄여 통로를 확장시키고 일련의 공공 프로그램을 도입함으로써 이 교량은 강이 보이는 탁월한 전망을 지닌 시민들의 거실 역할을 수행할 수 있다. 이로써 금교는 단지 통과하는 공간이 아닌 '목적지'가 되는 것이다.

→ 271 **교통섬 폴리**

　　역설적이게도 광주의 교통섬은 사막에서의 오아시스 같은 역할을 할 수 있다. 녹지와 함께 거울로 이루어진 벽면을 세우면 보행자는 끝없이 펼쳐진 자연을 경험할 수 있는데, 바로 동구청 앞 교차로가 그 예이다.

→ 272 **부활하는 마을 폴리**

　　동명로 67번길은 한 마을의 일부였다. 2013년도부터는 주차를 위한 공간을 만들어내야 한다는 이유로 이 지역의 주택들이 철거되기 시작했다. 과연 이게 최선의 방법이었을까? 우리가 이를 바로잡을 수는 없을까? 현재의 포장도로를 변경하면 자동차의 진입을 막을 수 있으며 놀이를 위한 공간을 만들어낼 수 있다. 이곳저곳에 있는 보도를 들어내는 것은, 마치 보도 아래서부터 마을이 부활하듯 옛 마을이 다시 나타나고 그것을 기리기 위한 것이다. 예룬 코에이만스가 들려주는 듀엣 사랑노래는 이전에 살던 이들의 (사랑)이야기를 전한다.

아이 러브 스트리트 폴리

　　제봉로 82번지는 자동차 통행이 차단되었다. 서석초등학교와의 긴밀한 협업을 바탕으로 학생들의 바람이 실현되었다. 그 결과 다양한 재료의 바닥은 학생들이 앉거나, 그림을 그리거나 트램폴린 위에 뛰어놀거나 모래를 가지고 놀 수 있도록 구성되었다. 글자들을 통해 이 바닥을 형상화하면서 사람들이 실제로 사랑하는 것들을 가리키는 진정한 문장이 나타나게 된다. 바로, '나는 …를(을) 사랑한다' 이다. 글자의 끝자락에 있는 바닥의 사각의 공간은 모든 사람들이 개인적으로 사용할 수 있으며 캔버스 삼아 그림을 그릴 수도 있다. '나는 …를(을) 사랑한다'는 결과적으로 '나는 한국을 사랑한다, 나는 김00를 사랑한다, 나는 걷는 것을 사랑한다, 나는 시장을 사랑한다, 나는 광주를 사랑한다, 나는 당신을 사랑한다'가 될 수 있다. 이 글자들은 도로 시작점에 있는 계단에서 만 볼 수 있는데 5미터 높이의 이 트리뷴(계단)에는 벤치와 테이블도 놓여 있어 이곳에서 서석초등학교의 교원도 한눈에 볼 수 있고, 셀카도 찍을 수 있다. 바닥의 칠판 공간은 매일 저녁 특별한 조명과 함께 댄스 플로어로 탈바꿈하여 예룬 코에이만스가 연주하는 러브송(사랑노래)를 통해 사람들을 춤추게 할 것이다. '나는 춤추는 것을 사랑한다'처럼.

→ 273 **다음의 계획은?**
주어진 예산과 시간 안에서

우리는 '아이 러브 스트리트'라는 광주폴리 작품을 완성하였다. 하지만 이 외의 남은 것들 그리고 그보다 더 많은 것들도 만들어갈 수 있을 것이다. 우리는 다시 돌아와 걷고 탐험하고 만나며, 이 폴리타운 광주로의 귀환을 꿈꾼다…

　　위니 마스,
　　2017년 11월 17일

Gwangju Folly Town, Small Things Do Help!

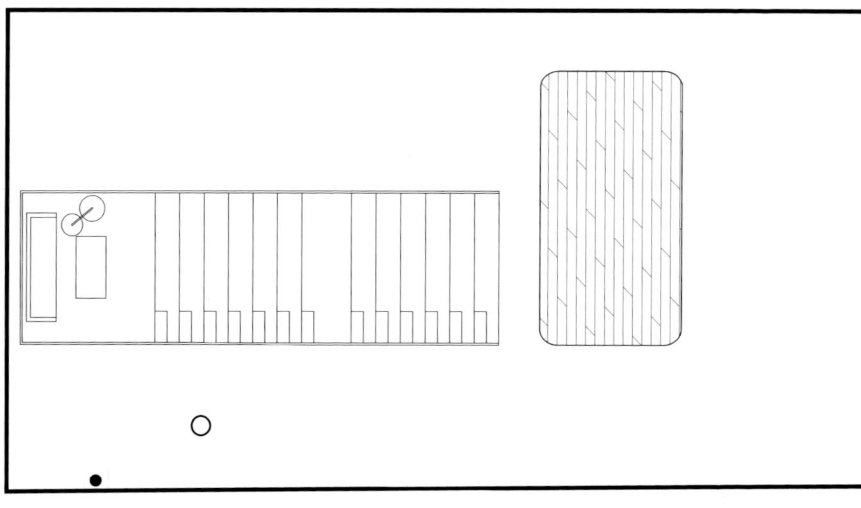

walk

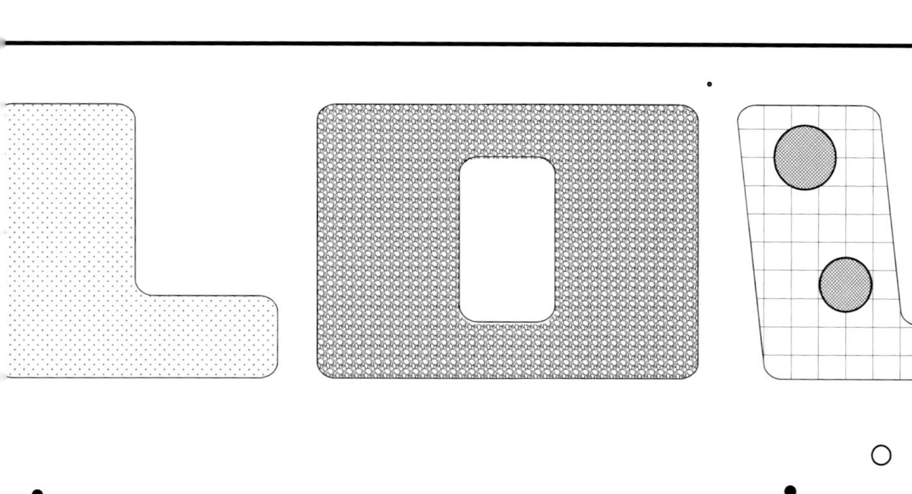

Gwangju Folly Town, Small Things Do Help!

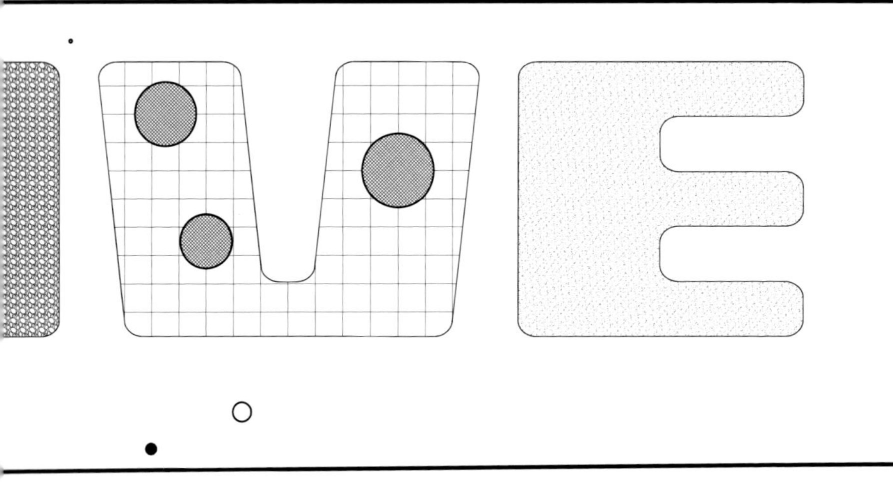

walk

Walking

walk

I Love to Dance

Jeroen Kooijmans

나는 춤을 사랑한다
예룬 코에이만스

I Love to Dance Working on
the GD Folly in collaboration with MVRDV was an interesting
adventure. I love adventures. My trip to Gwangju —and
learning about Korean culture—has inspired me in many
ways. The people I met, the expressive way of communicating that I didn't expect: The food, the karaoke bars, the
protest history, the fullness of all the visuals, and the sounds
of so many products and moments have all stayed with me.
Hearing Vivaldi's Four Seasons when the train arrived,
a futuristic song when the water boiled, car alarms, and lift
noises usually all combined with a colourful light or other
visuals. To me, Koreans seem to be visually very hungry.

Love song One of the first proposals
of MVRDV for the Gwangju Folly was a concept named
The Emerging Village. The villages (neighbourhoods) had
been demolished to make place for high-rise buildings
and car park. The Emerging Village was a concrete street,
half sunk into the pavement, and meant to serve as a monu-
ment for the villages and a tribute to times past. My contribution was "A Love Song" (duet), in which a love story
is told between a man and a woman who once lived there.
As part of this, I suggested the duet be spread out over
the neighbourhood and connect with the high-rise buildings.
It would then be broadcast daily at a fixed time to create
a special moment at the end of the day. The repetition
of this loud love song and the connection with the high-rise
buildings seemed interesting to me. The Emerging Village
was also meant to block all cars from driving and parking,
and after a protest by residents from nearby buildings, we
had to develop a new plan for a new location.

I Love Street I LOVE Street is a playground shaped like the words "I LOVE," a place where you can write words or make drawings behind "I LOVE" on a big chalkboard, whether it is someone or something you love, a personal or a public message. Gwangju is famous for its protests and demonstrations, and this is maybe an anti-protest, but even when you are against something, you still have wishes. You can take a selfie here and send it to someone or post it to the world.

The first designs of the new concept revolved around "I LOVE Ur Street," and my contribution to this concept was to change "YOU" into a green chalkboard (on the ground) in front of the primary school where people can express themselves. I like the idea that it's a constantly changing sentence, literally a "moving image." (The green chalkboard = the school board.)

My media contribution for I LOVE Street is to transform
the chalkboard into a temporary dance floor. Every evening
at 9 pm, light beams will project a light pattern on the
chalkboard and a song will be played to invite people to
dance. I Love to *Dance*.

The song is an edited version of a song
by Leonard Cohen, "Dance Me to the End of Love (by coincidence at the end of THE I LOVE Street :-) The lyrics are
translated into Korean and the music will be close to the original, but with some added Korean elements. The lyrics
are very poetic and the song seemingly right out of a movie.

I like the idea of transforming the kids'
playground in the evening into an adult "playground,"
a meeting point of sorts, if you will. The light on the dance
floor comes from above. I am still looking into a moving
light pattern and a light text for the dance floor, as the designs are still a work-in-progress as of right now. By the
time you are reading this book, the dance floor will be ready,
so please check it out and feel free to dance!

I Love To Dance: A Dance Floor for Adults
I Love To Dance: A Dance Floor for Adults

I LOVE to Dance

→ 288 　MVRDV와 함께 작업한 GD 폴리는 굉장히 흥미로운 모험이었다. 나는 모험을 사랑한다. 광주와 한국 문화로의 여행은 다방면에서 내게 영감을 주었다. 내가 만났던 사람들, 전혀 예상치 못했던 남다른 표현력의 소통 방식, 음식, 노래방, 시위의 역사, 시각적 충만함 그리고 다양한 존재와 순간들이 내는 소리들–기차가 도착할 때는 비발디의 사계가, 물이 끓을 때는 초현대적 음악이, 자동차 경보장치가 내는 소리 그리고 엘리베이터까지. 이들은 또 대체로 화려한 불빛과 시각적 효과를 동반한다. 한국인들은 시각적인 것들을 매우 갈구하는 듯하다.

사랑 노래

MVRDV의 초기 광주폴리 제안 중 하나는 '부활하는 마을'이라는 제목의 콘셉트였다. 고층 건물 주차장을 짓기 위해 (이웃)마을들이 허물어졌다. '부활하는 마을'은 포장이 반쯤 내려앉은 콘크리트 길로, 그 마을들과 과거의 시간에 대한 추모를 나타낸다. 여기서 나는 한 때 그곳에 살았던 한 여성과 남성의 '사랑 노래'(듀엣곡)를 제안했다. 주변에 퍼져 나가는 이 곡은 그 지역과 고층 건물들을 이어주는 것으로 정해진 시간에 틀어져 하루의 끝에 특별한 순간을 부여하도록 설정되었을 것이다. 크게 울려 퍼지는 이 사랑 노래의 반복성 그리고 고층건물들과의 관계 맺음에 초점을 맞췄다. '부활하는 마을'은 차량의 통행과 주차를 금지할 예정이었는데, 주민들의 반대로 인해 우리는 새로운 계획과 장소를 찾아야 했다.

MVRDV의 '아이 러브 스트리트(THE I LOVE STREET)'는 'I LOVE' 형상의 놀이터로, 'I LOVE' 다음에 위치한 대형 칠판에 글귀를 써넣거나 그림을 그릴 수 있도록 설계되었다. 즉, 당신이 사랑하는 사람 또는 무언가, 지극히 사적인 이야기부터 공개적으로 알리고 싶은 메시지까지도 담을 수 있다. 항쟁과 시위의 상징이기도 한 광주, 그러나 이 폴리는 일면 반-시위적이다. 그러나 무언가에 반대한다는 것은 무언가를 간절히 바란다는 의미이기도 하다. 당신은 셀카를 찍을 수도, 누군가에게 그를 보낼 수도, 또 그를 세상이 볼 수 있도록 포스팅할 수도 있다.

새로운 콘셉트의 초기 디자인은 '아이 러브 유어 스트리트(I LOVE Ur street)'였고, 여기서 내 역할은 '당신(YOU)'을 초록색 칠판으로 바꾸는 것이었다. 사람들이 자신을 표현할 수 있는 대형 칠판을 초등학교 앞에 설치한 것이다. '움직이는 이미지'로서 문장이 끊임없이 변화한다는 점이 아주 매력적이었다.

나는 엘스페스를 사랑해요
I LOVE Elspeth
나는 파랑을 사랑해요
I LOVE blue
나는 시간을 사랑해요
I LOVE time
나는 영감을 주는 것을 사랑해요
I LOVE to inspire
나는 기린을 사랑해요
I LOVE giraffe
나는 비밀을 사랑해요
I LOVE secrets
나는 눈썹을 사랑해요
I LOVE eyebrows
나는 치즈를 사랑해요
I LOVE cheese

레오나르드 코헨의
'사랑의 끝까지 나를 춤추게 하라'

 매일 밤 9시면 빔 조명이 이 칠판에 무늬를 만들어내, 사람들을 무대로 불러 모아 '나는 춤을 사랑한다'를 추도록 할 것이다.

이의 음악을 위해 레너드 코헨의 '사랑의 끝까지 나를 춤추게 하라(Dance me to the end of love)'를 편곡하였다. 우연의 일치로 '아이 러브 스트리트'의 끝에 위치해 있기도 하다 :-)

가사는 한국어로 번역했고, 곡은 원곡에 가깝되 일부 한국적인 요소들을 추가했다. 가사는 매우 시적이며 극적이다.

특히 아이들의 놀이터를 밤에는 어른들의 '놀이터'이자 만남의 장소로 변모시킨다는 지점이 굉장히 좋다.

무대 위의 조명은 위에서 비춰진다. 지금 이 순간 나는 이 무대를 비출 움직이는 빛의 패턴과 빛으로 만들어지는 글자들을 연구하고 있다. 이들의 디자인은 이 도록의 마감 기한이 오도록 아직 완성 중에 있다. 당신이 이 책을 읽을 즈음에는 무대가 준비되어 있을 테니, 꼭 그곳을 찾아 마음껏 춤춰주길 바란다.

GD Folly Blazes a Culture Trail for Gwangju

Lee, KiHun

문화도시 광주의 활로(活路)를 개척한 GD폴리

이기훈

1. Achievements and Challenges of Gwangju Folly I, Folly II & Folly III

Gwangju Folly I focused on the restoration of the identity and locality of Gwangju through intangible historical resources like Gwangju Eupseong Town Wall, which was destroyed in the past, showing the possibility of urban renewal through cultural interventions. However, it also faced opposition. While installing the folly, it inevitably imposed changes in the way people used existing lands, and the whole process lacked sufficient discussion and interaction with citizens.

Gwangju Folly II sought both plasticity and actual usage, suggesting a new way of using public space. However, the weight of the theme 'human rights & public space' became a burden in selecting sites and works based on imagination and creativity. Thus, an analysis on the pattern of the sites being used by participants (i.e. citizens) was overlooked, which, as a result, diminished the purpose and intention of Gwangju Folly II. However, it created various channels of engagement with the community through the Folly Citizens Committee, operation partners for each work that included citizen representatives, which was a significant advancement in realizing follies.

Gwangju Folly III started from a totally different point. In a workshop titled 'Folly & Everyday Life', Director Chun, Eui-Young claimed that Gwangju Folly III should be an indefinite 'activating device for the city' that embodies the future of the city, defining it as an urban space device for citizen and community engagement and interaction.

For this, the theme 'Folly & Everyday Life: Taste & Beauty' was selected, as these are the elements through which visitors usually experience a city while travelling. Also, in titling the works View Folly, Cook Folly, FunPun Folly and GD Folly, it attempted to make it more accessible and familiar to the public by using relatively light but relevant words.

In Cook Folly, the collaboration of renowned chef and young entrepreneurs starting their own businesses breathed life into the folly. At the same time, GD Folly was collaboratively created by Korea and the Netherlands, while FunPun Folly suggests a solution to the usual questions of public engagement and collaborating with local artists through a survival-based open-call judged by local residents. These were indeed the highlights of realizing Gwangju Folly.

Gwangju Folly III demonstrates the potential and possibility of defining and firmly establishing Gwangju Folly, and that it can contribute to the city's future as well as further developing Gwangju's brand as a cultural city.

2. A Story about GD Folly

After coming up as a possible site for GD Folly (i.e. Gwangju Folly III), Seoseok Primary School Street, where I would casually pass by in the past, grew to have social significance.

The 130m road in front of the school was the only pedestrian zone in front of any Gwangju school that prohibited all automobile traffic to ensure the safety of children. However, it could no longer function as a pedestrian zone after plans were unveiled for a two lane road for the new parking lot attached to the Asia Culture Centre. It appears that the Traffic Effect Evaluation Committee reached its conclusion in May 2015 and Dong-gu Office approved the construction

permit in December that year. Yet the Gwangju Folly Department, part of the Gwangju Biennale Foundation where public servants from the city government worked, only found this out later, and had to subsequently ask for cooperation from the Folly Citizen Committee.

Of course, the plan to install GD Folly in the pedestrian zone was also affected. Though barriers among different administrative departments was nothing new, the attitude of the city government and the Asia Culture Centre was difficult to understand.

Local civic groups that learned about this became aware of the gravity of the situation after visiting the site with Gwangju Biennale staff members. Starting from six groups, including the Regional Cultural Exchange Honam Foundation, the Korean Federation for Environmental Movement, the Gwangju Eco Bike, Children and Youth Familiar with the City of Gwangju Association, Architects Who Plant, and Parents for True Education various collaborative activities with local affiliates aunched an initiative to overturn the decision to create the two-lane road. Regardless of the installation of GD Folly, the issue was seen as a matter of value in setting an urban vision for Gwangju.

Replacing the pedestrian zone with a two-lane road was first, as increasing safety risks to children went contrary to the city's idea of making a human rights city and its children-friendly policies. Second, it went completely against the architectural concept of the Asia Culture Centre, which claimed to envision a square that symbolises democracy and materialises future values such as ecology and the environment. Third, it jeopardised damaging the urban renewal point that has infinite possibilities of creating new culture. Finally, it opposed the direction of the 6th elected city government to develop a safe and human-oriented city in that the pedestrian accident rate on two-lane roads was more than 50 percent higher than pedestrian-only zones.

However, the activities and efforts of the civic groups was not enough to overturn the city government's decision, which by then had been already made. After multiple gatherings and discussions, they realised that the parties that were directly concerned with the campaign against the road construction—namely the primary school, parents and neighbours—had not been involved. This proved a limit in the way civic society approaches issues, in that they put too much focus on the values, idea and appropriateness of a road.

Fortunately, local residents, parents and teachers from the school, and city councilors thought no differently. With everyone on the same page, things moved swiftly from there.

Finally, in January 2017, the Civic Group to Protect the Seoseok Primary School Pedestrian Zone was officially launched with the participation of local residents, the Parents' Association, the Dong-gu City Council Steering Committee, local representatives, and civic groups. We worked hard to ask for the cooperation of nearby shopping centres, residential complexes, people working in the area, and the general public. In only three days, we collected over 3,000 signatures.

The voice of the civic group resonated, forming social consensus and attracting media attention. The Asia Culture Centre and the city government, both of which had been adamant about their stance, also changed their position and decided to engage in a conversation. This was already a big step forward and raised hope, but the process was not easy.

Civic groups, the city government and the Asia Culture Centre met several times, but ended up reconfirming their differences without reaching any meaningful agreement.

Apparently, it was the parents and local residents who had the key to solving this deadlock. Local residents decided to respect the decision of parents, who

afterwards decided to keep the pedestrian zone through
a general meeting where over 90 percent of the people
voted in favour of it. With this, they strongly argued for it and
eventually the city government and the Asia Culture
Centre agreed to keep the pedestrian zone.

Afterwards, those who requested
to keep the pedestrian zone, including civic groups, parents
and teachers at Seoseok Primary School and locals, came
together to discuss the use of the space. With the condition
that the input of local residents and parents of children
who would be affected by this be reflected in the final out-
come, they agreed to have GD Folly installed.

By keeping the pedestrian zone in
front of the primary school, not only the safety of the children could be secured, but also fresh and bold ideas
could be realised, transforming a barren space into one
full of vitality.

In April 2017, the city government held
a Traffic Effect Evaluation Committee meeting and after
conducting a review, decided to keep the pedestrian road
in front of the school's entrance. This was significant
because the administrative procedures had finally wrapp-
ed up all of the efforts over the past year, including
the recent drawing event, The GD Folly I Want, in which

walk

40 students participated in. Since then, the follow-up process has been going smoothly.

3. Conclusion

Although it took a long time to confirm the pedestrian zone in front of the school as the site for GD Folly, it was clear there was much passion and devotion on the part of many different people. I hope this serves as momentum that policy-making procedures and projects that damage the values of the city will not be repeated in the future.

From the hope of the children, parents, teachers and local residents, this space will be transformed into an attractive place with the imagination and creativity of the world-renowned Dutch architect Winy Maas, who also designed Seoullo 7017.

Though walking the city as it is can be nice, it would be even better if it becomes a space with limitless cultural potential that facilitates the communication and interaction of its residents.

Gwangju Folly III is ongoing, but I hope the story behind the GD Folly site will mark a turning point for the Gwangju Folly, which is slowly being woven into the everyday life of many people.

→ 293 문화도시 광주의
활로(活路)를 개척한
GD폴리

→ 294 1. 1, 2차 폴리의
성과와 아쉬움, 그리고
3차 광주폴리

1차 폴리는 사라진 광주읍성 속 무형의 역사적 자원을 드러내 도시 정체성과 장소성을 복원하고자 했으나 기성 토지이용 행태에 변화를 강요하는 폴리의 설치가 시민들의 반발을 사기도 했다.

2차 폴리는 조형성과 사용성을 고려하고자 했으나 시민들의 접근성이 떨어져 결과적으로 '인권과 공공공간'이라는 2차 폴리 사업의 특성과 취지가 반감되었다. 하지만 폴리 시민협의회, 작품별 운영파트너, 시민참여단 등을 구성하여 지역사회와 다양한 소통 채널을 확보해 폴리 추진 과정이 진일보했다.

3차 폴리는 1, 2차 폴리와는 전혀 다른 방향으로 출발하였다. '폴리와 도시의 일상성'이란 주제로 열린 워크숍에서 천의영 총감독은 3차 폴리가 광주의 미래를 담는 새로운 비규정 형식의 '도시 활성화의 장치'가 되어야 하며, 동시에 시민과 커뮤니티의 참여와 소통의 도시공간장치가 될 것이라고 정의했다.

그런 의미에서 일반적으로 여행자들이 도시를 경험하는 요소들인 '도시의 일상성-맛과 멋'이라는 주제를 통해 새로운 폴리를 진행하고자 했다. 또한 뷰폴리, 쿡폴리, 뻔뻔폴리, GD폴리 등 너무 무겁지 않으면서도 각각의 의미가 담겨있는 네이밍을 선택하여 시민에게 보다 친숙하게 다가가고자 노력했다. 3차 폴리는 광주형 폴리의 개념과 방향을 정립하고, 폴리가 도시 발전 및 문화도시 광주의 브랜드 제고에 기여할 수 있다는 잠재력과 가능성을 보여주었다.

→ 295 2. GD폴리 장소에
얽힌 스토리

일상의 소소함을 즐기고자 무심코 지나다니던 서석초등학교 앞 도로가 필자에게 사회적 가치와 의미로 다가온 것은 3차 광주폴리의 하나인 'GD폴리' 장소로 회자되면서부터다.

서석초등학교 정문 앞 130m 도로는 광주에서 유일한 학교 앞 보행자 전용도로로 어린이들의 보행 안전을 위하여 도로의 차량 운행을 제한하는 지역이었다. 그러나 국립아시아문화전당 부속 주차장 건립으로 이 공간에 왕복 2차로 도로가 개설되어 보행전용도로로 기능할 수 없게 되었다.

확인해보니 이미 지난 2015년 5월에 광주시 교통영향평가심의위원회가 마무리되었고, 2015년 12월에 동구청의 건축허가도 승인되었다. 그럼에도 불구하고 광주시 파견 공무원이 근무하는 광주비엔날레 광주폴리부는 이러한 과정을 나중에 파악하고 폴리시민협의회에 협조를 요청하였다.

→ 296 당연히 서석초등학교 앞 보행전용도로에 'GD폴리' 작품을 설치하고자 하는 계획에도 차질이 생겼다. 행정 부서간의 칸막이식 업무야 어제 오늘의 이야기가 아니지만 납득할 수 없었던 것은 광주시와 국립아시아문화전당의 태도였다.

이러한 사실을 알게 된 지역의 시민문화단체는 광주비엔날레 관계자와 현장을 방문하면서 상황의 심각성을 인식하고 공동 행동에 들어갔다. 지역문화교류호남재단, 광주환경운동연합, 광주에코바이크, 어린이청소년친화도시협의회, 나무심는건축인, 참교육학부모회 광주지부 등 6개 단체부터 의기투합하고 해당 지역의 단체와 연대하여 왕복 2차로 도로 개설 결정을 철회하기 위한 다양한 활동을 전개하였다. 이는 'GD폴리' 설치 여부를 넘어 광주라는 도시의 미래상을 어떻게 정립하느냐, 하는 가치의 문제가 되었다.

서석초등학교 앞 보행전용도로에 왕복 2차로의 도로를 개설하겠다는 것은, 첫째로 어린이 안전을 포기하는 결정이자 광주가 지향하는 인권도시 및 어린이 친화도시 정책에 부합하지 않는다. 둘째로 민주주의를 상징하는 광장, 생태와 환경이라는 미래적 가치를 구현하고 있다는 국립아시아문화전당의 건축 취지에도 반하는 것이다. 셋째로 새로운 문화를 창출할 가능성이 무궁무진한 문화와 도시재생의 거점 공간을 훼손한다. 넷째로 보행자 사고의 50% 이상이 왕복 2차로의 도로에서 발생한다는 점에서 사람중심의 안전한 도시를 만들겠다는 민선 6기 시정 방향에 근본적으로 배치되는 것이기도 했다.

→ 297 하지만 시민문화단체의 활동과 노력만으로 이미 결정된 광주시의 결정을 되돌리기에는 역부족이었다. 여러 차례 논의와 모임을 거치면서 왕복 2차로 도로 개설 반대 운동의 직접적 이해당사자인 서석초등학교, 학부모, 지역 주민이 빠졌다는 것을 인지하였다. 가치와 철학, 당위성의 문제로만 사안을 바라보고 접근한 시민단체의 한계였다. 다행히 지역 주민, 서석초등학교 학부모와 선생님, 지역 의원들의 생각도 다르지 않았다. 이심전심, 마음과 뜻이 통하고 목표가 같아지니 일사천리로 일이 진행되었다.

드디어 2017년 1월에 지역주민, 서석초등학교 학부모회·운영위원회·학교, 시민문화단체, 동구 의원 등 이해당사자가 참여하는 '서석초등학교 보행전용도로 지키기 시민모임(이하 시민모임)'이 공식 출범하였다. 주변 상가 상인들과 주택 거주민, 직장인을 비롯한 시민들에게 보행전용도로 존치의 필요성에 대하여 열정을 다해 설득하고 협조를 구했다. 불과

3일 만에 받은 서명도 3천 명 분이 훌쩍 넘었다.

　　시민모임의 외침은 울림이 되어 시민들과 공감대를 형성했고 언론 역시 주목하기 시작했다. 요지부동이던 국립아시아문화전당과 광주시도 입장을 바꿔 시민모임과의 대화에 참여했다. 공식적인 만남을 성사시킨 것 자체가 절반의 성공이었으므로 좋은 방향으로 결과가 도출될 것이라는 기대를 가졌으나 과정은 만만치 않았다.

　　시민모임, 광주시, 국립아시아문화전당 측과 수차례의 만남이 이어졌지만 서로의 입장 차만 확인했을 뿐 별다른 접점을 찾지 못했다. 광주시와 국립아시아문화전당은 책임을 떠넘기기에 바빴으며 오히려 시민모임과 학부모, 주민과의 틈새를 파고 들어 연대의 끈을 흔들고자 했다.

→ 298 역시 해답은 학부모와 주민에게 있었다. 주민들이 학부모의 결정을 존중키로 하고, 학부모회는 전체 총회를 개최하여 90%가 넘는 비율로 아이들의 안전을 위한 보행전용도로의 존치를 결정하고 이를 관계 당국에 강력히 주장하였다. 결국 광주시와 국립아시아문화전당은 시민모임이 요구하는 보행전용도로를 보존하기로 합의하기에 이르렀다.

　　그 이후로 시민모임, 서석초등학교 학부모와 선생님, 지역주민 등 서석초 보행전용도로 존치를 요구했던 이해 당사자 들이 모여서 공간을 어떻게 활용할 것인가를 논의했다. 주민과 학부모, 어린이들의 의견을 충분히 반영하는 것을 전제로 'GD폴리' 작품을 설치하는 데 목소리가 모였다. 서석초등학교 정문 앞 도로를 보행전용도로로 두어 아이들의 안전을 확보하고, 학부모와 아이들의 발칙한 아이디어가 현실이 되어 생명력이 꿈틀거리는 공간으로 변모하는 일석이조의 효과를 기대할 수 있게 되었다.

　　2017년 4월에 광주시는 교통영향평가심의위원회를 개최하여 서석초등학교 정문 앞을 보행전용도로로 존치키로 심의·의결했다. 지난 1년간의 활동을 마무리할 수 있는 행정 절차가 완료되었다는 점에서 의미 있는 순간이었다. 최근에는 서석초 학생 40여 명이 참여한 '내가 원하는 GD폴리 그림그리기'가 열리는 등 차질 없이 후속조치가 진행되었다.

→ 298 우리 아이들을 위한
'안전한 스쿨존'을 지켜내자!

→ 299 **3. 마치며**

　　서석초등학교 정문 앞 보행전용도로는 먼 길을 돌고 돌아 'GD폴리' 장소로 정해졌지만, 이는 긴 시간 많은 이들의 열정과 헌신이 더해졌기에 가능한 일이었다. 이번 일을 계기로 정책과 사업을 이행하는 과정에서 광주를 위한다는 명분으로 도시가 지향하는 가치를 훼손하는 어리석은 일이 더 이상 반복되지 않았으면 한다.

　　앞으로 이 공간은 아이들과 학부모, 교사, 주민들의 바람에, '서울로 7017' 설계자인 네덜란드의 세계적인 건축가 위니 마스의 창의력과 상상력이 더해져 매력적인 공간으로 변모할 것이다. 있는 그대로의 도시를 걷는 것도 좋지만, 시민들의 소통 공간으로 새롭게 태어나는 문화적 잠재력이 풍성한 공간을 누릴 수 있다면 이보다 더 좋을 수 있을까?

　　3차 폴리는 여전히 진행형이지만 GD폴리의 장소가 선정되기까지의 이 이야기가 광주폴리가 지역민의 삶과 일상에 스며들어 바람직한 문화예술과 행정의 예로 자리매김하는 전환점이 될 것이라 기대한다.

WE WANT A SAFE SCHOOL ZONE
FOR OUR KIDS!
우리 아이들을 위한
안전한 통학로를 지켜내자!
2016 겨울방학 영어캠프
2016 Winter Vacation English Camp
서석초 캠프 : 2017. 1. 2.(월) ~ 1. 11.(수)
영어센터 캠프 : 2017. 1. 17.(화) ~ 1. 26.(목)
광주서석영어센터
안 전 한 등 하 교 길 화 이 팅
A Signature-collecting Campaign
to preserve a Pedestrian Zone
In front of the School
학교 앞 보행로를 지키기 위한 서명 운동
보다 사람이 우선입니다.

Gwangju GD Folly

Cho, ByoungSoo

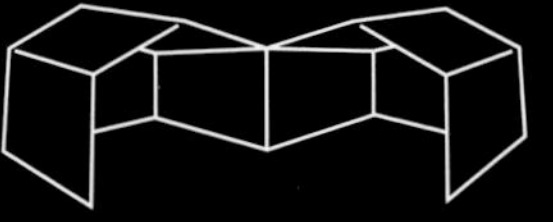

광주 GD폴리
조병수

Dream House

The Dream House from my dreams
is somewhere we
long for each other,
where we look into each other's eyes,
where we laugh together,
the house where we love each other.

The Dream House from my dreams
is at times twisted,
at times distorted,
at times deformed.
We are nevertheless there,
loving each other,
looking into each other's eyes,
tightly embracing one another.
That is why
we are blissful
in the house in our dreams.

Dream House

Gwangju GD Folly

GD Folly's Dream House is a small folly, 22m² (6.5 pyeong) in size and three meters high, situated in a small park located in Gwangju (23, Dongmyeong-ro, 67beon-gil, Dong-gu). Pureungil Park, which was converted from old railroad tracks, can be reached from the city's cultural hub, the Asia Culture Centre, by walking past Dong-gu City Hall and Jungang Library, then going straight through the residential area of Dongmyeong-dong. Dream House is in a small park situated in between the residential area near Pureungil Park. Despite being the former city centre area of Gwangju and featuring many old residential houses, it is losing this characteristic due to the large-scale development and transformation of alleys into roads that run through rows of flat, roof-tiled houses. Together with MVRDV, we focused on the daily lives of local passersby, the gradual disappearance of the old town, and scenes of back alleyways. Although narrow streets have now become wide and parking lots conveniently located, the pleasure of walking though the alleys can no longer be experienced. Perhaps that is because the strange yet familiar sight of local residents sitting on small wooden benches sharing their stories or of little children running after street cats no longer exists. Therefore, we sought to bring back memories of the old town and generate a once-known but odd experience of walking down the streets.

Dream House appears as a single house divided into two and opened up. Depending on your position, the building looks like a closed house, or a set of completely opened-up homes. As with a mirror reflection, the two houses are symmetrical. Their roofs are similar to traditional gable roofs from old Dongmyeong-dong houses. However, Dream House seems unrealistic because the gable structure is slightly distorted and deformed, almost as if it is in a dream.

The sharp corners of Dream House appear like depthless walls from afar. As you walk in, the walls gradually become thicker, eventually forming a small but cozy space for audiences of average height.

The familiar yet strange—or strange yet familiar—shape of Dream House introduces a sense of vitality to the city, while also serving as a meeting site for local residents or as a signpost. The façade of Dream House is made up of 850 brass plates, with 680 titanium plates used for the inner skin. The brass façade reflects the green trees and clear blue sky of the park, as well as the local landscape. The pinkish surface of the titanium plates are produced by reflections of light rather than paint, and their thin layers of oxidisation formed through a special colouring procedure reacts to the

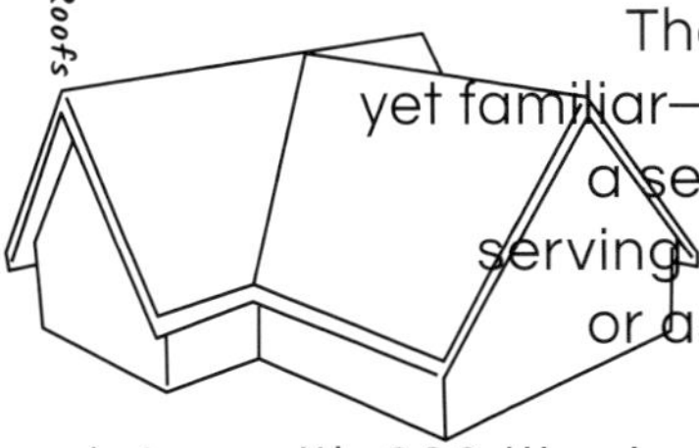

 Gwangju GD Folly

frequency and reflection of light at different angles, thereby generating a diverse array of pure colours.

In addition, the outer and inner skins have been produced by folding the corners so that all the plates hold each other tightly, rather than supporting themselves individually. As these plates were installed to fit the declining angle of the mass structure, they appear to be connected smoothly. In addition, since such materials are unusual in the surrounding neighbourhood, they lead to curiosity on the part of local residents and people walking by.

A media artwork screening takes place at Dream House after the sun goes down. Sensors detect movements of all the people passing through the park and they are transformed into special videos and sound through computer programming. These images are then projected onto the titanium surface. Overall, it creates a mysterious effect, as if looking and listening in a dream. Depending on the magnitude of the movement, the projection creates larger and more splendid images, emanating beautiful colours by reflecting off the titanium plates.

Media artwork (Time Slices; Song, JooGwan) Description
The concept of this interactive camera work is about recording a subject's movement in real-time and then regenerating the image into a projection and sound energy. Depending on how much time passes, the energy of each movement changes. In this work, 900 individual cube fragments depict the movement in one millisecond, turning them into fragmented images of each movement's waves. As a result, if the energy of the movement is stronger, the range at which the corresponding sound changes also becomes greater. The change in sound includes volume, pitch, and the speed of movement from both right and left. Consequently, audiences can witness the magnitude and traces of their movements (with a small delay that comes with transitioning from the past into the present), and begin to understand how the movement of each body in the space is affecting the flow of energy.

→ 304   꿈속에서 집 '꿈 집'
그 안에서 우리는
서로를 그리워하고,
서로를 바라보고,
서로를 웃고,
서로를 행복해하는 집

꿈속에서 '꿈 집'
때론 일그러지고,
때론 왜곡되고,
때론 변형되어도,
그 안에서 우리는
서로를 사랑하고
서로를 마주보고
서로를 부둥켜안는
그래서
서로를 행복해하는
우리 꿈속의 집,
'꿈 집'

→ 304   **광주 GD폴리**

GD폴리 '꿈 집'은 광주 동구 동명로67번길 23 소공원 내 위치한 넓이 22㎡(6.5py), 높이 3m의 작은 폴리다. 광주 문화예술의 중심지인 국립아시아문화전당으로부터 동구청과 중앙도서관을 지나 동명동 주택가를 가로지르면 옛 광주 기찻길을 공원화한 푸른길공원에 다다른다. 꿈 집은 이 푸른길공원 근방 낮은 주택가 사이의 소공원에 있다. 광주의 구도심이며 오래된 주택지였던 이곳은 지가상승과 대규모 단지개발로 인해 낮고 작은 기와 건물들 사이로 나 있던 골목길이 차도로 바뀌는 등 점점 예전 마을 풍경을 잃어가고 있다.

MVRDV와 우리는 이렇게 사라져가는 옛 마을과 골목의 풍경 그리고 그 속을 보행하는 주민들의 일상에 관심을 가졌다. 이제 골목길은 넓어지고 곳곳에 주차장이 생겼지만, 어쩐지 지금은 옛 골목길을 걷던 즐거움이 더 이상 느껴지지 않는다. 골목길 어귀에 놓인 작은 평상에 동네 주민들이 모여 앉아 나누던 이야기들, 어린 나비 고양이를 쫓아 동네를 모험하던 중 마주친 낯선 골목의 향기들이 없어서일까. 사라져가는 옛 동네의 모습을 기억하고 동네 골목길을 거닐며 느끼던 익숙하지만 낯선 체험들을 만들고자 했다.

→ 305   꿈 집은 하나의 집이 반으로 나뉘어 열린 모습을 하고 있다. 어느 각도에서 보는가에 따라 하나의 닫힌 집처럼 보이기도 하며 완전히 열린 두 집처럼 보이기도 한다. 두 집은 거울에 반사된 듯 대칭적으로 꼭 닮았다. 또한 지붕 형태는 동명동 옛 집들의 박공 모양과 비슷하다. 그러나 꿈 집의 박공 형태는 사라진 옛 집들이 꿈속에서 보이듯 약간 왜곡되고 변형된 것처럼 기울어져 비현실적으로 보인다.

꿈 집의 날카로운 모서리는 먼 거리에서 보았을 때 마치 두께가 없는 벽처럼 보인다. 안으로 들어갈수록 점점 두꺼워지는 벽체는 내부에 도달하여 보통 사람 키 높이의 낮고 작은 아늑한 공간을 만들어낸다.

익숙하지만 낯선 혹은 낯설지만 익숙한 형태의 꿈 집은 도시의 일상에 생기를 불어넣는 동시에 주민들의 모임장소나 이정표와 같은 역할을 할 수 있을 것이다.

꿈 집의 외피는 850개의 황동색 판으로, 내피는 680개의 티타늄 판으로 만들어졌다. 황동색 외피는 공원의 푸른 나무와 맑은 하늘 그리고 동네 풍경을 반사한다. 연분홍색 티타늄 외피는 칠이 아닌 재료 본연의 빛 반사에 의해 만들어지는데. 특수발색공정을 통해 티타늄 표면에 얇은 산화 피막을 형성하고, 이 산화 피막에 맞히는 빛의 간섭과 반사로 각도에 따라 다양한 천연색이 보이게 된 것이다. 따라서 꿈 집의 내부 색은 인공적인 색이 아닌 빛 자체의 순수한 색이라 할 수 있다. 꿈 집에서 아침 햇살부터 저녁노을까지 햇빛의 방향에 따라 오묘하고 풍부한 자연의 색을 볼 수 있다.

→ 306   또한 외피와 내피의 모든 판들은 모서리부분을 접어 붙이는 방법으로 만들어져 단 하나의 독립적인 판 없이 연결되어 서로를 붙잡고 있다. 이 판들은 매스의 기울어진 각도에 맞게 회전되어 있어 매스의 꺾인 면들에서도 자연스럽게 연결된다. 동네에서 쉽게 접할 수 없는 이 재료들은 주민들에게 활력을, 걷는 이들에게 보는 즐거움을 줄 것이다.

해가 저문 저녁부터 꿈 집엔 미디어아트가 상영된다. 센서를 이용해 공원을 지나가는 보행자들의 움직임을 포착하고 이를 컴퓨터 프로그램을 통해 소리와 특수 영상으로 변환하여 꿈 집 내부 티타늄 판에 영사하는데, 이는 마치 꿈속에서 듣고 보는 신비한 경험처럼 느껴진다. 보행자의 움직임이 클수록 더 크고 화려한 피사체가 나타나며, 티타늄 판에 맺힌 이 영상은 아름다운 색으로 반사된다.

미디어작품(Time Slices: 송주관 작가) 설명

카메라 인터렉티브 작품으로서, 피사체의 움직임을 카메라로 받아들여 실시간으로 변화하는, 즉 영상과 소리의 에너지로 환원시키는 콘셉트를 가지고 있다. 시간의 흐름에 따라서 움작임은 그 에너지를 달리한다. 이 작품에서는 900개의 큐브로 나뉜 파편들이 피사체의 영상을 1밀리세컨드 단위의 시간차로 나누어서 움직이는 순간둘을 파동의 이미지로 파편화해 보여주고 있으며, 움직임의 에너지가 강할수록 그에 수반되는 사운드의 변화 폭도 커진다. 사운드의 변화에는 소리의 크기, 음의 높낮이, 소리의 좌우 움직임의 속도 등이 포함되어 있다. 이로써 관객은 자신의 움직임의 크기와 동선(과거에서 현재로 이어지는 작은 시간차에 의한)의 변화를 관찰하면서 본인 스스로 움직이고 있는 그 공간에 파동을 일으키는 에너지의 흐름을 유도해낼 수 있다.

walk

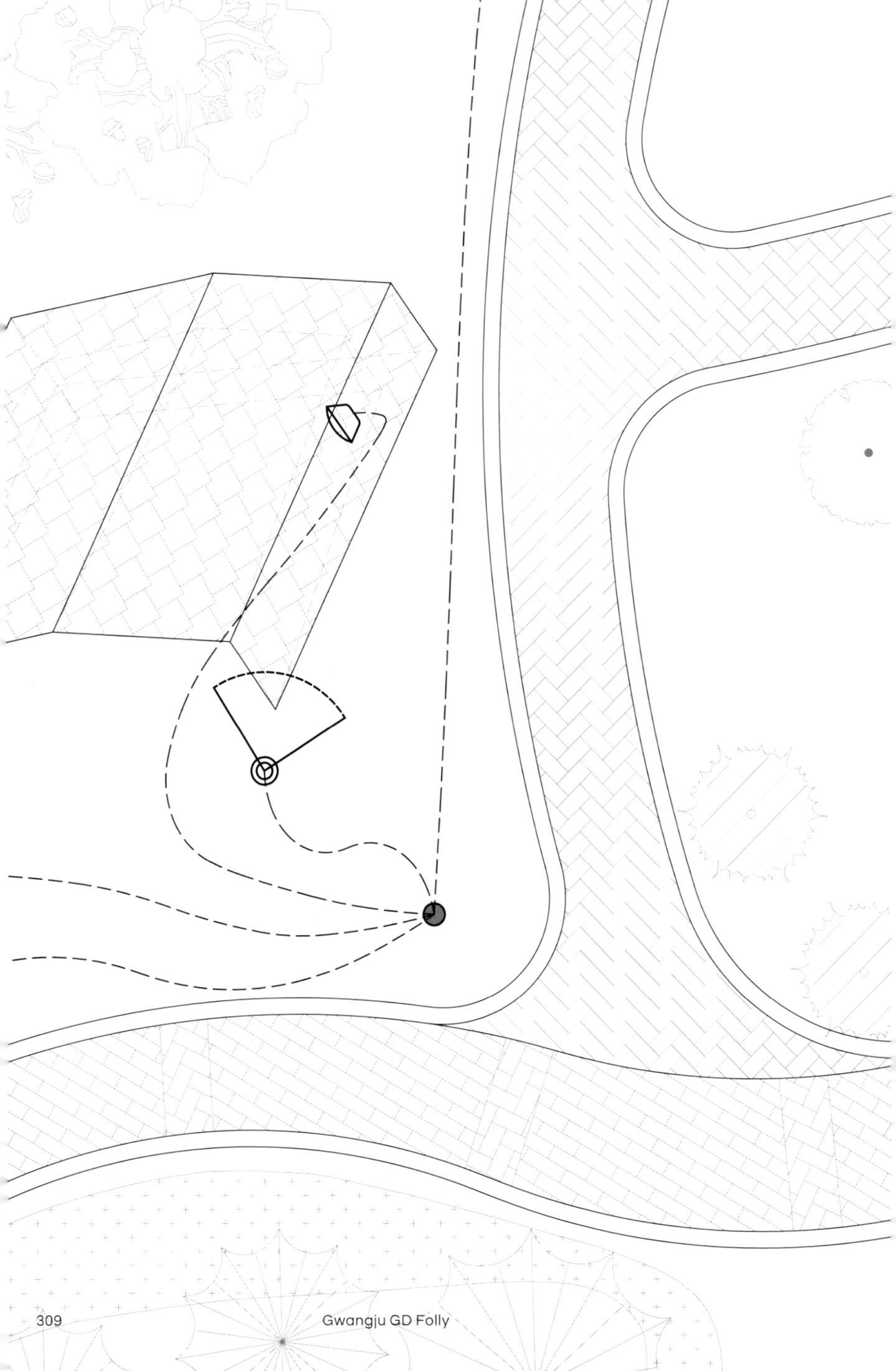

Gwangju GD Folly

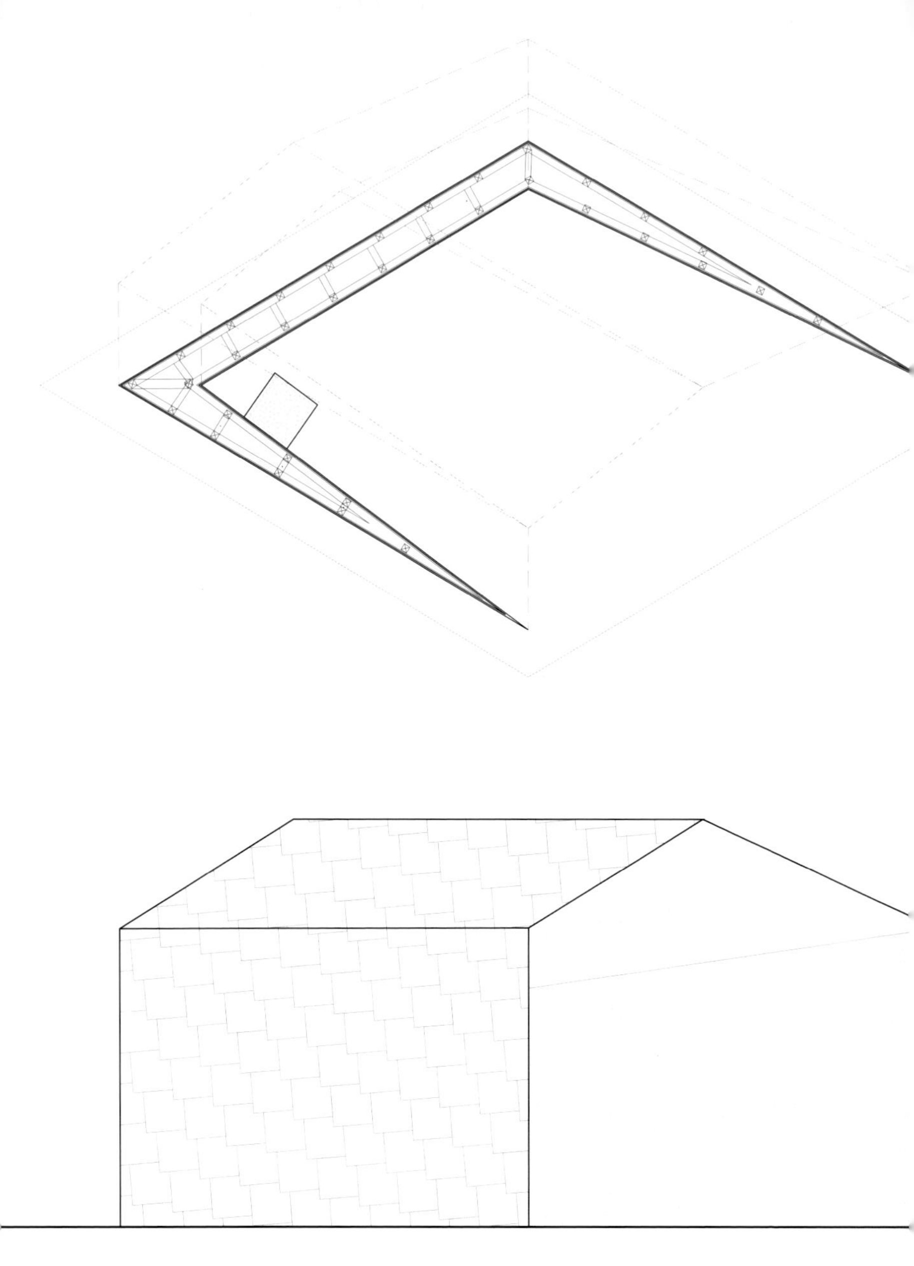

walk

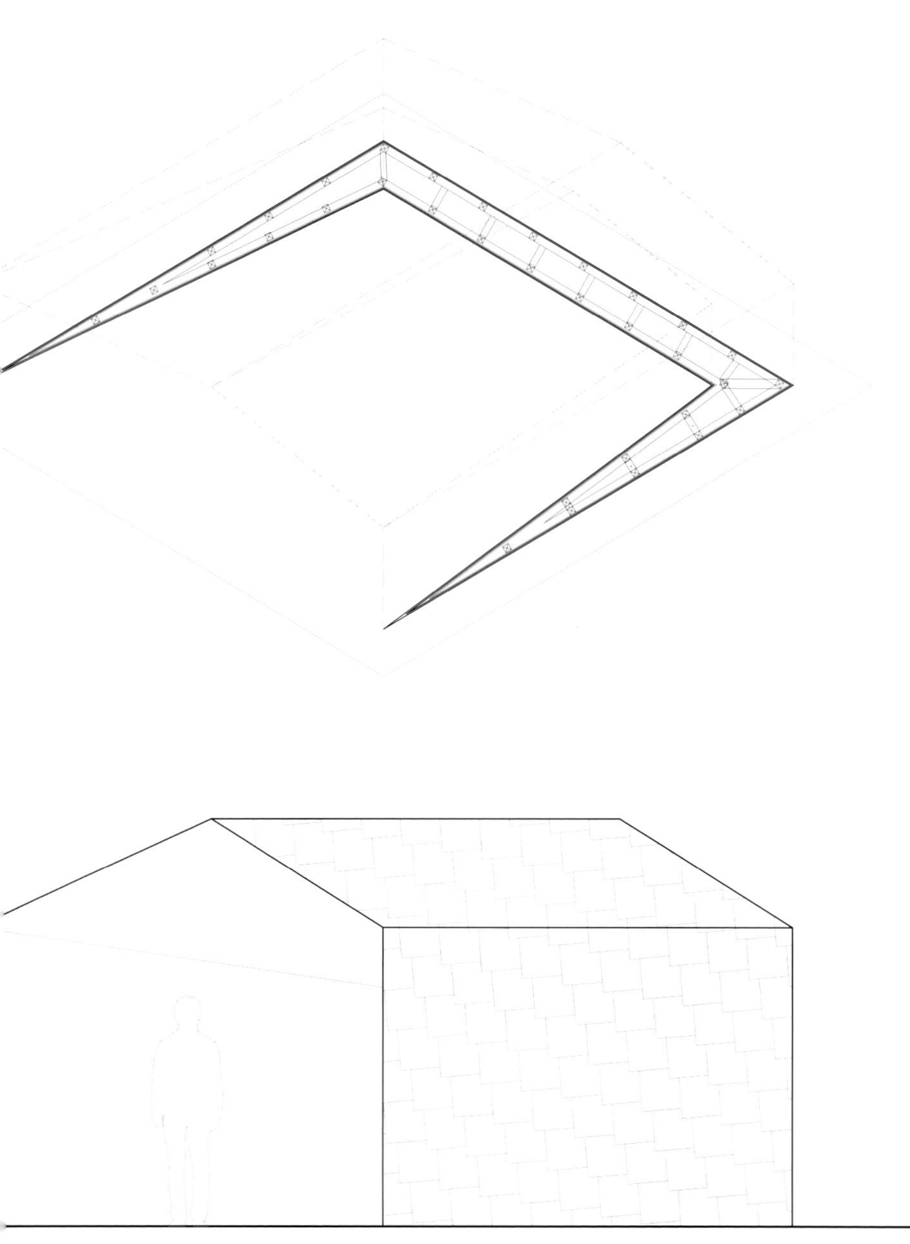

Gwangju GD Folly

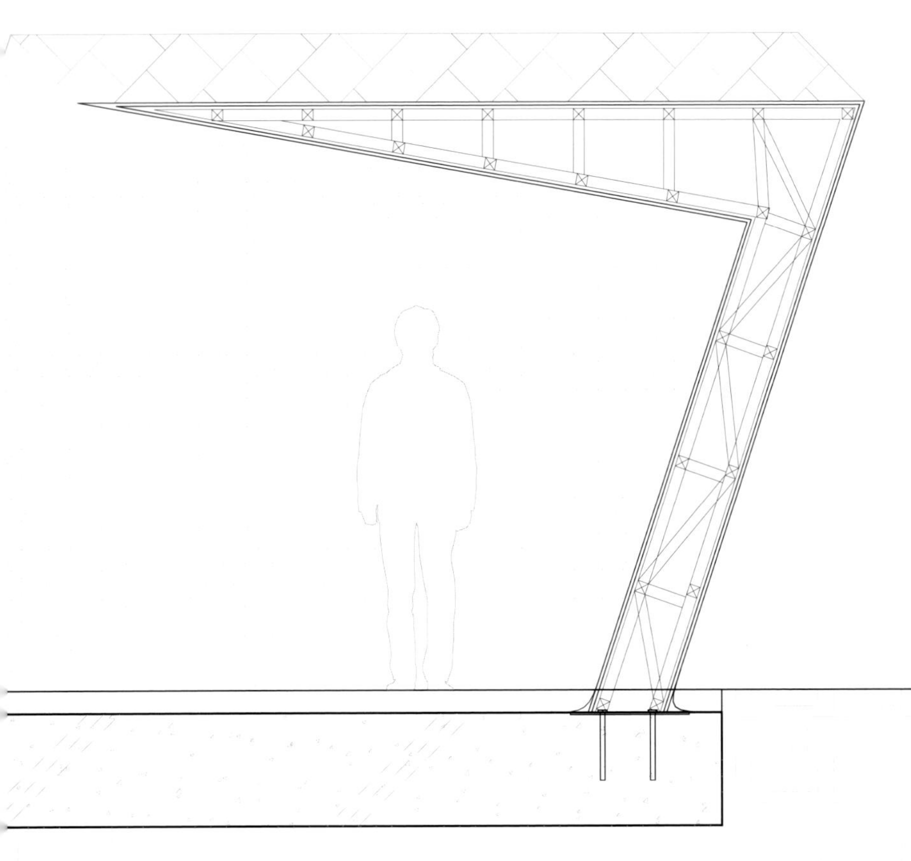

walk

External Voices
play
see
eat
walk

Mark Pimlott

Mark Pimlott is an artist, architectural designer and teacher. His work in photography, film, installation, interiors and public art attempts to make the specific characteristics of places visible and available to new uses and understandings. He is the author of *Without and Within: Essays on Territory and the Interior* (episode publishers, 2007) and *The Public Interior as Idea and Project* (Jap Sam Books, 2016). www.markpimlott.com

마크 **핌롯**은 작가이자 건축 디자이너, 교사이다. 그의 작업은 사진, 영화, 설치, 인테리어, 공공예술 등 다양한 시도를 통해 장소가 지니는 특질에 대한 새로운 이해와 용도를 제시한다. 저서로는 ‹위드 아웃, 위드 인: 영역과 실내에 대한 소고 *Without and Within: Essays on Territory and the Interior*›(episode publishers, 2007), 개념과 프로젝트로서의 공공 실내 *The Public Interior as Idea and Project* (Jap Sam Books, 2016) 등이 있다. www.markpimlott.com

Harry den Hartog

Harry den Hartog is an independent urban designer and critic. In 2004, he founded Urban Language in Rotterdam. Since 2008 he has been based in Shanghai, the heart of the Yangtze Delta Region. Through Urban Language he gives advice regarding urban design and architecture issues. He regularly publishes critiques and essays for various local and international magazines. Since mid-2012, he has been a faculty member at Tongji University Shanghai, where he teaches urban design and housing.

하리 덴 하르토흐은 프리랜서 도시 디자이너이자 비평가로, 2004년 로테르담에 도시의 언어(Urban Language)라는 싱크탱크를 설립하였다. 2008년 이래 장강 삼각주 지역의 핵심인 상하이에 거주하고 있으며, 도시의 언어(Urban Language)를 통해 도시 설계 및 건축 문제에 관한 자문을 제공하고 있다. 다양한 국내외 매거진에 정기적으로 비평문과 에세이를 기고하며, 2012년 중순부터 상하이 통지대학교 교수로서 도시 설계 및 주거를 강의하고 있다.

Kas Oosterhuis

Kas Oosterhuis is a Dutch architect. Currently, he is a Professor at Qatar University and a Professor Emeritus at Delft University of Technology. He is the director of ONL, working together with visual artist Ilona Lénárd. He was the director of Hyper body and the Proto-space Laboratory for Collaborative Design and Engineering at TU Delft. He is the author of *Towards a New Kind of Building* (NAi Publishers, 2011), and *HYPERBODY. First Decade of Interactive Architecture* (Jap Sam Books, 2012).

카스 오스터하위스는 네덜란드 출신의 건축가이다. 현재는 카타르 대학교(Qatar University)에서 교수직을, 델프트 공과대학교(Delft University of Technology)에서 명예교수직을 맡고 있다. ONL의 설립자로서 시각 예술가인 일로나 레너드(Ilona Lénárd)와 협업하고 있다. 그는 또한 델프트 공과대학의 협력적 디자인 및 엔지니어링을 위한 하이퍼바디 및 프로토 스페이스 연구실(Hyperbody and the Proto space Laboratory for Collaborative Design and Engineering)의 디렉터이다. ‹새로운 종류의 건축을 향하여(*Towards a New Kind of Building*›(NAi Publishers, 2011)와 ‹하이퍼바디, 인터랙티브 건축의 첫 10년(*HYPERBODY. First Decade of Interactive Architecture*›(Jap Sam Books, 2012)›의 저자이다.

Wim Nijenhuis

Wim Nijenhuis is a writer and architect. He is Associate Professor Emeritus Theory in Arts. He is the author of *The Riddle of the Real City, or the Dark Knowledge of Urbanism* (1001 Publishers, 2017).

빔 네이엔하위스는 작가이자 건축가이다. 예술이론학과의 명예부교수이고, ‹실제 도시의 수수께끼. 혹은 도시성의 어두운 지식(*The Riddle of the Real City, or the Dark Knowledge of Urbanism*›)(1001 Publishers, 2017)의 저자이다.

Q1. Can you give some examples of contemporary follies that have stimulated new ideas within the urban contexts?

Mark Pimlott

The Two Houses

The Stadhal Stadmarkt

The Monkey Puzzle Pavilion

Carlos Ramos Pavilion

The Stadhal/Stadmarkt in Ghent, Belgium, designed by Robbrecht en Daem, with Marie Jose Van Hee (2015) presented a sheltered yet open room in the midst of the historical centre. It can be used for many things, which are undefined, but given character by citizens. Furthermore, it is a place within the centre in which one becomes conscious of one's place in the city, and the 'room' becomes the most special room in the city, open to all.

The Monkey Puzzle Pavilion, Aberdeen, designed by Jonathan Woolf (2007) was similarly a temporary structure containing a series of beautifully proportioned rooms that transformed the central open space of Aberdeen into a meaningful space, in which the pavilion became a sort of treasure.

In that city, which is very business-like and dour, this provided a moment of grace and pleasure, and so changed the character of the city. The Two Houses of the Schilderswijk West housing project in The Hague, designed by Alvaro Siza (1988), set two functional structures containing local businesses and an entrance to an underground car park in the midst of a large-scale social housing project. Unlike the housing, which relied on repetition of accommodation, form and representative elements, the houses read as pavilions that were luxuries, more likely associated with grand ensembles. Their special expressions were sculptural and pleasurable, and they had a civilising effect on the whole project, giving it and its residents legitimacy within the city and to themselves. In the cases of Siza's Carlos Ramos Pavilion of the First Year Studio,

Architecture School, Porto (1986), and the Swimming Pool at Leça da Palmeiria, Matosinhos,
The structures reveal the city (and the alterations to the world) wrought by modernity. In the first case, the small pavilion, set in a garden, forces students to be aware of themselves as they learn. The one window onto the world looks out to the landscape beyond, with bridges, industrial buildings, and the natural forms of the mouth of the Douro into the Atlantic Ocean.
In the second case, the building, which is a series of walls and shelters, moves the swimmers through a series of spaces that culminate in a view of rocks and the sea, apparently natural, yet interwoven with low walls. When one finds oneself on a platform having lunch, an angled wall of the pool complex echoes an industrial jetty at a great distance. The world the swimmer occupies is one in which all aspects of human activity are drawn together and made visible.

Kas Oosterhuis

Bernard Tschumi's follies in La Vilette in Paris meant a rethinking of the romantic folly. In that context they fulfilled a perfect role as they organised the reclaimed urban site with a stimulation grid thanks to their abundant presence and their consistent unified appearance. Basically it was one large distributed folly, fragmented into 42 pieces. For me the power of his proposal is not deconstructivist at all; it is the power of a consistent urban strategy rather than the virtue of a philosophy. Just one folly in an urban context—in any urban context—will quickly get lost and will not have the power to stimulate the urban context; it would not be not much different from kiosks or works of public art. My own iWEB pavilion at the TU Delft campus is an example how isolated follies may get lost, and eventually are no longer supported by the community.
The iWEB became isolated after the big fire in 2008, which destroyed the Faculty of Architecture.
The iWEB became disconnected. Up to the moment of the big fire it was a successful intervention in the fabric of the campus.

Only when there would have been a subsequent urban strategy as to build a series of stimulation points at the TU Delft Campus, the iWEB would have survived and could have played a constructive role.

Harry den Hartog

The first one that comes to mind is of course Parc de la Vilette in Paris, but that was 20 years ago, thus not contemporary. In China, where I live, there have been several parks established with a collection of follies by various artists. The most famous and influential ones are probably Jinhua Architecture Park (Jinhua), the China International Practical Exhibition of Architecture (Nanjing), and the West Bund (Shanghai). In these three cases, it is not one individual folly but the collection of follies as a whole that matter.

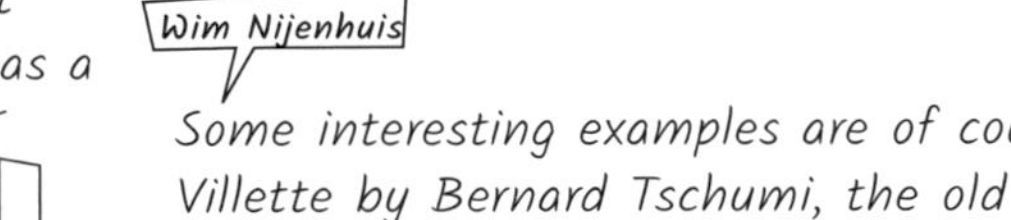
The Old Mines
in the Ruhrgebiet

The West Bund

Jinhua Architecture Park

Wim Nijenhuis

Some interesting examples are of course Parc de la Villette by Bernard Tschumi, the old mines in the Ruhrgebiet since the Ruhr Area was European Cultural Capital, as well as the old bunkers in the same area, the Gasholder in Dusseldorf, the old Bahnhof in Osnabruck, the harbour area, and some harbour buildings in Rotterdam and Amsterdam.

Q1. 도시라는 맥락 안에서 새로운 아이디어를 제시한 동시대 폴리의 예시를 살펴본다면?

마크 핌롯 로브레흐트 엔 댐(Robbrecht en Daem)과 마리 호세 반 히(Marie Jose Van Hee)가 벨기에 벤트에 제작한 슈타드할/슈타드마크트(Stadhal/Stadmarkt, 2015)는 역사적인 장소에 막혀 있으면서도 열려 있는 방을 구축했다. 이는 미리 정해진 방식이 아니라 시민들이 의도에 따라 다양하게 활용될 수 있다. 더욱이, 사람들이 도시를 특별한 시각으로 인지하게끔 하는 장소에 위치함으로써 이 '방'은 모두에게 열린, 도시 내 가장 특별한 방이 된다.

조나단 울프(Jonathan Woolf)가 애버딘에 설치한 몽키 퍼즐 파빌리온(Monkey Puzzle Pavilion, 2007)은 이와 일면 유사한데, 이상적으로 균형 잡힌 일련의 방으로 구성된 임시 구조물로 마치 보물과 같은 존재가 되어 애버딘 중심의 광장을 의미 있는 장소로 변모시킨다. 사무적인 회색 도시에 우아한 유희의 순간을 만들어내며 도시의 이미지까지 바꾸었다.

알바로 시자(Alvaro Siza)가 설계한 헤이그 쉴더 슈바이크 웨스트(Schilderswijk West) 주거 프로젝트의 두 집(Two Houses, 1988)은 대규모 사회적 주거 공간 프로젝트에서 지역 기업체 수용과 지하 주차장 입구라는 두 가지의 역할을 상정한다. 시설, 형식, 상징적인 요소가 반복되는 주거공간과 달리 이들은 더 큰 앙상블을 고려한 듯 사치로 느껴지는 파빌리온적 접근을 취했다. 이들만의 표현 방식은 조각적이고 유쾌하며 프로젝트를 보다 세련되게 만들어 프로젝트 자체와 거주민들에게 당위성을 부여했다.

또 다른 예시로는 포르투건축학교 퍼스트 이어 스튜디오의 카를로스 라모스 파빌리온(알바로 시자, 1986)과 마토지뉴스에 위치한 레카 다 팔메이라(알바로 시자, 1966)가 있다. 둘 모두 근대화에 의해 폐허가 된 도시(와 변화)를 드러낸다. 첫 번째 사례는 정원에 세워진 작은 파빌리온으로 학생들이 자신들의 존재를 자각하게끔 한다. 세상을 향해 난 단 하나의 창문은 그 너머의 풍경, 다리, 산업 시설 그리고 대서양으로 이어지는 도루강 어귀 자연 그대로의 형태를 보여준다.

벽과 막으로 이루어진 건축물인 두 번째의 사례는 몇 단계에 걸쳐 수영하는 이들을 바다와 암석으로 이루어진 자연의 광경, 그러나 그것이 낮은 벽들과 조화를 이루는 곳으로 안내한다. 플랫폼 위에서 점심을 먹으며 수영장의 기울어진 벽과 멀리 보이는 방파제의 울림을 경험할 수 있다. 수영을 하는 자가 접하는 세계는 모든 인간 행위가 집결해 시각화된 바로 그 곳이다.

카스 오스터하위스 파리의 라빌레트 공원에 있는 베르나르 추미의 폴리들은 로맨틱한 폴리의 새로운 발견이다. 라빌레트 공원 안의 스티뮬레이션 그리드(stimulation grid)에 설치된 폴리들은 그 풍성한 숫자와 일관되게 통일감 있는 모습으로 낙후된 지역에서 재생된 도시 공간(공원) 전체를 재조직한다. 이들 폴리들은 하나의 거대한 폴리로써, 42개 조각으로 분산되어 있다.

개인적으로 추미의 프로젝트는 전혀 해체주의적으로 느껴지지 않는다. 철학이라기보다는 일관적인 도시 전략의 힘을 보여준다고 생각된다. 도시 맥락(어떤 종류이든)에 단 하나의 폴리만이 존재한다면 이는 금세 의미를 잃을 것이고, 도시의 분위기를 자극하는 그 힘도 잃게 된다. 결국 키오스크나 공공미술 작품과 다를 바 없어질 것이다.

델프트 공과대학에 있는 내 작품인 'iWEB 파빌리온'은 고립된 폴리가 의미를 잃고 결국은 그가 속한 지역사회와의 연결이 끊어질 수 있음을 보여주는 예이다. 2008년 델프트 공과대학의 건축대학이 큰 화재로 인해 소실되었다. 화재가 나기 전까지 캠퍼스의 연결적인 구조에 개입해오던 iWEB은 그 후 고립되었고 결국 접속이 끊어졌다. 만약 델프트 공과대학 캠퍼스에 일련의 자극점(stimulation points)을 만들어낼 수 있는 화재 이후의 도시 전략이 존재하였다면, i-WEB은 살아남아 본연의 건설적인 역할을 해냈을 것이다.

하리 덴 하르토흐 가장 먼저 떠오르는 예는 당연히 파리의 라빌레트 공원이지만, 이미 20년이나 되었기 때문에 현 시대의 폴리라고 하긴 어렵다.

현재 거주하고 있는 중국에는 다양한 아티스트가 제작한 폴리의 컬렉션이 있는 공원이 여러 개 생겨났다. 가장 유명하고 영향력이 큰 공원을 꼽자면, 진화 건축공원(Jinhua Architecture Park), 중국 국제건축실용박람회(the China International Practical Exhibition of Architecture), 웨스트 번드(West Bund)가 있다. 이들 공간에는 하나의 개별적인 폴리가 아닌 폴리의 집합체들이 있다. 이들 폴리들은 집합으로서만 의미가 있다.

빔 네이엔하위스 베르나르 추미의 라빌레트 공원은 언급하지 않을 수 없고, 그 외에도 독일 루르 공업지역(the Ruhrgebiet)의 오래된 광산들, EU가 선정한 유럽 문화수도인 루르 지역(the Ruhr Area)의 폐광과 벙커들, 뒤셀도르프의 가스탱크(the Gasholder), 오스나브뤼크의 오래된 기차역(The old Bahnhof), 로테르담과 암스테르담의 항구 지역과 건물들이 흥미로운 예가 될 수 있겠다.

Q2. Can you give your vision on the theme of Gwangju Folly III: 'The Critique of Everyday Life'?

Mark Pimlott

Gwangju Folly III might, in relation to the theme, be able to be a platform or shelter in which occupants have a heightened consciousness of the superimposition of effects in the grounds of the exhibition, a consciousness that might involve the magnification those effects simply by presenting an absence of effects in its own realisation.

The folly, after all, is a building apparently without a purpose other than the completion of a pre-ordained view, or a shelter for pause from the elements, from which one may appreciate its setting. Occasionally, it might contain a dissonant effect of its own, such as a table for drinking as set in the folly of the ogre's gaping mouth at Bomarzo, or the many grottos lined with shells typical of Italian gardens. But we have also seen that the folly might be a building of extravagant size, ready for all sorts of interpretations and all sorts of uses, such as Cedric Price's proposal for a Fun Palace. This latter example was intended to be a place where occupants could, through inter-subjectivity, reinvent current social relations by moving elements of the structure. In fact, Price thought it a place in which one might 'start a riot'.

Kas Oosterhuis

I do not believe in follies giving a "critique of everyday life." Follies don't talk. They are what they are and are either attraction points for relevant activities that contribute to the community, or they are meaningless and take more from the community than they give.

Harry den Hartog

I haven't visited Gwangju, but I would love to go. Thus, with my limited knowledge about the context, my feeling is that this third edition is more interactive and already programmed, which is nice but different from the idea of the folly as an empty space with a 'decorative role after losing its original function' and meant to 'facilitate communication'. In fact, a folly is a form of public space that can be used for all kind of unplanned activities, similar to a square or a park. The themes ('to walk', 'to see', 'to eat', 'to play') are very related to everyday life and perhaps could be extended with 'to rest' and 'to hang out' or 'to perform'.

Wim Nijenhuis

I know the concept of the critique of everyday life from the theories and concepts of the International Situationists. In their opinion it is very difficult for a visual element in an urban space to have an influence that can compete with visual media. We must not forget that the critique of everydaylife was first and foremost a critique of life ruled by consumerism, particularly the consumerism of images and object-related images. It is for these reasons that the International Situationists focused on the human body in an effort to bypass the visual impulse that was already wasted by media-oriented cultural industries. Their so-called 'situations' were social conditions that tried to evoke and involve bodily social actions from by-standers. I believe that all other strategies will be second rate as far as it concerns an effective critique of everyday life.

마크 핌롯 광주폴리 III 역시 전시 속 효과의 중첩에 대한 증대된 자각을 제공하는 플랫폼 또는 셸터가 될 수 있을 것이다. 이러한 자각이 구현되면 오히려 효과의 부재를 보여줌으로써 이들 효과를 확대시키는 과정을 수반한다.

결국 폴리는 정해진 시각의 완성 외에는 목적이 없는 건축물이자 주변을 바라보는데 이용되는 요소들로부터의 일시적인 정지이자 피신처이다. 때로는 보마르초에 있는 오거의 입에 자리한 테이블이나 이탈리아 정원 특유의 조개껍데기로 장식된 동굴들과 같이 내재적으로 불협화음을 지니는 경우도 있다.

하지만 우리는 세드릭 프라이스(Cedric Price)의 펀 팰리스(Fun Palace) 제안과 같이 폴리가 온갖 해석과 용도를 지닌 거대한 규모의 건축물일 수도 있다는 것도 안다. 이 후자의 예시는 장치와 파티션의 이동을 통해 기존의 사회적 관계를 재구축할 수 있는 공간으로 창안되었다. 프라이스는 이를 누군가 '폭동을 시작'할 듯한 곳이라고 생각했다.

카스 오스터하위스 폴리가 '일상에 대한 비판'을 할 수 있다고는 생각하지 않는다. 폴리는 말도 할 수 없다. 폴리는 그저 폴리일 뿐으로, 공동체에 기여할 수 있는 관련 활동을 위한 명소인 것이다. 그렇지 못한 폴리는 의미가 없고 공동체에 기여하기는커녕 의존하게 될 것이다.

하리 덴 하르토흐 꼭 방문해보고 싶으나 아직 광주에는 가본 적이 없다. 따라서 질문에 대해 제한적인 지식밖에는 없다. 이번 세 번째 폴리는 더욱 인터랙티브하고 이미 프로그램되어 있는 느낌이다. 다 짜여져 있는 것도 좋지만, '본연의 기능을 잃은 후 장식적인 역할을 하고; '커뮤니케이션을 촉진'하기 위해 만들어진 빈 공간이라는 폴리 본연의 관념과는 다른 것 같다.

사실 폴리라는 것은 공공 공간의 한 형태로서, 계획되지 않은 각종 활동에 이용되는 광장이나 공원과 같은 공간이다. 이번 테마('걷고; '보고','먹고; '노는')는 일상과 밀접히 관련되기 때문에 '쉬고; '어울리고' 혹은 '공연하는' 등으로 확장될 수 있겠다.

빔 네이엔하위스 나는 국제 상황주의자들(Inter-national Situationists)의 이론 및 인식 측면에서 일상에 대한 비판이라는 주제를 이해하였다. 그들은 도시 공간의 시각 요소가 시각 매체와 겨룰 수 있을 정도의 영향력을 가지기는 매우 어렵다고 생각한다.

여기서 잊지 말아야 할 것은 일상에 대한 비판이란 소비주의, 특히 이미지 및 상품과 관련된 이미지의 소비주의가 좌우하는 일상에 대한 비판이란 점이다.

이러한 이유로 국제 상황주의자들은 인간의 몸에 집중하여 미디어 위주의 문화 산업으로 인해 이미 소비되어 버린 시각적 충동에 현혹되지 않고자 하였다.

이들이 말하는 소위 '상황'은 주변 사람들의 신체적 사회 활동을 이끌어내고 이들을 참여시키기 위한 사회적인 조건이다. 일상을 효과적으로 비평하기 위해 이보다 더 좋은 전략은 없다고 생각한다.

Q3. Can you respond to the text by Chun, Eui-Young on urban regeneration?

Mark Pimlott

The neighbourhoods that were eradicated in the service of new high-rise, high-density, high-yielding developments simply cannot be reproduced; they developed, and then acquired their lives and their language of use over many, many generations. The expectation that such spontaneity can be re-staged seems almost far-fetched: these large developments have caused profound cultural damage, displacing populations and their knowledge.

A strategy may be possible that encourages uses under and between high-density developments, but it requires that any notion of distance or exclusivity that those developments might entertain should be dismissed in favour of a principle of propinquity. One of the problems of a continuous conurbation is that moments of pause or distance and opportunities for consciousness (of oneself and of the entire urban project) is never possible: one is trapped in an environment whose fictions are never revealed, which leads to a condition of complete subjugation. It is an extremely dangerous condition, one in which singularity becomes but a distinguishing feature in a total, interiorising, controlled environment, more likely a city-state than a one-city nation.

Kas Oosterhuis

The issue raised is a serious one, but has nothing to do with the concept of follies. It does relate to the definition of the functional use of spaces. What will be mandatory for enriching community life in and around the super blocks is to free them from strict and restrictive planning rules. It is a question of rule-based design. A particular block should never be residential alone, or function as an office building alone. One should allow a mix of multiple functions. The functions should not even be defined beforehand, only their performance in terms of production of noise and other elements that might hinder their neighbours. In essence it comes down to stimulating 24 uses of a substantial number of buildings as to revive the neighbourhoods. Follies alone are not able to fulfil that role.

Harry den Hartog

This is very broad, and many books can be (and have been) written about this, but follies could play a role in place making and adding a sense of identity.

Wim Nijenhuis

Terms like 'revitalisation', 'regeneration', and the like descend from the 19th-century discourse on urbanism, which was heavily influenced by biological discourse. This was due to the primacy of medicine as part of the first strategies to improve cities and city life. Biological discourse cooperated very well with history and was capable of installing an image of the city as the accidental appearance of a core principle that had to be continuous, and that was called 'life'. It is very questionable these days that the city would be the accidental appearance of 'life'. Further, we should note that many of the summarising categories we use to think of the city stem from sociology (that emerged in the wake of the discourse of biology and medicine). This sociology has been heavily criticised in French theory as an arrogant, hegemonial discipline that commonly functions as a force to eliminate spontaneous actions of the people. In my opinion it is time for urbanism to abandon the totalising visions of sociology and move to another kind of self-understanding.

마크 핌롯 간단히 말해, 고층·고밀도·고수익 개발에 의해 사라진 지역들을 재생산 하는 것은 불가능하다. 그들은 수많은 세월을 거쳐 발전을 거듭하고 그들의 삶과 사용 언어를 갖게 되었기 때문이다. 그러한 자발성이 다시 연출될 수 있다는 기대는 현실성이 없어 보인다. 이러한 대규모 개발은 사람들과 그들의 지식을 몰아 내 심각한 문화적 손상을 초래했기 때문이다.

고밀도 개발 지역 아래에, 그리고 그 사이사이에 기존의 토지이용을 장려토록 하는 전략은 가능하다. 그러나 이를 위해서는 고밀도 개발이 추구하는 거리와 배제에 대한 개념이 근접성의 원칙으로 대체되어야 할 것이다.

연속적인 광역 도시권의 문제는 멈춤 또는 거리 두기의 순간, 그리고 (자신과 전체 도시 프로젝트에 대한) 자각의 기회가 허락되지 않는다는 것이다. 사람들은 허구가 절대 드러나지 않는, 그리하여 완전한 종속의 상태가 되는 환경에 갇히게 된다. 특이성이 전체 내 구별점밖에 되지 않는, 통제된 환경을 내면화시켜 단일-도시 국가가 아닌 도시 국가가 될 확률이 더 높은 굉장히 위험한 상황이다.

카스 오스터하위스 제기된 이슈는 매우 진지한 것이나 폴리의 콘셉트와는 아무런 관련이 없다. 그보다는 공간의 기능적인 활용의 정의에 관한 것이다. 슈퍼 블록 안팎에 존재하는 커뮤니티의 삶의 질을 높이기 위하여 꼭 필요한 것은 이들에게 엄격하고 제한적인 도시 계획 규정을 적용하지 않는 것이다. 어떤 블록은 절대 거주용으로만 사용되어서는 안 된다거나 사무용 빌딩으로만 기능하여서는 안 된다, 어떤 블록은 복합적인 기능을 사용할 수 있도록 허락되어야 한다 등등. 이런 식으로 각 블록의 기능이 미리 정의되어서는 안 되며, 오직 소음이나 기타 요소 등 주변 이웃들을 불편하게 할 만한 요소에 대하여만 규정이 적용되어야 한다. 결국 지역을 활성화시키기 위해서는 상당한 숫자의 건물이 24시간 활용되도록 하는 것이 중요하다. 그리고 폴리만으로는 이러한 목적을 달성할 수 없다.

하리 덴 하르토흐 천의영 교수의 글은 매우 광범위한 내용을 담고 있기 때문에, 여기에 관하여는 책이 몇 권씩 쓰일 수 있을 것이다(그리고 실제로 쓰여진 것으로 알고 있다). 공간에 정체감을 추가하여 장소메이킹의 역할을 할 수 있다.

빔 네이엔하위스 활성화, 재생과 같은 단어들은 생물학 담론에 크게 영향을 받았던 19세기 어바니즘 담론 이래로 점점 덜 쓰이는 추세이다. 당시 도시와 도시 생활을 개선하기 위한 최초의 전략의 하나인 의학의 우월성으로 인하여 생물학 담론의 영향력이 컸다. 생물학 담론은 역사에 협조적이었고, 계속되어야만 하는 '삶'이라고 불리는 핵심 원리의 우연적인 등장이라는 도시의 이미지를 만들어 낼 수 있었다.

그러나 오늘날 과연 도시가 '삶'의 우연한 등장이라고 볼 수 있는지는 의문이며, 도시 연구의 여러 하부 범주들이 실은 생물학과 의학 담론의 발생에 이어 나타난 사회학에서 비롯된 것임을 명심하여야 한다.

이러한 사회학은 프랑스 이론가들에 의해서 오만하고 패권적이며 사람들의 자연스러운 행동을 없애버리는 힘으로 작용한다고 강하게 비판되었다.

개인적으로는 어바니즘이 사회학의 전체적인 시각을 포기하고 다른 종류의 자기 인식을 해야 할 때라고 본다.

Q4. In what direction should Gwangju Folly develop in the future? What is your advice for the team of curators of future editions?

The folly as a type is an exceptional structure—exceptional, in that it stands outside the rules of other structures, even though it might be known within cultural conventions. It provides the opportunity for aberrant uses, dissonant notes, pleasure, and heightened consciousness of individual experience in relation to the total environment in which it is set. It can be, therefore, at once familiar and unfamiliar, special, and linked to desires within individuals that are only rarely given an opportunity to be expressed. They are simultaneously useless and necessary structures that need to find a place within the urban fabric. There was a moment when telephone booths and bus shelters could play the role of follies within the city; occupying them meant being within the city and apart from it, at a privileged distance. Perhaps it is possible to entertain the idea of structures at a range of scales in which citizens could be offered different scales of unprogrammed activity, ranging from the most private or individualised to the most public. One can imagine the folly at these varying scales being deployed as a kind of infrastructure for the city in which citizens become aware of themselves, and others, and their situation in society and in the world.

I think designers—artists and architects—need to intervene in the basic rules of master planning, including infrastructural projects and large-scale building developments. The paragraphs of the laws that are related to building codes and land use are where the conditions are sculpted for a possible prosperity of the neighbourhoods. To me it would be interesting to see whether the creative sector would be able to propose rules that facilitate the emergence of a more engaged community. I believe in simple rules leading to complex outcomes. The challenge is to find those simple rules that really work. It is like the rules of cellular automata: some rules lead to boring results, and only a few rules lead to interesting complexity. Perhaps the intuition and instincts of the invited designers can find those rules that create buzz and excitement.

Harry den Hartog

It would be interesting to make some follies that are foldable and/or mobile, that can travel all over the world, to test how they work out in different contexts.

Wim Nijenhuis

I do not feel I am in a position to give a professional opinion here. I only can say people should read the right books, read books from the angle of your eyes, and try to be on the level of the time in a true manner. Look deep into yourself and try to be as personal as possible in your involvement when you develop new strategies.
I am of the opinion that we should start to develop a critical sense of ethics (ethics understood as the way we behave and the accompanying effort to rule our lives in the face of the overwhelming control by modern technology). To do well in the future will depend on our ethical power, and that can be developed by means of strategic reading and writing. It will all depend on the kind of personality (a personality at all) we are able to develop.

마크 핌롯 종으로서의 폴리는 매우 이례적인 구조물이다. 비록 문화적 관습 내에서 이해되더라도, 다른 구조물들에 적용되는 원칙 밖에 존재한다는 점에서 그렇다. 일탈적인 사용, 불협화음, 유희, 개인의 경험 그리고 그 경험이 존재하는 주변 환경과의 관계에 대한 자각의 기회를 제공한다.

따라서 폴리는 친숙함과 동시에 낯설 수 있고 특별하며 표현할 기회가 거의 없는 개인의 욕망들과 연결된다. 무용한 동시에 필요한, 도시 구조 속에 자리를 찾아야 하는 구조물이다.

공중전화 박스와 버스 정류장이 도시 속 폴리의 역할을 할 수 있었던 때도 있었다. 도시 안에 있다는 것은 그 안에 있으면서도 동시에 특권적인 거리를 두고 분리되어 있다는 것을 의미했다.

어쩌면 가장 사적이고 개인적인 것부터 가장 공적인 것까지 서로 다른 차원의 정해지지 않은 활동들을 시민들에게 제공할 수 있는 수준의 건축물을 생각해 볼 수도 있다. 이렇듯 다양한 규모의 폴리를 도시의 기반시설로서 배치해, 시민들이 그들 자신과, 타인과, 사회와 세계 속 그들의 상황을 자각하게끔 하는 것도 상상해 볼 수 있을 것이다.

카스 오스터하위스 디자이너들, 즉 예술가들과 건축가들이 인프라 프로젝트나 대규모 건축 개발과 같은 종합계획(master planning)의 기본적인 규정 수립에 참여해야 한다고 생각한다. 건축 법규 및 토지 이용을 구성하는 내용은 공동체의 번영을 도모하는 방향으로 만들어지는 것이다. 창조 부문(the creative sector)이 제안하여 만들어진 규정으로 인해 구성원들이 더욱 활발히 참여하는 커뮤니티가 만들어진다면 재미있을 것이다.

나는 단순한 규칙이 복합적인 결과로 이어질 수 있다고 믿는 사람이다. 여기에서 어려운 부분은 실제로 잘 작동할 단순한 규칙들을 찾아내는 것이다. 이는 셀룰러 오토마타(cellular automata)의 규칙과도 비슷하다. 즉, 어떤 규칙은 따분한 결과로 이어지고, 오직 소수의 규칙만이 흥미로운 복잡성을 만들어낸다. 어쩌면 초대된 디자이너들의 직관과 본능이 매우 흥미로운 규칙을 찾아낼지도 모른다.

하리 덴 하르토흐 전 세계를 돌아다닐 수 있는 접히는 폴리 혹은 이동식 폴리를 만들면 흥미로울 것 같다. 폴리가 각 국의 상이한 맥락에서 어떻게 어울리는지 시험해볼 수 있기 때문이다.

빔 네이엔하위스 내가 전문적인 조언을 줄 수 있는 위치에 있다고는 생각지 않는다. 해줄 수 있는 말이 있다면, 적절한 종류의 책을 읽으라는 것이다. 자신의 시각으로 책을 읽고 진정으로 당시의 수준에 올라서도록 하라. 자신을 자세히 들여다보고 새로운 전략을 개발하고 사회에 개입할 때는 최대한 자신만의 주관과 방식을 갖도록 하라.

나는 사람들이 저마다 자신만의 윤리-우리가 행동하는 방식에 따른 윤리이자, 현대 과학의 압도적인 지배를 받는 현 상황 속에서도 자신의 삶을 스스로 지배하고자 하는 노력에 따른 윤리-를 개발해야 한다고 생각한다.

향후에 이로운 사람이 될지의 여부는 전략적인 읽기 및 글쓰기로 개발될 수 있는 각자의 윤리적 힘에 달려 있다. 우리가 어떤 인격을 가지게 될지-인격 자체가 있기라도 한다면-에 따라 미래가 결정될 것이다.

Q4. 향후 광주폴리가 어느 방향으로 발전되어야 하는가? 다음 폴리의 큐레이터 팀에게 해주고 싶은 조언이 있다면?
team of curators of future editions?

피르요 사낙세나호
건축가, 교수
핀란드

Pirjo Sanaksenaho
Architect, Professor
Finland

Gwangju Folly Workshop

광주폴리 워크샵

2016년 4월, 광주폴리 워크숍에 초청을 받게 되었다. 나로서는 한국에도 광주에도 첫 방문이었고, 그곳에서 받은 환대는 정말 감동적이었다. 동료 연사들과 함께 광주 곳곳에 위치한 폴리를 돌아보며 이토록 작은 건축물들이 얼마나 놀라운 도시공간과 네트워크를 창조해낼 수 있는지 확인할 수 있는 기회가 되었다. 폴리는 단순한 구조물, 그 이상의 의미를 지니고 있었다. 그 곳에서 머무르며 무언가 할 수 있는, 즉 보고, 듣고, 휴식을 취할 수 있는 공간을 시민들에게 제공해주고 있었다. 아주 인상 깊었던 작품 중에 하나는 건축가 후안 헤레로스의 '소통의 오두막'이었는데, 원래 그곳에 있던 나무들을 재활용해 새로운 공간을 창조한 작품이었다. 이 현대적인 느낌의 오두막은 지나가는 행인들에게 앉을 수 있는 벤치와 조명, 음악 그리고 무료 무선인터넷까지 제공하고 있었다. 공중에 자유롭게 부유하는 이 작품으로 인해 평범한 거리 한편이 특별한 공간으로 재탄생하게 된 것이다.

마치 고대의 문을 연상시키는 듯한 계단과 책꽂이로 구성된 데이비드 아자예(David Adjaye)의 '광주천 독서실(Gwangju River Reading Room)' 또한 굉장히 놀라웠다. 작품의 배경이 도심의 강가라는 위치적 특성으로 인해, 사실상 독서를 위

I had a chance to visit Gwangju Folly Workshop in April 2016. It was my first trip to Korea. Koreans' hospitality impressed me. Visits to the existing follies with fellow speakers showed how small architectural installations can create remarkable urban spaces and a network within a city. More than sculptures, they offer people space to do something: to listen, to watch, or to relax for a while. One of the most interesting was Huan Herreros Architect's urban folly Communication Hut, which created a space with existing trees at the site. A contemporary hut, it offered benches, lights, sounds and free Wi-Fi connection to passersby. The free-formed piece which was hanging in the air made the ordinary street corner special.

David Adjaye's Gwangju River reading room was as also remarkable, like an ancient gate with stairs and bookshelves. The meaning of the architectonic was on an even bigger scale and more dominant in the urban riverside than its function as a reading place.

A folly can be understood as a building without purpose, a decoration which can encourage people to use their imagination and even how to use it. The French word folie means "madness" or "silliness." A folly in an urban space tempts

Writing Staff

한 기능적인 공간의 의미보다는 건축학적인 의미가 훨씬 더 지배적으로 다가왔다.

어떻게 보면 폴리는 그 자체로서 목적이 없는 건물, 즉 사람들에게 그 활용방법을 구상하게 함으로써 새로운 상상력을 불러일으키는 장식물로도 볼 수 있다.

프랑스어로 'folie(폴리)'는 광기 또는 어리석음의 의미를 가지고 있는데, 사실상 광주라는 도시공간 속의 폴리는 바쁘게 지나가는 사람들에게 잠시 멈추어 긴장을 풀고, 그 공간이 의미하는 바를 생각할 수 있게끔 하는 기능을 한다.

나는 이전 워크숍의 발제에서 핀란드의 도시공간에 위치한 몇 가지 폴리를 예시로 소개한 적이 있었는데, 그중 일부는 핀란드의 알토대학교와 오울루대학교의 건축 전공생들에 의해 지어진 것이었다.

핀란드의 투르쿠에 위치한 폴리 중, 오울루대학교와 컬럼비아대학교의 학생들의 협업으로 제작된 폴리를 Pudelma(푸델마)라고 부른다. 투르크는 오래 전, 핀란드의 수도였으며, 2011년에는 유럽문화수도로도 선정된 바 있다.

폴리의 전체적 구조는 뉴욕 컬럼비아 대학의 워크숍에서 단기간에 집중적으로 디자인되었고, 목재 부분은 핀란드에서 제작되었다. 총 3일간 약 스무 명의 학생들이 직접 폴리를 탄생시켰는데, 그 중 목재 텐트의 구조는 알고리즘 방식으로 제작되었다. 이 파빌리온의 면적은 약 70m² 이며, 도심의 활기가 넘치는 시청과 버스정류장 옆에 자리 잡고 있다.

passersby to release for a moment, relax, stop and wonder what this is about. In my presentation in the workshop, I showed some examples of follies in a Finnish urban context, some of which were built by architecture students, both from Aalto University and Oulu University.

A folly made in collaboration with architecture students from Oulu University and Columbia University for Turku, Finland is called Pudelma. Turku is the old capital of Finland, and was the European Capital of Culture in 2011. The structure was designed in a workshop at Columbia University in New York City in an intensive week of work, while the wooden parts were cut in Finland. It was built up in three days by 20 students. The structure of the wooden tent was designed with algorithmic methods. The pavilion covers an area of about 70m² and is situated beside a lively bus stop and city hall.

The students from Oulu hold a workshop for one week every year, at which time they build a folly on the centre of an island near its marketplace that is close to Oulu. The pavilion is made out of recycled planks, and after the summer the folly is torn down and the planks are used again. It is a wonderful little place for sitting down and chatting with friend.

오울루대학의 학생들은 매년 일
주일간의 워크숍을 진행하는데, 이때
오울루센터와 시장 인근의 섬에 폴리
를 제작하는 프로젝트가 주된 임무
이다. 폴리 건축물들은 이미 사용되
거나 재활용된 널빤지나 판자 등을
재료로 지어지며, 여름이 지나고 폴
리가 철거되면 나무들은 재사용된다.
이렇게 만들어진 폴리들은 잠시 멈
추어 친구들과 앉아 담소를 나눌 수
있는 공간으로서 기능한다.

2015년 오울루대학 학생들에 의
해 지어진 폴리의 경우 버드나무 가지
를 엮어서 만들어졌다. 건물 안에 들
어가면 공간의 모양과 안에 비추어지
는 빛을 느낄 수 있으며, 마치 곤충의
고치와 같은 구조를 하고 있다.

The folly made by Oulu architecture students in 2015 was weaved of willow branches. You could walk through it and feel the light and shape of the space. The form was like a cocoon for insects.

'Willow Branch: Folly',
Designed by Oulu University
Architecture Students
오울루 건축학교 학생들이 디자인한
'버드나무 가지' 폴리

Pudelma: Folly 2011, Turku, Finland
푸델마: 폴리 2011, 투르크, 핀란드

'A Folly Made out of Recycled Planks'
Designed by Oulu University Students of
Architecture
오롤루 건축학교 학생들이 디자인한 재활용된
판자들로 만들어진 폴리

Writing Staff

알토대학교의 나무 스튜디오는 캐노피 형태의 파빌리온을 제작했는데, 이 건축물은 핀란드 헬싱키 건축 박물관과 디자인 박물관 사이에 위치해 있다. 이 공간은 2012년 여름 헬싱키가 세계디자인수도로 선정되었을 당시, 요가 수업부터 강의에 이르기까지 다양한 목적으로 활용되었지만 여름 한 철 동안만 운영되었다.

이 건축 공간의 전체적 구조는 합판으로 이루어져 있다.

Students from the wood studio at Aalto University designed and built a pavilion, a canopy between the Museum of Finnish Architecture and Design Museum, which served as a vibrant place in the summer of 2012, when Helsinki was serving as World Design Capital. Everything from yoga lessons to lectures were organised as well. The pavilion was only used temporarily for one summer.

The structure of the pavilion was made out of plywood.

'World Design Capital (WDC) Pavilion' designed by Pyry-Pekka Kantonen and Aalto University Wood Studio. Helsinki, 2012
피리-페카 칸토넨과 알토대학교 우드 스튜디오가 디자인한 '월드 디자인 캐피탈 파빌리온', 헬싱키, 2012

핀란드의 도시 문화는 아직 태동기라고 할 수 있다. 핀란드에서는 전통적인 농업형태가 오랫동안 이어져 왔으며, 급격한 산업화는 주로 1960년도에 집중적으로 일어났으나 아직까지 국가 면적의 상당수는 숲과 호수들로 구성되어 있다.

Urban culture is quite young in Finland. The country has a long agricultural tradition, with rapid urbanisation taking place mainly in the 1960s. The main part of the land is forest and lakes. A folly in a forest is a study of a pure space, like the one made by my partner, the architect Matti Sanaksenaho. It is a study of volume, material, light and space, and essentially a work between architecture and sculpture. It is a quiet room open to anyone. One can find a square box in the woods, in stark contrast to the forms of nature, where you can also walk around and find a tiny door.

Gwangju Folly Workshop

숲속에 위치한 폴리는 동료 건축가 인 마티 사낙세나호(Matti Sanaksenaho)의 순수공간에 대한 연구의 일환으로 제작되었다. 부피와 소재, 빛과 공간에 대한 연구이자 건축과 조각의 경계를 넘나드는 작품으로 볼 수 있다. 이 공간은 황무지에 위치하며, 그곳을 방문한 사람들을 위해 하나의 조용한 방이 된다. 사람들은 숲속 한가운데에서 자연의 형상과 대비되는 정사면체의 나무 박스를 발견하게 되며, 그곳을 통과하여 다시금 공간을 돌아볼 때 작은 문 하나를 발견하게 된다.

빈 공간(Empty Space)에서 우리는 벽과 천장을 만져보고, 느슨한 나무 바닥의 소리를 들어보고, 벽에 깃든 타르의 냄새를 맡으면서 어두운 방을 경험하게 된다. 문을 닫는 순간 방은 어둠으로 가득하게 되고, 그 순간 우리는 일상생활과 보여지는 것들, 즉 물질적인 공간에서 마음의 공간으로 들어서게 된다.

At Empty Space, you can sense a dark room just by touching the walls and the ceiling, hear the sound of loose floor planks, and smell the tar in the walls. When you close the door, it becomes pitch black. You move from everyday life and the visual, physical space to a space of the mind.

'Empty Space in the Forest' Designed by Matti Sanaksenaho
마티 사낙세호가 디자인한 '숲 속의 빈 공간'

Writing Staff

헹 치에 키앙 + 이반 나수티온
싱가포르 국립대학교 교수, 싱가포르,
싱가포르 국립대학교 연구원, 싱가포르

HENG Chye Kiang + Ivan Nasution
Professor, National University of Singapore
Research Associate, National University of Singapore

Singapore's Urban Folly

싱가포르의 어반폴리
본 기고를 처음 요청 받았을 때 우리에게 떠오른 첫 질문은 이것이었다. '과연 싱가포르에 폴리가 존재하는가?' 싱가포르 건축계에서 '폴리'라는 용어의 사용은 흔치만은 않다. 따라서 폴리의 지역적 정의나 일상에서의 역할을 규정하는 것은 쉽지 않다. 지역적 맥락에서 폴리에 대한 새로운 정의를 내리는 대신 본 글은 섬 내에서 우리가 발견한 장식적이거나, 사용자들의 일상성에 즐거움, 동기, 전환 또는 새로운 균열을 만들어내는 상호작용 건축물을 다루고자 한다. 글을 쓰는 데 있어서의 최대 난제는 고도로 실용적인 싱가포르 사회 내에서 명확한 기능이 없는 건축물을 찾아내는 것이었다.

실용주의 이념
실용주의는 싱가포르에서 국가적인 이념이다. 정치적인 개념이며 그 의미가 긴 논쟁의 대상이 되기도 한다. 이 격론을 다루는 대신, 본 글은 실용주의를 싱가포르의 만트라이자 싱가포르가 작동하는 방식으로서 차용하며 건축 환경에서의 영향을 논의한다. 싱가포르에서 가장 중요한 것이 '그것이 실제로 어떻게 나타나는가'라는 사실은, 특정 이념이나 신념만을 고수하지 않는다는 것을 뜻한다. 이는 급속도의 발전과 경제성장 그리고 안정적이면서도 잘 정돈된 사회의

Does Singapore have any follies? This was our first question upon receiving an invitation to contribute an article to this book. The term (architectural) 'folly' is rarely used in the context of Singapore's built environment; it is therefore difficult to pinpoint its local definition or the roles that it may play in the daily life of people here. While the article will not offer any local definition of folly, we went around parts of the island to discover built structures that may be decorative, user-interactive and/or with the ability to cheer up, motivate, divert or create a rupture in the everydayness of people's lives The challenge in writing this article was to discover the existence of built objects that have no apparent function in the very pragmatic society of Singapore.

Ideology of pragmatism

Pragmatism is the national ideology of Singapore. The concept is political and its implications are subject to lengthy debates. Without engaging the polemic, this article accepts pragmatism as the mantra and modus operandi of Singapore, and discusses its effect on the built environment. The fact that what matters to Singapore is what works in practice means not

구축에 지대한 공헌을 하기도 했지만, 건축 환경, 사회 그리고 사람들의 일상에 있어서는 장점뿐 아니라 역설적으로 단점도 함께 지닌다. 단일한 공공 주거와 다변적 도심부라는 두 가지 도시 구조를 만들어내기도 했다.

실용주의는 싱가포르인들의 일상에서 '공유된 가치'로 공공 주거의 기반에 깊이 박혀 있다. 1960년 도입 이후 싱가포르 공공 주거는 필요한 보금자리를 제공하는 것에서 시작해 프라이드, 국가, 정치적 성취, 시민들에 대한 정부의 자비를 상징하며 진화했다. 오늘날 공공 주거는 전체 인구의 80% 정도를 수용한다. 이토록 빠른 진보는 고도로 밀집된 주거지에 '모든 시민들에게 건실한 주거 공간을 제공'하고자 하는 '현실적이고 실용주의적인' 접근에 기인한다. 이는 물리적 풍경과 주거 환경의 사회적 구조에도 영향을 미치게 된다. 공통적으로 들리는 것이 단조로운 주거 환경에 대한 불평이다. 놀이나 공용 시설은 주거 지역 그리고 블록 수준에서 균일하게 제공된다. 공공 주거 당국 또한 소수 민족 집단 거주지의 형성을 막고 인종 다양성과 통합을 추구하기 위해 인종 쿼터(중국, 말레이시아, 인도)를 적용하고 있다.

sticking to any ideologies or beliefs. While this contributed to the rapid development and economic progress of the country and made a stable and well-ordered society, it does, paradoxically, has advantages and disadvantages for the built environment, society, and the daily life of the people. It is arguably responsible for creating two distinct urban fabrics: the homogeneous public housing fabric and the heterogeneous urban fabric of the city centre.

Pragmatism is a 'shared value' in the everyday life of the Singaporean, embedded in the foundation of the nation's public housing. Since its inception in 1960, Singapore's public housing has evolved from providing much-needed shelter to a symbol of pride, of nationhood, of political achievement, and of benevolent governance. Today, it houses about 80 percent of the population. Such quick progress is due to the 'realistic and pragmatic' approach to 'house every citizen decently' in a high-density housing environment. This has also impacted the physical landscape and social makeup of the housing environment. Commonly heard are complaints of monotonous housing environments. In terms of amenities and facilities for recreational and communal use, they are uniformly provided at the level of housing precinct and block. The public housing authority also imposes a racial quota in its housing blocks to ensure ethnic (Chinese, Malay and Indian) diversity and integration, preventing racial enclaves.

Writing Staff

싱가포르 경제 발전의 원동력 또
한 이 공공 주거 프로그램의 성공을
이끈 실용주의이다. '실용주의'와 '생
존의 필요'는 문화적 규범과 가치를
보다 넓은 글로벌 환경에 맞춰 진화하
고 적응할 수 있도록 만들었고 도시—
국가의 경제 발전을 도왔다. 천연 자
원이 부재한 상황에서 국가의 초점
은 국민들의 물질적·비물질적 발전
과 웰빙에 맞춰졌다. 가능한 모든 측
면에서 싱가포르는 '바퀴'를 재발명
하는 것이 아닌, 다른 국가들로부터
배우고 최선의 방식들을 차용, 적용
하는 것을 선택했다. 공공 주거, 환경
보호 및 친환경, 교통 등 특정 분야에
서 싱가포르는 최고의 해법을 고안해
내기도 했다.

끊임없는 글로벌 시티들의 경쟁구
도에서 실용적인 싱가포르는 높은 생
활수준과 세계적 수준의 시설을 제공
하는 것에 성공했다. 다른 글로벌 시
티들처럼 싱가포르의 도심 지역은 상
징적인 구조물, 건축물, 유흥 및 생활
시설 그리고 문화예술 시설 등을 갖
추어 해외의 재능 있는 이들을 세계
적 생활수준의 싱가포르로 불러들였
다. 실용주의는 다른 글로벌 시티들
과 그 정체성을 공유하는 이종적 건
축 환경을 만들어내기도 했다.

Singapore's economic development is driven by the same pragmatism that drives its successful public housing programme. 'Being practical' and 'the need to survive' push cultural norms and values to evolve and adapt to the larger global environment and help to propel the economic development of the city-state. For a country without natural resources, the task of nation-building focuses primarily on the development and well-being, material and otherwise, of its people. Wherever possible, Singapore tries not to reinvent the wheel, instead learning, adopting and adapting best practices from other countries. In certain areas, such as public housing, environmental protection and greening, as well as traffic management, it invents solutions that have, in turn, become best practices.

In the relentless competition of global cities, pragmatic Singapore strives to provide high living standards and world-class facilities. Like other global cities, Singapore's city centre is equipped with iconic structures and architecture, entertainment and lifestyle centres, as well as arts and

Singapore's Urban Folly

cultural centres to attract foreign talents to the world-class living of Singapore. Pragmatism also creates a heterogeneous built environment that shares an identity with other global cities.

실용주의는 기능이 없는 건축 또는 오브제를 낳을 수 있는가? 답은 '그렇다' 이다. 사실 우리는 폴리라는 기준에 부합하는 건축물을 발견할 수 있었다. 흥미롭게도 이들 구조물들은 서로 다른 두 맥락, 즉 단일한 공공 주거 풍경에 영구적으로 뿌리내리거나 다변적인 도심 공간에 일시적으로 삽입되어 작동하고 있다. 단순한 장식용이 아니라 이들 영구, 임시 구조물/오브제들은 (이하 오브제로 통일) 시민들의 일상성에 대해 질문하고 또 그와 상호작용한다. 아래 섹션들에서 또한 실용주의 맥락으로 이들 오브제를 논하고자 한다.

Can pragmatism give rise to structures and objects with no function? Yes. In fact, we found several structures that fulfill the criteria to be a folly. Interestingly enough, the structures operate differently in the two contexts. One type of structure is permanently implanted within the homogeneous public housing landscape, while the other is temporarily inserted to the heterogeneous city centre. More than simply serving a decorative function, the permanent and temporary structures/objects (simply referred to as 'objects' hereinafter) attempt to question and interact with the everydayness of the people. In the following section, we will continue to use the concept of pragmatism as a context to discuss the objects.

Writing Staff

영구 오브제는 공공 주거의 차원에서 보다 자주 발견된다. 특유의 성질을 지닌 이들은 특정한 기준을 따르지 않고 선천적으로 꼭 기능을 내재하고 있지도 않다. 이들의 미적 가치(재료와 형태)는 이들을 환경으로부터 구분 짓는다. 본 연구에 나타나는 오브제들은 서 주롱(Jurong West), 우드랜드(Woodlands), 탬파인 신도시(Tampine new towns) 세 지역에 위치한다. 이들 신도시들의 개발은 모두 1970년대에 시작되었다. 각각의 오브제들은 원형 램프, 잔해, 그리고 타워 형태의 구조물이다.

Permanent objects

Permanent objects are found more commonly within the fabric of public housing neighbourhoods. They are unique, non-standard and not necessarily functional in nature. Their aesthetic quality (e.g. material and form) distinguishes them from their surroundings. The objects identified in this study are situated in three different neighbourhoods: Jurong West, Woodlands, and Tampines new towns. The development of these new towns all began in the 1970s. The objects are a circular ramp, a ruin and a tower-like structure, respectively.

Circular Ramp at Tampines Avenue 1, Team Design Architects
탬파인 애비뉴 1의 원형 램프, 팀 디자인 건축소(Team Design Architects)

1980년대 서 탬파인(Tampines West)에 후반 형성된 지역 끄트머리 쪽 1헥타르 잔디밭의 모서리에는 영구적인 원형 오브제가 자리한다. 2014년 완성된 이 오브제는 경사로와 금속 구조물을 원형으로 활용하고 있다. 이는 배경과 같은 역할을 하는 슬라브 블록과 대치되며, 동시대적인 특유의 미적 표현을 보여준다. 주거 단지의 재활성화를 위한 지역 보수 프로그램의 일환인 이 오브제는 지역의 표식으로 활용하고자 한 의도가 있었던 듯하다. 화분이 모여 있는 곳으로 이어지는 경사로 상단에는 벤치가, 하단에는 원형 극장이 위치한

A circular object sits prominently at a visible corner on a lawn one-hectare in size at the edge of a neighbourhood built in the late 1980s in Tampines West. Completed in 2014, the object merges a ramp and metallic sculpture in a circular form. It has a contemporary and unique aesthetic expression that contrasts with the modernist slab blocks of flats that serve as a backdrop. As part of a neighbourhood renewal programme to rejuvenate the residential estate, the object was perhaps intended to serve as a distinct marker of the neighbourhood. It has a rampway leading to a rib-

Singapore's Urban Folly

bon of planter boxes that terminates with a seating area at the upper level and encloses a circular amphitheatre at the lower level. The seating area comprises two sets of tables and stools overlooking a twisted rib-like sculpture. Being publicly accessible, the grated floor of the ramp renders it less slippery and safer, especially after it has rained.

Ruins at Jurong West Street 81, Unknown
서 주롱 81번가의 터, 건축가 미상

Eight Tuscan columns arranged in a half circle surrounding a hard court give the impression of the remains of a circular Roman temple. The 'ruin' nestled in a neighbourhood park in Jurong West stands out from the surrounding 11-storey housing blocks built in the early 1990s. Aligned with the public housing vision at that time, the object was constructed to give an aesthetic character and identity to the neighbourhood. It acts as a focal point and landmark in the park.

The 'ruin', however, bears little relation to the aesthetic quality of the context or any historical event of the site.

A two-storey tower-like structure sits in the middle of a neighbourhood park at Woodland new town. Like the earlier example, the object

Writing Staff

베르나르 추미의 라빌레트 공원 폴리들을 연상시킨다. 놀이터 옆에 자리한 이 오브제는 필로티 위 고가 보도와 좌석을 갖추면서 놀이 공간의 확장을 암시하는 듯하다.

Tower-like Object at Woodlands Circle, Unknown
우드랜드 서클의 탑 형태 오브제, 건축가 미상

임시 오브제
이 글에서 다루는 임시 오브제의 설계는 글로벌 도심의 국제적 특징을 담고 있다. 이들 작업들은 예술의 일시성과 변화 가능성을 활용해 글로벌 생활의 일상성 탓에 자칫 소원해질 수 있는 공동체들을 포함한다. 상징적인 미학을 통해 사람들 불러들여 자연, 집단적 기억, 그리고 공동체와의 재연결을 시도하기도 한다. 본 글에서 다룰 오브제들은 인도네시아 작가 겸 건축가 에코 프라워토가 설계한 웜홀과 더 템플이다.

웜홀 웜홀은 2013 싱가포르비엔날레 참여 작품이다. 3개의 원뿔 모양 대나무 구조물 ─ 또는 웜홀 ─ 들이 싱가포르국립미술관 앞 잔디밭에 설치되어 있다. 지역의 특산 식물을 재료로 활용한 이들 원뿔들은 주변의 콘크리트 철근 구조물들과 재료와 형태 모든 면에서 뚜렷한 대비를 이룬다. 겪인 대나무의 밀도가 원뿔 내부로 들어오려 하는 신비한 빛을 한 번 걸러내고, 의도적으로 불규칙적인 마

sitting in the neighbourhood built in the late 1990s focuses on creating an aesthetic identity. Its architectural quality reminds us of Michael Graves's architectural articulations as well as the forms of Bernard Tschumi's Parc de la Villette follies. Located next to a playground, the object suggests an extension of the play space with an elevated walkway and seating area on pilotis.

Temporary objects

The temporary objects chosen are constructed to integrate the international nature of global identity in different parts of the city centre. These are artworks that utilise the ephemeral and changeable meaning of the art to include communities that may be alienated by the everydayness of global life. The objects attempt to reconnect people with nature, collective memories and the community by using iconic aesthetic qualities to attract people to them. The objects are Wormhole and The Temple, both designed by Indonesian architect-artist Eko Prawoto.

Wormhole *Wormhole* was originally an art installation for the Singapore Biennale 2013. Three conical bamboo structures—the wormhole—are planted on the lawn in front of the Singapore National Museum. Using local plant materials, the cones contrast starkly with the surrounding concrete and steel buildings in both material and form. The dense bamboo plaits sieve a mysterious light into the interior of the cones, the tips of which are deliberately left irregular to give a dramatic 'wormhole' view of the sky. The object is perhaps a critique of an instrumentalist and

Singapore's Urban Folly

materialistic society that regards nature only as the raw materials for the building industry.

By hiding the busy city from sight, the structure provides a temporary refuge to be alone with nature (grass and the sky), to engage nature and to contemplate.

The Wormhole at Singapore Biennale, Eko Prawoto, 2013
웜홀, 싱가포르 비엔날레,
에코 프로토(Eko Prawoto), 2013

더 템플 더 템플은 마리나 베이에 의해 2010년 에스플란데에 임시 건축물로 지어졌다. 일련의 대나무 파빌리온들이 기존의 나무들 사이사이에 전략적으로 자리한다. 하늘로 열려 있는 메인 파빌리온으로는 대나무 문들이 이끄는 대로 3가지 방향에서 입장할 수 있다. 점진적인 과정을 통해 이들 일련의 문은 방문객들을 도심이라는 맥락에서 보다 원시적이고 평화로운 시공간으로 안내한다. 대나무의 사용은 현대적이고 글로벌한 주변 환경에 일시적이면서 지역적인 성질을 추가하고 한때 어촌 마을이었던 싱가포르와 다시 만나게끔 한다.

The Temple *The Temple* was built as a temporary installation in 2010 at the Esplanade by the Marina Bay. It is a series of bamboo pavilions strategically situated in between the existing trees of the site. The main open-to-sky pavilion is entered from three different directions by pathways defined by bamboo portals. Via a gradual transition, the rows of portals funnel visitors from an urban context through time and space to a more primordial and serene environment. The use of bamboo contributes to the ephemeral and local character with the modern and global context of the surroundings, and attempts to resuscitate the connection with the fishing village that was once Singapore.

340

Writing Staff

The Temple at Esplanade Bay, Eko Prawoto
에스프라나데 베이의 더 템플, 에코 프로토(Eko Prawoto)

싱가포르의 어반폴리
흥미롭게도 여기에서 선정하고 2가
지-영구 및 비영구-로 분류한 이들
폴리들은 임시적인 '무기능' 오브제
들이다. 도심부의 레저 및 업무 시설
에 위치한 반면, 영구적인 오브제들
은 생활 및 주거 지역에 위치해 있음
을 암시하고 있다. 이는 우연일 수도
있겠으나 사회 저변의 실용주의 이론
에 대한 우리의 초기 논의에 잘 부합
하기도 한다. 즉, 명백히 '기능이 없
는' 폴리들이 여전히 미적 오브제 또
는 랜드마크로서 보다 영구한 기능
을 가진다는 것이다. 건축적 표현 또
한 특정 구성 민족의 전통적인 미적
정체성을 담아내는 대신 새로운 정체
성을 제공하는 동시대적 건축 언어를
사용하는 것 또한 매우 의도된 점으
로 보인다. 또한 맥락이나 공동체의
지역적 역사와의 연결고리가 강하지
않은 경우도 많다. 일면, 오브제의 특
수성과 정치적으로 옳다고 여겨지는
미적 기준 덕분에, 확연히 드러나지
않는 경우에도 이들 오브제의 실용
주의적 측면은 명확하다.
　　임시 오브제의 경우 그들이 위치
한 맥락에서 의미를 가져오는 경우가
많다. 구조의 임시적 특질은 사용된

Singapore's Urban Folly

Interestingly, the current selection and categorisation of the follies into two groups—permanent and temporary—seem to suggest that the temporary 'functionless' objects are located in the leisure and work spaces within the city centre, while the permanent ones are situated within the living environment of our housing neighbourhoods. This may be coincidental, but does fit well in our initial elaboration of the ideology of pragmatism that underlies the society so that the apparently 'functionless' folly still serves a more permanent function as an aesthetic object or even a landmark. The architectural expression is perhaps also deliberate in not embracing any specific traditional aesthetic identity of the constituent ethnic groups, but instead uses a contemporary architectural idiom to offer a new identity. Often times it also does not have any relation to the local history of the context or community. In a sense, thanks to the uniqueness of the object and the politically correct aesthetic choice, the utility of such an object is still manifest even if in a less obvious utilitarian way.

Singapore's Urban Folly

재료와 형태가 영구성, 내구성, 구조적 안정성이 아닌 다른 가치들을 고려해 선택될 수 있었음을 뜻한다. 즉, 흥미를 배가시키거나 질문을 이끌어내기 위해 선택에 대해 생각하고 역사, 환경, 사회, 개인적 집단적 선택 그리고 우리 사회를 끌어가는 실용주의에 대해 고민하도록 하고자 선정되었을 수 있다.

이제, 첫 번째 질문으로 돌아가보자, 싱가포르에는 폴리가 있는가? 만약 폴리가 글로벌 시티 내의 예상 가능한 표준적 일상 환경을 넘어서는 오브제로 해석될 수 있다면 모든 오브제들이 폴리라는 분류에 해당한다. 하지만, 폴리가 기존의 맥락에 대한 질문을 던질 수 있는 능력으로서 규정되는 것이라면 일부만이, 특히 우리가 논의한 임시 구조물들만이 이 분류에 부합한다. 하지만, 실용주의와 폴리의 수사를 넘어 모든 오브제들이 꾸미고, 놀리고, 조롱하며, 맥락을 맥락화-비맥락화해 사람들의 일상에 균열을 만들어내고 있다는 점만큼은 분명해 보인다.

The temporary objects, more often than not, derive their meaning from the context in which they are located. The temporary nature of the structures meant that the material and forms used could be chosen for values other than permanence, durability and structural integrity. Rather, they could be chosen to kindle interest in, evoke questions, interrogate choices, and encourage contemplation of our history, environment, society, personal and collective choices, and even of the pragmatism that drives our society.

So, let us return to the first question: Does Singapore have any follies? If a folly can be seen as an object beyond the expected and the standard environment of our daily lives in a global city, then all the objects previously mentioned fulfil the criterion. However, if a folly is defined by its ability to question the existing context, then only some objects, particularly the temporary ones discussed, fulfil the criterion. Yet beyond the rhetoric of pragmatism and folly, all the objects do decorate, tease, ridicule, and contextualise-decontextualise the context to create a rupture in the daily life of the people.

Writing Staff

모종린
연세대학교 국제대학원 교수
한국

Mo, Jongryn
Professor, Yonsei Graduate School of International Studies
Republic of Korea

Culture City Gwangju is a City of Public Art

공공미술의 도시 문화도시 광주
문화도시 광주는 공공미술의 도시다
국립아시아문화전당, 광주시립미술
관 등 미술관이 전시하는 공공미술
과 더불어 광주시가 폴리 사업을 통
해 기획한 작품이 도시 거리를 장식한
다. 광주폴리는 도시 거리에 세계적
인 건축가와 예술가의 소형건축예술
(Folly)을 설치하는 사업이다. 2011
년에 시작해 현재 제3차 사업이 진행
되고 있다.

Culture City Gwangju is a city of public art. Works exhibited by Asia Culture Centre and the city's museums, as well as those organised by the city government through the Gwangju Folly project, light up city streets. The Gwangju Folly project has installed small architectural artworks created by international architects and artists around the city. First published in 2011, it is now in its third edition.

Asia Culture Centre, a Key Cultural Asset in Gwangju
문화도시 광주의 중심 문화 자산 국립아시아문화전당

Public art quickly became one of the most frequent choices of projects aiming at revitalising lagging neighbourhoods and alleys in Korea. The most popular example of this is Mural Village, a project started at Dongpirang Hill, Tongyeong in 2007, which then spread nationwide. Successful cases in other countries, such as the Guggenheim Museum in Bilbao, Spain and Angel of the North in Gateshead, England, had a large influence on the boom of public art in Korea.

This begs the question: Should public art necessarily be artworks? Though some public artworks like the In-between Hotel and Cubic Meter Food Cart at Gwangju Folly exhibited practical functions, they are more artistic than anything else. There must be a way that public art can make a more direct contribution to the lives of the people. *There aren't any other tools that have more importance than public art in urban re-generation that revitalises the local community and creates attractive urban culture.*

When you walk the streets and pass by any number of buildings, from convenient, high-end public facilities to cute little stores, there is hardly a single piece of urban infrastructure that does not require public art.

Design is especially crucial in commercial facilities that enrich people's lives and offer unique experiences with different sentiments. In an age of SNS marketing, stores that successfully attract customers are those with architecture, signage, interiors, and products that people want to share on Instagram. In other words, it is the Instragram-able stores that survive today.

*Communication Hut,
a Folly installed
at a Jang-dong Intersection
in Gwangju*
광주 장동 사거리에 설치된
광주폴리 '소통의 오두막'

Writing Staff

특히, 삶의 질을 윤택하게 하고 특별한 경험과 감성을 제공하는 상업시설에서 디자인의 중요성은 절대적이다. SNS 마케팅 시대에 인스타그램에 잘 나올법한 건축, 사인, 인테리어, 상품 디자인을 가진 가게들이 성공적으로 고객을 유인한다. 한마디로 'Instagramable(인스타그램에 올릴만한)'한 가게만이 살아남을 수 있다.

색다른 경험과 취향을 기록하는 도시여행자에게 거리와 건물 디자인은 도시의 매력을 평가하는 중요한 기준이다. 특색 있는 디자인과 건축으로 상권의 정체성을 구현하고 점포의 외관을 장식해야 주민의 지역경제에 중요한 관광객을 유치할 수 있다.

그러나 아쉽게도 대부분의 지역 정부는 상권 조성과 재생을 자신의 업무로 생각하지 않는다. 제조업 공장의 유치를 위해서는 온갖 재정적 지원을 다 하면서 장기적으로 지역경제에 더 중요할 수 있는 상업시설을 방치하는 것은 구시대적인 사고방식이다. 그러나 정부가 직접 상업시설을 매입하고 운영하는 것은 시장경제에서 성공하기 어렵다.

도시를 새롭게 경험하는 공간,
광주 쿡폴리
전국의 모든 도시가 낙후 지역의 상권을 활성화하기 위해 고민하는 와중에 광주에 혁신적인 상업시설 유치 모델이 등장했다. 경기대 천의영 교수가 총감독하는 3차 광주폴리가 '먹고 마시는' 쿡폴리를 오픈한 것이다.

3차 광주폴리는 '도시의 일상성-맛과 멋'을 주제로 뷰(View)폴리, GD(Gwangju Dutch)폴리, 쿡(Cook)폴리, 뻔뻔(FunPun)폴리, 미니(Mini)폴리 등 도시의 일상과 밀접한 관계가 있는 작품으로 구성되어 있다. 산수동과 충장로에 들어설 3차 폴리 작품은 총 11개소에 달한다. 1, 2차 사업도 기능성과 예술성의

To urban travelers who document different experiences and tastes, the design of a street and its architecture are important standards in evaluating a city. ***Attracting tourists is important to the locals and local economy, and it can be done when we embody the identity of the area through unique design and architecture and decorate the exterior of the stores.***

However, most city governments do not consider this as their duty, to create, and instead focus on regenerating business areas. This is an outdated view to neglect business facilities that could be more important to the local economy in the long term, while giving full financial support to lure factories to the area. Yet in a market economy, it can be difficult to be successful if a government purchases and runs commercial businesses by itself.

Gwangju Cook Folly: A Space Offering Different City Experiences

While all the cities in the country were trying to vitalise the economy of lagging areas, Gwangju presented a creative model to attract commercial businesses. Gwangju Folly, which was led by Chun Eui-Young, a professor at Kyonggi University, opened Cook Folly, somewhere we can eat and drink to our heart's content.

Under the theme Folly & Everyday Life—Taste & Beauty, Gwangju Folly consists of works that closely relate with the daily lives or urban dwellers, including View Folly, GD (Gwangju Dutch) Folly, FunPun Folly and Mini Folly. For the project, 11 works will be installed around Sansu-dong and Chungjang-ro. Although Gwangju Folly and

조화를 목표로 삼았지만 실제로는 예술성에 방점을 찍은 작품 중심으로 설치했기 때문에 3차 쿡폴리의 시도에 귀추가 주목된다.

흥미롭게도 카페 '콩집'과 음식점 '청미장'이 입점한 2개의 건물로 구성된 쿡폴리는 한 사람의 작품이 아니다 천의영 교수는 광주시가 확보한 공폐가를 재생 건물로 설계했고, 서울 이태원 경리단길에서 '장진우거리'를 조성한 장진우 대표가 쿡폴리의 콘셉트와 콘텐츠를 제공했다. 실제 카페와 식당을 운영하는 기관은 지역 청년 협동조합(맛있는골목협동조합)이다.

쿡폴리의 건축은 구도심 활성화와 관련하여 긍정적 의의를 갖는다 무엇보다, 쿡폴리는 상업시설과 공공미술을 융합한 건축물로서의 가치를 초월한다.

공공미술을 통해 도시의 일상성을 회복한다는 목표를 식생활과 외식 문화에서 실현하고자 하는 기획자의 담대성에서 더 큰 의의를 찾아야 한다 도시의 일상생활에서 식생활만큼 중요하고 현실적인 문화를 찾기 어려움에도 불구하고 그동안 공공미술가들은 공공미술을 식생활 상업시설에 접목하는 작업을 적극적으로 추진하지 않았다.

also tried to balance practical functions and artistic aspects, they installed works that shed more light on their artistic value. This is why there is a keen interest in Cook Folly.

Consisting of two structures that house the café Congzib and the restaurant Chungmijang, it is also notable that that Cook Folly is not a work created by just one person. Chun redesigned an empty and abandoned house bought by the City of Gwangju, while Chang, Jinwoo, who brought about Chang, Jinwoo Street on Gyeongridan-gil (Road) in Seoul, provided the concept and contents of Cook Folly. Today, Gwangju's Young Startup Cooperative actually runs the café and restaurant. ***Blending public art into a commercial facility, Cook Folly goes far beyond the value of architecture.***

Cook Folly has already had a positive impact in the regeneration of the old city centre area. Above all, it is in the boldness of the curator where we can find a larger significance, to choose the culture of food and food service in seeking to embody the idea of rebuilding everydayness through public art.

Collaboration between a Restaurant, Chang, Jinwoo, and Public Art for the Alleys of Gwangju
광주 골목길을 위한 공공미술과 장진우 식당의 콜라보

Writing Staff

In an interview, Chun displayed his ambition in linking art, diet and business, saying, "As a restaurant-folly focusing on urban regeneration, Cook Folly will breathe new energy into the hollowed out and declining area, while also rebranding the taste of the old days." **Cook Folly offers a new channel of urban experience.**

The people of Gwangju can experience the publicness of public art and everydayness as well as consumption through Cook Folly. Instead of the rhetoric of a metadiscourse or nationalistic ideas, it permeates the daily lives of people and epitomizes the culture of the city. Thus, it stands right at the frontier of small urbanism.

Front Yard of Cook Folly Chungmijang
쿡폴리 청미장 앞마당

쿡폴리 장소에 있던 2개 가옥 중 하나는 본래 공폐가였다. 광주시가 동네에서 방치됐던 가구를 폴리로 재생한 것이다. 도심재생의 관점에서 쿡폴리는 혁신적이다. 서울 경리단 지역에 '장진우거리'를 개척한 장진우 대표를 초빙해 음식점과 카페의 콘셉트를 잡은 것도 다른 지역에서 보기 힘든 민관 협업 모델이다.

음식점과 카페를 운영하는 주체로 지역 청년이 설립한 협동조합을 선정한 것도 긍정적으로 평가할 수 있다. 광주시가 세금으로 조성한 폴리 시설을 기업이나 기존 자영업자에게 임대했다면 과연 지역 주민들이 이를 납득했을까? 쿡폴리를 청년창업가들에게 임대함으로써 시당국은 상업시설에 대한 지원의 정당성을 찾았다.

쿡폴리 모델은 새로운 상업시설 재생 모델로도 주목해야 한다. 그동안 지역 정부가 전통시장에 입주한 청년창업 가게를 보조한 적은 있으나 골목상권의 재생을 위해 상업시설에 직접 투자한 사례는 필자가 아는 한 쿡폴리가 처음이다.

Reflecting on Cook Folly through Two Key Words: Regeneration and Cooperation

Houses that used to be at the Cook Folly site were empty and abandoned. These two deserted houses that were not being used were renovated into a Folly. From the perspective of urban regeneration, Cook Folly is progressive. At the same time, inviting Chang, Jinwoo, the man responsible for developing Chang, Jinwoo Street in the Gyeongridan area and adopting the concepts of restaurant and café, was an unusual model of collaboration between the public and private sectors.

Another positive element is that it chose a cooperative formed by local young people to run the café and restaurant. If the Folly, which was created by using tax money, was rented out to other entrepreneurs or companies, would it be acceptable to the locals? By renting them out to young locals running their own startups, the city government could justify the investment to a commercial facility.

Cook Folly should be seen as a different model of regeneration commercial facility. While there have been cases when the local government subsidised stores in traditional markets rented out by young people starting up their own businesses, this is the first case of it investing directly into a commercial facility to revitalise the economy, as far as I know.

A Quiet, Peaceful Alley in Sansu-dong
고즈넉한 광주 산수동 골목길

Writing Staff

도시 개척에 나선
쿡폴리 기획자들

쿡폴리에 참여한 장진우 대표는 창업으로 도시를 재생하는 일종의 도시 기획자다. 골목대장이라는 타이틀을 지닌 그는 "외국인들에게 명동 광장시장, 가로수길이 다가 아니라는 걸" 보여주고 싶어 한다. 이태원 '스핀들 마켓', 대구 '마린타코', '영등포 케이크 공장', 세종시 카페 'I got everything' 등 국내 여러 지역에서 새로운 상업시설을 창업해 우리나라의 전국적 문화 콘텐츠 개발을 꿈꾼다.

장진우 대표를 쿡폴리 작가로 추천한 것은 다름 아닌 쿡폴리 총감독 천의영 교수다. 천교수의 궤적을 따라가면 쿡폴리 사업이 우연이 아님을 발견할 수 있다. 그는 1990년대 말 방영된 MBC '일요일 일요일 밤에'의 업소와 주택 재생 프로그램인 '신장개업'과 '러브하우스'에 출연해 대중적으로 많이 알려진 인물이다. 최근에는 성수동 수제구두 거리를 기획하는 등 도시 일상 속의 건축을 오랜 기간 꾸준히 추구해왔다. 건축과 디자인이 어떻게 소상공인 업장을 재생시킬 수 있는지.

Cook Folly Participants Help Develop the City

Chang, Jingwoo, who participated in Cook Folly, is sort of a city planner who regenerates the city through start-up businesses. Also referred to as the "boss among the neighbours," Chang hopes to show that "Myeong-dong, Gwangjang Market and Garosu-gil Road aren't the only things in Seoul." Having already created new businesses in different cities, such as Spindle Market (Itaewon), Marine Taco (Daegu), and the cake factory in Yeongdeungpo, café 'I got everything' in Sejong-si, he now dreams of **developing our own culture contents nationwide.**

The one who recommended Chang as an artist for Cook Folly is in fact, Director Chun. If you go through Chun, it is easy to see that the Cook Folly project is not a coincidence. He is well known to the public for appearing in the TV series Sunday Night in the 1990s, especially the segments titled "New Opening" and "Love House," both of which helped renovate small businesses and houses. Including his most recent project where he curated Seongsu Handmade Shoe Street, architecture in our daily lives has long been his primary focus. **How architecture and design can regenerate small businesses and enterprises.**

Culture City Gwangju is a City of Public Art

그가 보여준 '신장개업'은 여러 측면
에서 시대를 앞선 프로그램이었다
프로그램 정신은 그 후 현대카드, 호
텔신라 등 디자인과 컨설팅을 통해 전
통시장과 자영업 음식점을 지원하는
대기업 사업으로도 이어졌다. 하지만
정부는 아직도 소상공인 역량 강화보
다는 소규모 융자와 골목상권 보호를
위한 규제 등 보호 중심의 소상공인
정책을 고수하고 있다.

쿡폴리는 2017년 1월에 개장해
이제 막 시작된 사업이다. 사업의 혁
신성에도 불구하고 아직 성공했다고
평가하기는 이르다. 상업시설인 쿡폴
리는 궁극적으로 시장에서 긍정적인
평가를 받아야 한다. 광주시 입장에
서도 많은 시민이 쿡폴리를 찾고 그
서비스에 만족해야 사업에 대한 지원
을 합리화할 수 있다.

*Estrella (Dong
myeong-dong
branch) by Chef
Kim Sungshik
who is Devel-
oping Spanish
Food in Gwangju*
광주에서
스페인 음식을 개척하는
김성식 쉐프의
에스트레아
(동명동점)

쿡폴리의 성공을 위해
남겨진 과제
첫째, 지역 소상공인의 지지를 확보하
는 것이 중요하다. 지역 소상공인들은
광주시가 서울의 기업인 주식회사 장
진우를 쿡폴리 파트너로 영입한 것에
대해 상당한 소외감을 표출했다고 한
다. 쿡폴리가 새로운 유동인구를 창

"New Opening," the TV show mentioned above,
was a program ahead of its time in many aspects.
The spirit of the program was succeeded by large
entrepreneurs, including Hyundai Card and
Hotel Shilla, which supported traditional markets
and individually owned restaurants through design
and consulting. However, the government is still
pursuing protective policies such as supporting
small-scale loans or implementing regulations to
protect local businesses instead of trying to
strengthen their capacities.

Opened in January 2017, Cook Folly is a
project that has just got off the ground. In spite of
its innovative features, it is still too early to say
whether it has succeeded or not. As a commercial
business, in the end it has to receive positive
feedback from the market. From Gwangju's point
of view, its support can only be justified when
many people visit and are satisfied with the service.

Tasks Left for the Success of Cook Folly

First, it is imperative to have the support
from owners of small local businesses. It is said that
local business people have expressed a sense of
alienation about the fact that the local government
invited Chang, Jinwoo and his company from
Seoul, for example. **Cook Folly is functioning as
an anchor in the local economy and attracting
a floating population.** The local community and
businesses will only change if those running
the small stores in the area can enjoy direct benefits.

Second, it is also a key issue how the
Gwangju government responds to the gentrification
problem that the Cook Folly project may bring
about. Sansu-dong, where Cook Folly is located, is

출하는 지역 상권의 앵커 시설로 기능
ᅦ 같은 지역에서 가게를 운영하는 소
상공인들에게 직접적인 혜택을 줘야
지역 주민과 소상공인들의 여론도 바
ᅵ 것이다.

둘째, 광주시가 쿡폴리 사업이 초
ᅢ 할 수 있는 젠트리피케이션 현상에
ᅢ해 어떻게 대응하는지도 관건이다
쿡폴리가 위치한 산수동은 이미 젠트
리피케이션으로 홍역을 치르고 있는
동명동과 인접한 상권이다. 쿡폴리의
위치를 고려할 때 이 사업이 성공하면
필연적으로 젠트리피케이션 확산을
유발할 것이다.

현재 광주시는 쿡폴리 주변의 건
물을 매입하고 여기에 폴리, 문화시설
등 공공시설물을 설치하는 방식으로
젠트리피케이션에 대비하고 있다. 하
지만 공익시설의 공급이 효과적인 반
젠트리피케이션 정책인지는 확실치
않다. 임대료 인상을 합리적으로 관
리할 수 있는 제도적 장치가 젠트리피
케이션 위험 지역의 미래를 결정한다.

기술 발전과 가치의 변화는 우리
를 공유경제, 탈물질주의경제, 제로
한계비용경제 등 아직 경험하지 못한
형태의 경제로 이끌고 있다. 미래의
경제 형태는 우리가 모르는 미지의 세
계지만, 또 한편으로는 새로운 실험
이 가능한 도전의 세계다.

새로운 공유경제로 진입하고 있
는 우리가 순수 상업 영역과 순수 정
부 영역을 무리하게 구분 지을 필요는
없다. 광주 쿡폴리 사례가 보여주듯
낙후지역을 지속 가능한 방식으로 재
생하기 위해서는, 경쟁력 있는 상업시
설을 유치하는 것 외에는 다른 방도
가 없다. 정부-민간 파트너십이 쿡폴
리가 우리 도시에 제시하는 상업시설
재생 모델이다.

near Dongmyeong-dong, which is already suffering from gentrification.

Currently, the city government is preparing for gentrification by purchasing adjacent buildings where it will build public facilities, including Follies or other cultural facilities. However, it is not sure if providing public facilities is an efficient anti-gentrification policy. *An institutional device that can reasonably manage increasing rent costs will decide the future of areas in danger of gentrification.*

Technological development and changes in values are leading us to an economy that has yet to be experienced, namely the shared economy, post-materialism economy, and zero marginal cost economy. Although the future of our economy is unknown, it will certainly be a challenge that we can experiment with.

By entering a new shared economy, we do not need to try too hard to distinguish the pure commercial sector an d pure government sector. As Gwangju Cook Folly suggests, government-private partnerships can be a sustainable business regeneration model for lagging areas of the city. *There is no other way to go than having effective commercial facilities.*

Reference

Intro

Text

→ 005 "The 'meaning' of life is not to be found in
anything other than that life itself."
– Henri Lefebvre, *Critique of Everyday Life*
"삶의 '의미'는 다름 아닌 그 삶 자체에서만 발견할 수 있다."
– 앙리 르페브르, ‹일상에 대한 비평
(Critique of Everyday Life)›

→ 011 For the quest for satisfaction and the fact of being
satisfied presuppose the fragmentation of
'being' into activities, intentions, needs, all of them
well-defined, isolated, separable and separated
from the Whole. Is this an art of living? A style?
No. It is merely the result and the application to
daily life of a management technique and a
positive knowledge directed by market research.
– Henri Lefebvre, *Critique of Everyday Life*
"만족에 대한 추구와 만족의 상태는 전체로부터 구분되고 분리
되며 격리된, '존재'의 쪼개진 파편들을 전제한다.
즉 분명하게 정의된 행위와 의도, 그리고 요구들인 것이다.
이것이 삶의 기술인가? 양식? 그렇지 않다. 이는 단지 결과이며
시장조사가 만들어낸 경영기술과 실증적 지식을 일상에
적용한 것에 불과하다."
– 앙리 르페브르, ‹일상에 대한 비평
(Critique of Everyday Life)›

→ 013 "Against an economism void of values other than
those of exchange, protest stood for reuniting
the festival and daily life, for transforming daily life
into a site of desire and pleasure.
The protesters were protesting against the fact,
simultaneously obvious and ignored, that delight
and joy, pleasure and desire, desert a society
that is content with satisfaction –that is to say,
catalogued, created needs that procure some
particular object and evaporate in it."
– Henri Lefebvre, *Critique of Everyday Life*
"교환 가치 이외에는 어떠한 의미도 두지 않는 경제주의에 반해,
시위대는 축제와 일상을 재결합하고, 일상을 욕망과 즐거움의
장으로 바꾸기 위해 거리로 나섰다. 시위자들은 기쁨과 즐거움,
쾌락과 욕망이 만족의 사회를 유기한다는 명백하고도 무시되어
온 사실에 항의했다. 즉, 특정 대상만을 구하고 결국 그 안에서
증발해버리는 목록화되고 만들어진 수요에 항의한 것이다.
– 앙리 르페브르, ‹일상에 대한 비평
(Critique of Everyday Life)›

Small Urbanism with Gwangju Follies

광주폴리와 스몰 어바니즘

Image

→ 020 Fig.1 Success Diagram of Place Marketing by
Seppo K. Rainisto
그림 1 세포 K. 라이니스토(Seppo K. Rainisto)의
성공적인 장소 브랜딩을 위한 요소 다이어그램

→ 024 Fig.2 Seongsu Station
~ 025 From SS to Public Handmade Shoe Stores,
Photo © Chun, Eui-Young
그림 2 성수역 하부 수제화 공동매장 프롬SS
사진 © 천의영

→ 028 Fig.3 The Follies of Parc de la Villette in Paris,
Photo © Chun, Eui-Young
그림3 파리에 있는 라빌레트 공원의 폴리
사진 © 천의영

→ 031 Fig.4 The Gwangju Folly III a Workshop Site Visit,
April 8th, 2016
Photo © Yeo, Gyunsoo
광주폴리 III 참여작가 워크샵 현장투어,
2016년 4월 8일
사진 © 여균수

→ 032 Fig.5 A View over the Asia Culture Centre
~ 033 from View Folly
Photo © Chun, Eui-Young
그림5 뷰폴리에서 본 국립아시아문화전당 전망
사진 © 천의영

→ 033 Fig.6 Urban Sketchbook Event with
Seoseok Primary School Students at GD Folly
(Sep. 18, 2017)
Photo © Chun, Eui-Young
그림6 GD폴리 앞 서석초 어린이 거리칠판 행사(2017.09.18)
사진 © 천의영

→ 034 Fig.7 The Public Ideas Poster Contest of
FunPun Folly
Illustration © Kerb
그림7 뻔뻔폴리 대국민 아이디어 공모전 포스터
일러스트레이션 © 커브

→ 035 Fig.8 Opening of the Cook Folly at Congzib
(Jan. 10, 2017)
Photo © Chun, Eui-Young
그림8 쿡폴리 오프닝, 콩집(2017.01.10)
사진 © 천의영

Text

Seppo. K. Rainisto., "Success Factors of Place
Marketing: A Study of Place Marketing Practices in
Northern Europe and the United States", Helsinki
University of Technology, Institute of Strategy and
International Business, Doctoral Dissertations,
pp.66, 2003/4.
세포 K 라이니스토., ‹장소 마케팅의 성공적 요인: 북유럽과
미국의 장소 마케팅 실태에 관한 연구›,
박사논문, 헬싱키 공과대학, 전략 및 국제 비즈니스 연구소,
pp.66, 2003/4.

Amy Cortese., Translated by Hong, Sun-Young.,
*Locavesting: The Revolution in Local Investing and
How to Profit from It*, Wisdom House,
Korea, 2013.
에이미 코테스, 홍선영 옮김 ‹로카베스트›, 위즈덤하우스, 2013.

Henri Lefebvre Translated by John Moore With
a Preface by Michel Trebitsch, *Critique of Everyday
Life Volume 1*, London, New York, VERSO, 1991.
앙리 르페브르, 존 무어 옮김, ‹일상생활비판론 제 1 권›,
런던, 뉴욕: 베르소, 1991.

Nikolaus Hirsch + Chun, Eui-Young + Philipp
Misselwitz, *Gwangju Folly II*,
Ostfildern: Hatje Cantz, Germany, 2013.
니콜라우스 히르쉬, 필립 미셀비츠, 천의영, ‹광주폴리 II›,
오스트필더른: 하체 칸츠, 독일, 2013.

Chun, Eui-Young., "A Study on the Place Branding
Strategy", *Journal of Architecture Institute of
Korea*, Volume 27, 2011.
천의영, ‹장소 브랜딩 전략에 관한 연구›,
대한건축학회 논문집 27권, 2011.

Gwangju Folly: Cultural Landscape and Place Marketing
문화 경관과 장소마케팅 관점으로 본 광주폴리
Image
→ 047 Gwangju Follies Map
광주폴리 지도

→ 052 Project Comparison Table
~ 053 by each Gwangju Folly 2017, 2013, 2011
광주폴리 I(2011), II(2013), III(2017) 사업별 프로젝트 비교 표

Text
Kim, Yu-Gyeong, Kim, Yu-sin, Lee, JinYong,
Lee, MuYong, Koo, Ja-ryoung,
Strategic Management of Public Brands,
Hangyeongsa, 2014.
김유경, 김유신, 이진용, 이무용, 구자룡,
‹공공 브랜드의 전략적 관리›, 한경사, 2014.

Lee, MuYong, "A Study on the Cultural Concept
and Methodology of the Place Marketing Strategy",
Journal of Korea Geography, Volume 41(1),
pp. 39-57, 2006.
이무용, ‹장소 마케팅 전략의 문화적 개념과 방법론에
관한 연구›, 한국지리학회지, 41권(1), pp.39-57, 2006.

Kang, Hyo-Jeong, "A Study on the Cases of
Folly Project in the Contemporary Architecture
After Parc de la Villette", *Journal of the Korean
Institute of Interior Design* Volume 23(3),
pp. 144-152, 2014. 6.
강효정, ‹라빌레트 공원 이후의 현대건축에서의
폴리 프로젝트의 사례에 관한 연구›,
한국실내 디자인학회지 23권(3), pp. 144-152, 2014. 06.

Gwangju View Folly
광주 뷰폴리
Image
→ 090 View Folly Drawing 1, Illustration © Moon, Hoon
뷰폴리 드로잉 1, 일러스트레이션 © 문훈

→ 091 View Folly Drawing 2, Illustration © Moon, Hoon
뷰폴리 드로잉 2, 일러스트레이션 © 문훈

→ 092 View Folly Drawing 3, Illustration © Moon, Hoon
뷰폴리 드로잉 3, 일러스트레이션 © 문훈

→ 093 View Folly Drawing 4, Illustration © Moon, Hoon
뷰폴리 드로잉 4, 일러스트레이션 © 문훈

Architecture of Autonomy
자율건축
Image
→ 106 The overall ensemble, which consists
of View Folly and Architecture of Autonomy
뷰폴리와 자율건축의 앙상블

→ 108 Chun, Eui-Young, Moon, Hoon and Wee, Jinbok
in front of Architecture of Autonomy,
Photo © Chun, Eui-Young
천의영, 문훈, 위진복 '자율건축' 앞, 사진 © 천의영

Architecture of Autonomy: Behaviour Image Caption
Architecture of Autonomy
Rotating the 33 triangular columns allows visitors to
create their own individual colour code
Credit: Illustration © 2017 realities:united, Berlin
자율건축: 행동
'자율건축', 서른 세 개의 삼각기둥을 회전시켜
관객들은 자신만의 색 조합을 만들 수 있다.
일러스트레이션 © 2017
리얼리티즈:유나이티드(realities:united), 베를린

Architecture of Autonomy: Interaction Image Caption
Architecture of Autonomy
Visitors entering the roof rotate columns individually.
Credit: Illustration © 2017 realities:united, Berlin
'자율건축: 교감'
'자율건축', 옥상에 들어선 관람객들이 기둥을 회전시키고 있다.
일러스트레이션 © 2017
리얼리티즈:유나이티드(realities:united), 베를린

→ 111 MuseumX
Video: http://vimeo.com/realitiesunited/museum-x
Photos © 2006 Natalie Czech, courtesy of
realities:united, Berlin
영상: http://vimeo.com/realitiesunited/museum-x
사진 © 2006 나탈리 체크(Natalie Czech),
리얼리티즈:유나이티드(realities:united), 베를린

→ 112 BIX
Video: http://vimeo.com/realitiesunited/bix
Photos © 2003 Paul Ott, courtesy of
realities:united, Berlin
영상: http://vimeo.com/realitiesunited/bix
사진 © 2003 폴 오트(Paul Ott),
리얼리티즈:유나이티드(realities:united), 베를린

Crystal Mesh
Video: http://vimeo.com/3473657
Photo (s) © 2009 Tim Griffith
Crystal Mesh
영상: http://vimeo.com/3473657
사진 © 2009 팀 그리피스(Tim Griffith)

Data 5) Urban Park Area per capaita (m²),
Statics per Each Municipality, 2008
자료 5) 1인당 도시공원 면적(m²),
자료: 각 지자체별 통계연보, 2008

→ 265 Data 6) Heatwave Days (Day),
The Meteorological Administration
자료 6) 폭염일수(일), 자료: 기상청

Data 7) Self-sufficient Electricity,
The Ministry of Trade Industry and Energy,
Korea Energy Economics Institute, 2014
자료 7) 전력 자급률, 출처: 산업통상자원부,
에너지경제연구원, 2014

→ 266 Data 8) Monthly Use Frequency of Public Library,
The National Survey on Reading, 2011
자료 8) 공공도서관 월 평균 이용 빈도,
자료: 국민 독서 실태 조사, 2011

→ 267 Data 9) Annual Exhibition Number,
The Korean Culture and Arts Committee, 2014
자료 9) 연간 전시 횟수, 자료: 한국문화예술위원회, 2014

Data 10) Number of Theatre (per 100,000),
The Ministry of Culture, Sports and Tourism, 2011
자료 10) 10만명 당 공연장수, 자료: 문화체육관광부, 2011

Data 11) Number of Gym, The Ministry of Culture,
Sports and Tourism, 2008
자료 11) 체력단련장 수, 자료: 문화체육관광부, 2008

→ 268 Data 12) Degree of Children's Happiness (rank),
Save the Chilidren & SNU Social Welfare
Institute, 2013
자료 12) 어린이 행복감 순위,
자료: 세이브더칠드런 & 서울대 사회복지연구소, 2013

Data 13) Number of Festival in 2012,
The Ministry of Culture, Sports and Tourism, 2009
자료 13) 2012 축제 총괄표, 자료: 문화체육관광부, 2009

→ 291 I Love to Dance: A Dance Floor for Adults
Photo © Lee, Bohyun
나는 춤을 사랑한다: 어른을 위한 댄스 플로어
사진 © 이보현

GD Folly Blazes a Culture Trail for Gwangju
문화도시 광주의 활로(活路)를 개척한 GD폴리
Image

→ 302 WE WANT A SAFE SCHOOL ZONE
FOR OUR KIDS!
Photo © Lee, KiHun,
Regional Cultural Exchange Honam Foundation
우리 아이들을 위한 안전한 '스쿨존'을 지켜내자!
사진 © 이기훈, 지역문화교류호남재단

A Signature-collecting Campaign to preserve
a Pedestrian Zone in front of the School
Photo © Lee, KiHun,
Regional Cultural Exchange Honam Foundation
학교 앞 보행로를 지키기 위한 서명 운동
사진 © 이기훈, 지역문화교류호남재단

Gwangju Folly Workshop
광주폴리 워크숍
Image

→ 330 'A Folly Made out of Recycled Planks' Designed
by Oulu University Students of Architecture,
Photo © Aleksi Rastas
오룰루 건축학교 학생들이 디자인한 재활용된 판자들로
만들어진 폴리, 사진 © 알렉시 라스타스(Aleksi Rastas)

'Willow Branch: Folly', Designed by Oulu University
Architecture Students, Photo © Ville-Pekka Ikola
오룰루 건축학교 학생들이 디자인한 '버드나무 가지' 폴리,
사진 © 빌라-페카 이콜라(Ville-Pekka Ikola)

→ 331 'World Design Capital (WDC) Pavilion'
Designed by Pyry-Pekka Kantonen and Aalto
University Wood Studio, Helsinki, 2012,
Photo © Tuomas Uusheimo.
피리-페카 칸토넨과 알토대학교 우드 스튜디오가 디자인한
'월드 디자인 캐피탈 파빌리온', 헬싱키, 2012.
사진 © 토마스 우쉬모(Tuomas Uusheimo)

→ 332 'Empty Space in the Forest' Designed by
Matti Sanaksenaho, Photo © Seppo Sarkkinen.
마티 사낙세호가 디자인한 '숲 속의 빈 공간',
사진 © 세포 사키넨(Seppo Sarkkinen)

Singapore's Urban Folly
싱가포르의 어반 폴리
Image

→ 334 Precinct pavilions, drop-off areas,
shelters/pergolas, seating, playgrounds,
elderly fitness stations and court
지구 파빌리온, 드롭오프공간, 셸터/페르골라, 좌석,
놀이터, 노인용 신체 단련 시설 또는 뜰

→ 335 Public Housing Landscape of Singapore
Some rights reserved by Jnzl's Photos
(https://www.flickr.com/photos/surveying/)
The file is licensed under the Creative Common
Attribution 2.0 Generic (CC BY 2.0) license
(https://creativecommons.org/licenses/by/2.0/)
© Creative Commons 2.0
https://www.flickr.com/photos/surveying/
https://creativecommons.org/licenses/by/2.0/
'싱가포르의 공공주거' 사진에 대한 일부 권리는
Jnzl(https://www.flickr.com/photos/surveying/)에게
있으며 이 파일은 Creative Common Attribution 2.0
Generic(CC BY 2.0)의 허가에 따라
(https://creativecommons.org/licenses/by/2.0/)에
따라 라이선스가 부여됩니다. © Creative Commons 2.0
https://www.flickr.com/photos/surveying/
https://creativecommons.org/licenses/by/2.0/

Text

→ 333 Bayley, S. (2016). Let's celebrate follies –
England's most distinctive contribution to world
architecture. The Spectator, available at:
https://www.spectator.co.uk/2016/06/lets-
celebrate-follies-englands-most-distinctive-
contribution-to-world-architecture/#
[Accessed 11 April 2017].
베일리, S., ‹세계건축에 대한 영국의 가장 독특한 기여
– 레츠 셀러브레이트 폴리›, 방문자(https://www.
spectator.co.uk/2016/06/lets-celebrate-follies-
englands-most-distinctive-contribution-to-world-
architecture/# [2017년 4월 11일 액세스]), 2016.

→ 333 Choy, C. L. (1987). "History and managerial culture
in singapore: "Pragmatism", "openness"
and "paternalism"". Asia Pacific Journal of
Management,
4 (3), 133-143. doi:10.1007/BF01732383
초이, C.L., ‹싱가포르의 역사와 경영 문화: "실용주의",
"개방성" 그리고 "온정주의"›, 아시아태평양 저널 매니지먼트,
4 (3), 133-143. doi: 10.1007/BF01732383, 1987

→ 333 Chua, B. H., & Murdoch University. Asia Research
335 Centre. (1995). Communitarian ideology
and democracy in Singapore. New York; London:
Routledge.
추아, B. H & 머독대학교. ‹싱가포르의 공동체 이데올로기와
민주주의›, 아시아 연구 센터, 뉴욕, 런던: 루트레지, 1995.

→ 333 GwangjuFolly (n. d.). Gwangju Folly Introduction.
Available at: http://gwangjufolly.org/en/about/
introduction/[Accessed 11 April 2017].
광주폴리(n. d.), 광주폴리 소개,
이용 가능: http://gwangjufolly.org/ko/about/
introduction/ [액세스: 2017년 4월 11일].

→ 333 Farrow, C. (2014). "Pure folly: a new generation of
artistic architecture". Design Curial, 17 June 2014.
Available at: http://www.designcurial.com/news/
pure-folly-4294810 Accessed 11 April 2017].
패로우, C., ‹완전한 폴리: 새로운 세대의 예술적 건축물›,
디자인 큐리얼, 2014년 6월 17일,
http://www.designcurial.com/news/pure-
folly-4294810
[액세스: 2017년 4월 11일].

→ 333 Headley, G. (1996). Architectural follies in America.
New York: John Wiley & Sons.
헤들리, G., ‹미국의 건축학적 폴리›
뉴욕: 존 와일리 & 선즈, 1996.

→ 333 Howley, J. (1993). *The follies and garden buildings of ireland*. New Haven [Conn.]: Yale University Press.
하울리, J., ‹폴리와 아일랜드의 정원건물›,
뉴 헤이븐: 예일 대학 출판부, 1993

→ 333 Jones, B. M. (1974). *Follies & grottoes* (2nd, heavily revised and enlarged.). London: Constable.
존스, B.M., ‹폴리와 그로토스›, (2번째 개정판).
런던: 콘스터블, 1974.

→ 333 Somjee, A. H., & Somjee, G. (1995). *Development success in asia pacific: An exercise in normative-pragmatic balance*. New York; London: St. Martin's Press.
솜지, A. H., & 솜지, G., ‹아시아 태평양에서의 발전 성공:
규범적 - 실용주의적 균형에서의 운동›,
뉴욕; 런던, 세인트 마틴 프레스, 1995.

→ 333 Tan, K. P. (2012). "The ideology of pragmatism: Neo-
336 liberal globalisation and political authoritarianism in Singapore". *Journal of Contemporary Asia*, 42 (1), 67-92. doi:10.1080/00472336.2012.634644
탄, K. P., ‹실용주의 이데올로기: 싱가포르의 신자유주의
세계화와 정치 권위주의›, 컨템포러리 아시아 저널,
42 (1), 67-92. doi: 10.1080/00472336.2012.634644
링크, 2012.

→ 333 Tschumi, B. (2014). *Tschumi parc de la villette*. London: Artifice Books.
베르나르 츄미, ‹베르나르 츄미의 라빌레트 공원›,
런던: 아트피스 북스, Link, 2014

→ 334 Mahbubani, K. (2016). "Youth here lack idealism". *The Strait Times*, 20 February 2016. Available at: http://www.straitstimes.com/opinion/youth-here-lack-idealism [Accessed 11 April 2017].
마부바니, K., ‹젊음 부족 관념론›,
스트레이츠 타임즈, 2016년 2월 20일.,
http://www.straitstimes.com/opinion/youth-here-lack-idealism [액세스: 2017년 4월 11일]

→ 334 Pow, C. P. (2013). "From Housing a Nation to Meeting Rising Aspirations: Evolution of Public Housing over the Years". In E. L. E Ho, C. Y Woon and K. Ramdas (eds.), 2013. *Changing Landscapes of Singapore: Old Tensions, New Discoveries*. Singapore: National University of Singapore Press, pp. 43-60.
파우, C. P., ‹주택에서 떠오르는 열망을 충족시키기:
공공 주택의 발전›, E. L. E 호, C. Y. 윤 및 K. 라마다스(편집),
2013. ‹싱가포르의 경관 변화: 오래된 긴장, 새로운 발견›,
싱가포르: 싱가포르 국립대학교 출판부, pp. 43-60, 2013.

→ 334 Wong, A. K., Yeh, S. H. K., & Housing and Development Board. (1985). *Housing a nation: 25 years of public housing in singapore*. Singapore: Maruzen Asia for Housing & Development Board.
웡, A. K., 예, S. H. K., & 주택 개발 위원회,
‹국민주택: 싱가포르 공공주택 25년›,
싱가포르: 마루젠 아시아 주택개발 위원회, 1985.

→ 334 Pugh, C. (1989). "The Political Economy of Public Housing". In K.S. Sandhu and Paul Wheatley (eds.), 1989. *Management of Success: the Moulding of Modern Singapore*. Singapore: Institute of Southeast Asian Studies. pp. 833–859.
푸, C., ‹공공 주택의 정치 경제›, K.S. 산두, 폴 휘틀리(편집),
1989., ‹성공의 관리: 현대 싱가포르의 변화›,
싱가포르: 동남아시아 연구소, pp. 833-859, 1989.

→ 334 Rago, D. (2013). Gwangju Folly Project 2013. *Domus*, 13 August 2013. Available at: http://www.domusweb.it/en/art/2013/08/13/nikolaus_hirsch_gwangjufollyproject.html [Accessed 11 April 2017].
라고, D., ‹광주폴리 프로젝트›, Domus, 2013년 8월 13일.
http://www.domusweb.it/en/art/2013/08/13/nikolaus_hirsch_gwangjufollyproject.html [액세스: 2017년 4월 11일]

→ 334 Singstat (2017). Statistics. Department of Statistics Singapore. Available at: http://www.singstat.gov.sg/statistics/latest-data [Accessed 11 April 2017].
사인스태트, ‹통계, 싱가포르 통계청›,
이용 가능: http://www.singstat.gov.sg/statistics/latest-data [액세스: 2017년 4월 11일], 2017.

→ 339 Li, Z. (2006). *Four Essays on Aesthetics*. Oxford: Lexington Books.
리, Z., ‹미학에 관한 네 가지 수필›
옥스포드: 렉싱턴 북스, 2006.

Culture City Gwangju is a City of Public Art
공공미술의 도시 문화도시 광주
Text

Chang, Jinwoo, *Chang's Kitchen*, Eight Point (8.0), Korea, 2016.
장진우, ‹장진우식당›, 에이트 포인트(8.0), 2016.

Chun, Eui-Young, *Destroy the Gird*, Sejong Books, 2016.
천의영, ‹그리드를 파괴하라›, 세종서적, 2016.

Overview

Project Duration	2014~Aug. 31, 2017 (3 years, 8 months)
Project Scale	4 main types (View, GD, Cook, FunPun) + subsidiary Mini Folly
Strategy	Night scenery, combining it with media art, concentrating on selected core contents, engaging the public
Director	Chun, Eui-Young (Professor, Graduate School of Architecture, Kyonggi University)
Curators	Yoo, Uoo Sang and Wee, Jinbok
Concept	Folly & Everyday Life—Taste & Beauty Helping Gwangju realise its future vision in which urban devices revitalise the city
Participants	11 participants from 4 nations

Major Progress

Jan. 2014	Organisation and operation of Gwangju Folly Citizen Committee (16 sessions)
Oct. 2014~Feb. 2015	Organisation and operation of Gwangju Folly Evaluation Group
Jun. 2015	Public hearing
Aug.~Dec. 2015	Appointed the director and curators
Dec. 2015	Meeting with City Council
Nov. 2015~May 2016	Site selection
Dec. 2015~Apr. 2016	Developed works selected from an open call and chose participants
Apr. 8, 2016	Participant workshop
May~Jun. 2016	Submitted basic design
Jul.~Aug. 2016	Final design and construction permission
Nov. 2016	Gwangju Folly III press conference
Dec. 2016	Gwangju City Council Industry and Construction Committee site visit
Dec. 2016	Completion of Cook, FunPun and GD Folly
Jan. 10, 2017	Gwangju Folly III Cook Folly opening event
Jan. 12~14, 2017	Artist workshop for View Folly installation
Feb. 2017	2nd presentation of GD Folly for residents of Sansu-dong
Feb. 2017	Completed deliberations on View Folly repairs and reinforcement; changed the state of cultural property
Mar. 3, 2017	Completed View Folly building agreement
Mar. 8, 2017	3rd presentation of GD Folly for residents of Sansu-dong
Apr. 4, 2017	1st presentation of GD Folly installation (Seoseok Primary School) for parents
Apr. 14, 2017	2nd presentation of GD Folly installation (Seoseok Primary School) for parents
May 16, 2017	GD Folly workshop (with local residents, parents, students, civic groups)
Jun. 30, 2017	Completion of View Folly
Jul. 10, 2017	Presentation of GD Folly's basic design at Dong-gu Office
Aug. 2017	Completion of GD Folly by Winy Maas

사업개요

사업기간	2014년~2017. 08.31(3년 8개월)
작품규모	4개 구성 유형(뷰·GD·쿡·뻔뻔) + 서브 미니폴리로 구성
추진방식	야간경관·미디어아트 접목, 선택과 집중, 핵심콘텐츠, 시민참여형
총감독	천의영(경기대학교 대학원 건축설계학과 교수)
큐레이터	유우상, 위진복
주제	도시의 일상성–맛과 멋, 광주의 미래를 담는 새로운 형식의 '도시 활성화 장치'로서 역할
참여작가	4개국 11명

주요 추진사항

2014. 01~	광주폴리시민협의회 구성·운영(16회)
2014. 10~2015. 02.	광주폴리운영평가단 구성·운영
2015. 06.	시민공청회 개최(1회)
2015. 08.~12.	총감독 및 큐레이터 선임
2015. 12.	의회 산업건설위원회 간담회
2015. 11.~2016. 05.	장소(부지) 선정
2015. 12.~2016. 04.	공모작 추진 및 참여작가 선정
2016. 04. 8	참여작가 워크숍 개최
2016. 05.~06.	기본디자인 제출 완료
2016. 07.~08.	실시설계 및 인허가
2016. 11.	광주폴리 III 기자간담회 개최
2016. 12.	광주시의회 산업건설위원회 현장방문
2016. 12.	쿡, 뻔뻔, GD폴리(조병수) 작품 준공 완료
2017. 01.10	광주폴리 III 쿡폴리 개막행사
2017. 01. 12~14	뷰폴리 작품설치를 위한 작가 워크숍 개최
2017. 02.	GD폴리 산수동 주민설명회 개최(2차)
2017. 02.	뷰폴리 건물 보수보강·문화재현상변경심의 완료
2017. 03. 03	뷰폴리 건축협의 완료
2017. 03. 08	GD폴리 산수동 주민설명회 개최(3차)
2017. 04. 04	GD폴리(서석초) 설치 학부모 1차 설명회 개최
2017. 04. 14	GD폴리(서석초) 설치 학부모 2차 설명회 개최
2017. 05. 16	GD폴리 워크숍개최(지역주민, 학부모, 학생, 시민단체)
2017. 06. 30	뷰폴리 준공 완료
2017. 07. 10	GD폴리 동구청 기본디자인 설명회 개최
2017. 08.	광주폴리 III 위니 마스 GD폴리 작품 준공

2017	Master Architect, Gyeonggi Hybrid Town New Provincial Office Building
2011	Designed the Architecture Department Building at Kyonggi University
2010	Visiting Professor at UCLA
2009	Director General, Seoul Design Olympiad 2009
2004	Designed the headquarters for Noblesse Ad. Seoul, Republic of Korea
1999	Guest designer for TV shows including MBC's Opening New Restaurants (Shinjanggaeup) and Love House

2015	Presented on behalf of Gwangju at International Design Congress
2014~2016	Head of Centre for Innovation in Engineering in Education, Chonnam National University
2014	Campus Master Plan for Mokpo National University
2014	Presented on behalf of South Korea at Asia-Europe Culture Ministers' Meeting
2010	Planned Kim Hwan Ki Museum
2007	Master Plan for Sadeung Culture and Historical Village

2015	Designed swimming pools for the Gwangju Universiade
2012	Assistant Curator for the Gwangju Biennale
2012	Designed temporary container dwellings for Yeongdeungpo shantytowns
2009	Founding partner/Head of UIA (Urban Intensity Architects)
2007	Named an ARB/RIBA Chartered Member Architect
2006	Completed an architectural professional course, Kingston University (UK)
2003	Graduated with an M.Arch. from AA (Architecture of Association) School of Architecture

Gwangju Folly III – "Folly & Everyday Life–Taste & Beauty"
Profile of Participating Architects & Artists

1984~1990	MA in Architecture, Delft University of Technology, NL
1984~1990	MA in Urban Planning, Delft University of Technology, NL
1980~1984	MA in Landscape Architecture, RHSTL, Boskoop, NL

· Professional Experience

2008~	Director and founder of The Why Factory, Delft, NL
1993~	Co–director and Co–founder of MVRDV, Rotterdam, NL
1990, 1993	Office for Metropolitan Architecture, Rotterdam, NL
1987~1989	DHV, Amersfoort, NL/UNESCO, Nairobi, KE
1984~1987	Municipality of Amsterdam, Amsterdam, NL
1983~1984	Bureau Bakker and Bleeker, Amsterdam, NL

· Awards: Winy Maas and MVRDV

2016	GCSC Award for European Innovation, Markthal, Rotterdam, NL
2015	Rotterdam Architecture Award, Markthal, Rotterdam, NL
2015	European Steel Construction Award of Merit, DNB Bank HQ, Oslo, NO
2014	Sign + Award–Public vote–Overall winner–Architectural Signage Category
2013	Red Dot Design Award 2013, Essen, Book Mountain, Spijkenisse, NL
2012	A&W Architect of the Year 2012, Hamburg, DE

· Educational Background

| 1991 | M.A. Architecture, Harvard University, US |
| 1986 | Bachelor of Architectural Studies, Montana State University, US |

· Awards

2014	KIA National Award for the design of Namhae South Cape Owner's Club Linear Suite
2013	AIA Honor Northwest and Pacific Regional for the design of L–shaped House
2010	Soo Kun Kim Prize for Earth House
2005	National Architectural Culture Award of Korea for the design of PaiChai University's College of Architecture

· Selected Works

2015	Namhae South Cape Owner's Club Linear Suite, Namhae, Republic of Korea
2014	5.18 Kwangju Memorial Hall, Republic of Korea (in progress)
2014	Jung–Geun An Memorial Hall, Republic of Korea
2008	TT Tower, Jongno, Republic of Korea
2002	PaiChai University, College of Fine Arts and Architecture building

· Publications

2010	Dwell–Four Box House, San Francisco, US,
2008	"Contemporary Korean Architecture," JOVIS Publishers Germany
2007	db (deutsche bauzeitlung) Embedded House, '口' Shaped Concrete Box House
2006	"Korea Style" Turtle Publishers. '口' Shaped Concrete Box House, H–House
2004	The *Phaidon Atlas* of Contemporary World Architecture Phaidon Press. AWA, Germany
2000	Pine Courtyard Apartment, Yong-in, Republic of Korea

· Exhibitions

2016	Marco, Monterrey, Mexico/Centre for Arts and Technology, Lisbon, Portugal,
2014	Art Museum Kloster Unser Lieben Frauen, Magdeburg, Germany
2014	artQ13, Rome, Italy
2014	German Academy Villa Massimo, Rome, Italy
2013	Urbane Künste Ruhr, Bergkamen, Germany
2013	Vitra Design Museum, Weil am Rhein, Germany
2013	Oslo Architecture Triennale, Norway
2012	Museum for Applied Arts, Cologne, Germany
2011	The Museum of Modern Art, New York, US
2009	Swedish Museum of Architecture, Stockholm, Sweden
2009	Bauhaus Archive, Berlin, Germany
2008	La Biennale De Venezia, Arsenal, Venice, Italy
2008	SAM–Schweizer Architektur Museum, Basel, Switzerland

· Awards

2016	Public Art Competition for the "Building of the Future", Berlin, Germany (1st Prize)
2015	North East Transit Garage Public Art Project, Edmonton, Canada, (1st Prize)
2015	Smart House Public Art Project, Toronto, Canada (1st Prize)
2012	Global Holcim Award (Bronze)
2011	Holcim Award Europe (Gold)
2011	Amagerforbraending Waste–to–Energy Plant, Copenhagen, Denmark (1st Prize with Bjarke Ingels Architects)
2009	Art Prize Berlin (Architecture Category)

· Educational Background

1993	M.A. Architecture, M.I.T., US
1988	B.A, School of Architecture, Inha University, Republic of Korea

· Selected Works

2014	Jeju Wind House
2014	Two Moon Junction
2013	K-POP Curve
2013	Roll House
2012	Lollipop House
2008	Rock it Suda
2006	S Mahal
2004	Sangsang Museum

· Exhibitions

2015	Inaugural Chicago Architecture Biennial (Participant Architect)
2014	14th La Biennale di Venezia Architecture Exhibition (Crow's Eye View: The Korean Peninsula)
2005	Architectural drawings for solo exhibition (Human Shaman), Gallery Pyundonamu

· Awards

2014	14th La Biennale di Venezia, Golden Lion for Best National Participation to Korea
2005	KIA National Award for Sangsang Museum

· Educational Background

2005	B.A Korean Classical Music & Photography, Chung-Ang University

· Selected Works

2015	Launched of Nikita Pasta & Burger
2015	Launched of Spindle Market food court
2015	Launched of Kalho & Diego (cafe and bar)
2015	Launched of Marine Tacos (Mexican restaurant)
2014	Launched of Mathilda (French-Italian restaurant)
2014	Operated Chang's Business Start-up School
2013	Launched Frank (bakery)
2012	Launched Bangbum Pocha
2011	Launched Chang's Kitchen

· Awards

2015	Korea Remodeling Association Award
2013~2014	Seoul City Architecture Award
2011	Hanhwa Galleria Foret, Good Design Award from the Korea Institute of Design Promotion (KIDP), Winner, Republic of Korea
2010	Samsung Raemian Gallery, Good Design Award from the Ministry of Knowledge Economy, Winner, Republic of Korea
2007	Design House, Designer of the Year, Architecture Division, Republic of Korea
2001	Brigham & Woman's Hospital Competition, Winner, Boston, USA

· Exhibitions

2013	Korean Cultural Centre in India Exhibition, invited architect, New Delhi, India
2012	National Museum of Contemporary Art personal exhibition, Art Folly Cubrick, Republic of Korea
2010	Harvard GSD special exhibition, invited architect, Cambridge, US
2009	Seoul Design Olympiad International Exhibition of 15 Architects, invited architect, Seoul, Republic of Korea
2007	Hong Kong-Shenzhen Bi-City Biennale, invited architect, Hong Kong, China

· Educational Background

2010	Ph.D. candidate in Art, Chosun University, Gwangju, Republic of Korea
2005	M.F.A in Art and Design, New Forms, Pratt Institute, New York, US
1996	B.F.A in Fine Art, Chosun University, Gwangju, South Korea

· Selected Exhibitions

2015	"Light Club" E–Land Space, Seoul, Republic of Korea
2015	"Humans are one of the Stars...FLOW" logos, Past Oral Gallery, Uiwang, Republic of Korea
2010	SIYON JIN's Video & LED installation, Crown Haitei Gallery, Seoul, Republic of Korea
2008	"Two Wheels," Taipei Artist Village Gallery, Taipei, Taiwan
2008	WAVE Brain Factory, Seoul, Republic of Korea
2007	Grand Art Tour (B.V.M.K) Docu Reportage, Lotte Gallery, Gwangju, Republic of Korea
2006	"DISTANCE," National Museum of Modern and Contemporary Art, ChangDong Residence Gallery, Seoul, Republic of Korea
2004	"DISTANCE," Steuben East Gallery, New York, US

· Awards

2011	Gwangju Award, Gwangju Art Award Committee
2007	Shinsegae Art Award, Gwangju Shinsegae Gallery
2005	Ha jung Woong Young Artist Award, Gwangju Museum of Art

· Selected Professional Background

| 2016~present | Adjunct professor, Seowon University |
| 2013~present | Adjunct professor, Kyunghee University |

· Educational Background

| 2009 | M.A in Planning and Preservation (GSAPP), Columbia University, New York, US |
| 2002 | B.A. in Architectural Engineering, Yonsei University, Seoul, Republic of Korea |

· Awards

2016	Honorable Mention, Design Competition for Rehabilitation of Namsan
2015	Yejangjarak, Seoul, Republic of Korea
2015	Winner for SOMA Outdoor Project S, Seoul Olympic Park Museum of Art, Seoul, Republic of Korea
2014	Finalist, Young Architects Program, MMCA (National Museum of Modern and Contemporary Art, Seoul, Republic of Korea
2014	Main Prize, Korea Wood Architecture Award, Seoul, Republic of Korea
2012	Honorable Mention, International Competition for Rehabilitation of Mapo Oil Depot, Seoul, Republic of Korea
	2nd place, Library at Yeongjong Hanul City

· Selected Journals and Publications

2015	Published "Re: thinking locality in architecture"
2014	"Digital Fabrication & Architectural Experiment," Architectural Institute of Korea
2012	Kook, Hyoung–Gul featured in Archistory section, Archiworld magazine

· Selected Exhibitions and Works

2016	Design Competition for Rehabilitation of Namsan Yejangjarak, Seoul, Republic of Korea
2015	Exhibition, Seoul Architecture Festival, Dynamic Relaxation, Seoul, Republic of Korea
2015	Urban Menifesto Archive, Art Council Korea, Seoul, Republic of Korea
2014	Exhibition "Part to Whole," MMCA (National Museum of Modern and Contemporary Art, Seoul, Republic of Korea
2013	Exhibition "Bilateral Theatre I," Interspace Dialogue at SeMA
2012	Exhibition "Floating Garden," Artificial Garden at SeMA
2012	Exhibition "Opening Chronometry," Campus Pavilion at Ewha Womans University
2011	Exhibition "Plis/Replis," La Fabrique Sonore at Pommery Champaign factory, Reims, France

2010	M.A. in Interactive Telecommunication, New York University, US
2003	B.A. in Communication Design, Korea National University of Arts, Republic of Korea

· Selected Exhibitions and Works

2015	Curated, Seoul, Republic of Korea
2013	'INTER. Act Reciprocity in Media', BRIC Media Museum, Brooklyn, New York, US
2012	Governor's Island Art Fair Artist Selection, Governor's Island, New York, US
2011	"Interconnected Segment," Artgate Gallery, New York, US
2011	"Hanji Metamorphosis," Space 475, New York, US
2011	"Desired SYNC," Gallery Korea of Korean Cultural Service New York, New York, US
2011	"Anxiety and Desire," Artgate Gallery, New York, US
2011	"All–Light," Digital Media Exhibition, Seo Art Gallery, Brooklyn, US
2010	SIGGRAPH "Space–Time," Los Angeles Convention Centre, Los Angeles, US
2009	Interactive VJ projection system, "Fashion Victim" fashion show, Jun Space, New York, US
2008	SIGGRAPH Asia Suntec International Convention Centre, Singapore
2008	Dumbo Art Festival, Brooklyn, US

Associate Professor, Aarhus School of Architecture, Denmark
Principal, Studio CONTEXT, Denmark, Italy and India
Vice President, DOCOMOMO, Denmark DOCOMOMO, Documentation and Conservation of buildings, sites and neighborhoods of the Modern Movement, Denmark

광주폴리 III - '도시의 일상성 & 맛과 멋'
참여작가 프로필

· 주요 약력

2010	국립현대미술관 서울관 현상설계 심사위원
2009	광주디자인비엔날레 건축부분 총 책임 큐레이터
2004	서울시 '한강 노들섬 오페라하우스' 현상설계 심사위원
1994	조병수건축연구소 개소
1991	미국 하버드대학교 대학원 건축학 석사
1986	미국 몬태나주립대학교 건축학 학사
1957	대한민국 서울에서 출생

· 수상경력

2014	한국건축가협회상 수상
2013	미국 몬태나주 건축가협회 최고상(Honor Award)
2013	영국 AR하우스어워드, Highly Commended 수상(L-shaped House)
2010	김수근문화상 수상
2005	영국 파이돈 출판사가 5년마다 선정하는 세계 100대 건축가 선정

· 주요 작품

2015	사우스케이프 주택단지 마스터플랜 및 주택(설계/감리/C.M)
2014	5.18 광주 민주인권평화기념관(진행 중)
2014	안중근기념관
2008	TT Project: 한국일보사 사옥 재개발 프로젝트
2002	배재대학교 예술대학, 박물관 및 채플

· 주요 수상

2016	'미래의 빌딩' 공모전 공공예술 1등상, 베를린, 독일
2015	로저스 아레나 공공예술 프로젝트 1등상, 에드먼턴, 캐나다
2015	스마트 하우스 공공예술 프로젝트 1등상, 토론토, 캐나다
2012	홀심 어워드 동상
2011	홀심 어워드 금상
2011	Amagerforbraending 쓰레기 재처리시설 현상공모 1등상(바르크 인겔스 공동), 코펜하겐, 덴마크
2009	베를린예술상(건축부문)

· 최근 전시

2016	마르코, 몬테레이, 멕시코
2016	예술 및 기술 센터, 리스본, 포르투갈
2014	성모수도원 예술박물관, 막데부르크, 독일
2014	artQ13, 로마, 이탈리아
2014	독일 아카데미 빌라마시모, 로마, 이탈리아
2013	Urbane Künste Ruhr, 베르크카멘, 독일
2013	비트라디자인뮤지엄, 바일암라인, 독일
2013	오슬로 건축 트리엔날레, 노르웨이
2012	응용미술박물관, 쾰른, 독일
2011	뉴욕현대미술관(MOMA), 뉴욕, 미국
2009	스웨덴 건축박물관, 스톡홀름, 스웨덴
2009	바우하우스 아카이브, 베를린, 독일
2008	라 비엔날레 드 베네치아, 아스날, 베니스, 이탈리아
2008	SAM 스위스 건축 박물관, 바젤, 스위스

· 주요 약력

2001	문훈건축발전소 설립
1993	MIT 건축대학원 졸업(M.Arch)
1988	인하대학교 건축과 졸업
1968	전주 출생

· 주요 수상

2014	베니스비엔날레 황금사자상
2005	건축가협회상 베스트7 수상

· 주요 전시

2015	시카고비엔날레
2015	한반도 오감도, 아르코미술관
2014	한반도 오감도, 베니스비엔날레 한국관
2009	예술의 새로운 시작–신호탄, 국립현대미술관(서울관)

· 주요 작품

2014	제주 윈드하우스(Wind House)
2014	투문정션(Two Moon Junction)
2013	케이팝 커브(K-POP Curve)
2012	롤리팝 하우스(Lollipop House)
2008	락잇수다(Rock It Suda)
2006	에스마할(S Mahal)
2004	상상미술관(SangSang Museum)

· 주요 저서

2016	기쁨의 건축
2014	달로 가는 제멋대로 펜

· 주요 약력

1986	출생
~현재	주식회사 장진우 대표

· 주요 학력 및 경력

2015	'니키타 파스타 앤 버거' 오픈
2015	'스핀들 마켓' 오픈(푸드코트)
2015	'칼로 앤 디에고' 오픈(카페 & 바)
2015	압구정 갤러리아 내 '프랭크' 입점
2015	'마린타코' 오픈(멕시코 음식점)
2014	'마틸다' 오픈(이탈리아, 프렌치 레스토랑)
2014	'장진우 창업스쿨' 운영
2013	'그랑블루' 오픈(재즈 비스트로)
2013	'프랭크' 오픈(베이커리)
2013	'문오리' 오픈(문어, 오리 음식점)
2012	'방범포차' 오픈(실내포차)
2011	'장진우식당' 오픈
2005	중앙대학교 국악관현악 및 사진학과 광고사진 복수전공 321 Studio 포토그래퍼로 활동

· 주요 약력

2012~현재	더 시스템 랩(THE SYSTEM LAB) 대표
2006	제10회 베니스비엔날레 한국 대표 건축가로 초청
2003~현재	경희대 건축대학원 초빙교수
2000	미국 하버드대학 건축학 석사학위
1999	스위스연방공과대학에서 수학
1995	고려대학교 건축공학과졸업

· 주요 수상

2015	리모델링 건축대전 수상
2014~2013	서울시 건축상 수상
2011	한화 갤러리아 포레, 굿디자인 디자인진흥원장상 수상

2010	삼성 래미안 갤러리, 굿디자인 지식경제부 장관상 수상 KHVatec 사옥 지명 현상설계 당선
2007	디자인하우스, 올해의 디자이너 건축부문 선정
2001	Brigham & Woman's Hospital 현상 설계 당선, 보스턴, 미국

· 주요 전시

2015	국립현대미술관 서울관 문화의 날 행사 초대작가, 서울
2013	인도 한국문화원 초청 전시, 뉴델리, 인도
2010	하버드 대학교 초청 한국의 현대건축 12인전, 캠브리지, 미국
2009	서울 디자인 올림피아드 세계 건축가 15인 초청 건축전, 서울
2007	홍콩-심천 국제 비엔날레 초청전시, 한강 르네상스 프로젝트, 홍콩, 중국

· 주요 작품

2012	SK 행복나눔재단 사옥
2011	폴 스미스 플래그십 스토어
2011	국립현대 미술관 큐브릭
2009	한강 보행자터널 프로젝트

· 주요 약력

2016~현재	서원대학교 융합예술학부 미술학과 겸임교수
2015~2013	중앙대학교 예술대학 미술학부 미디어기법연구 외래교수
2010	조선대학교 대학원 미술학과(서양화) 박사 수료
2007~2009	홍익대학교 미술대학 애니메이션전공 뉴미디어와 영상 외래교수
2005	프랫인스티튜트 졸업(석사), 뉴욕, 미국
1996	조선대학교 미술대학 회화과 졸업

· 주요 전시

2015	'Light Club' 이랜드 본사 이랜드 스페이스, 서울, 한국
2015	'인간은 하나의 별이다...FLOW' 로고스전원갤러리, 의왕, 한국
2010	'Video & LED Installation' 크라운해태갤러리, 서울, 한국
2008	'Two Wheels' 타이페이 아티스트빌리지갤러리, 타이페이, 대만
2008	'WAVE' 브레인팩토리, 서울, 한국
2007	'Grand Art Tour(B,V,M,K) 다큐르뽀' 롯데갤러리, 광주, 한국
2006	'DISTANCE' 국립현대미술관 창동갤러리, 서울, 한국
2004	'DISTANCE' 스투번이스트갤러리, 뉴욕, 미국
2011	광주미술상, 광주미술상위원회
2010	상징물 설계 현상공모 최우수상, 광주광역시 서구청
2007	신세계미술상, 광주신세계백화점갤러리
2005	하정웅 청년작가상, 광주시립미술관

· 학력

2009	컬럼비아건축대학원
2002	연세대학교 건축공학과

· 주요 수상경력

2016	남산 예장자락 재생사업 현상설계, 가작, 2016
2015	소마미술관 야외프로젝트 S, 최종당선,
2015	국립현대미술관 젊은건축가 프로그램 최종 후보
2014	대한민국목조건축대전, 본상, 2014
2014	마포 석유비축기지 국제설계경기, 가작
2012	LH 영종 하늘도시 제2공공도서관 현상설계, 최종후보

· 주요연구 및 저서

2015	저서, 건축의 지역성을 다시 생각한다(Re: thinking locality in architecture)
2015	기고, 알고리즘을 통한 자유곡면 쉘 구조물의 설계 및 시공
2014	기고, 디지털 제작과 건축적 실험-특집 'Digital Tectonics', 건축학회지

· 주요 전시 및 작품

2016	남산 예장자락 재생사업, 현상설계, 서울
2015	한강 건축 상상전 전시
2015	어반매니페스토 아카이브전, 문화예술위원회

2014	Part to Whole(설치구조물), 국립현대미술관 서울관
2013	Bilateral Theatre I(설치구조물), 서울시립미술관
2012	Floating Garden(설치구조물), 서울시립미술관
2012	Opening Chronometry(설치구조물), 이화여자대학교, 2012
2011	Plis/Replis(설치구조물), 프랑스 랑스(Reims)

· 학력

| 2010 | 한국예술종합학교, 커뮤니케이션 디자인(Communication Design) |
| 2003 | 뉴욕대 인터랙티브 텔레커뮤니케이션(Interactive Telecommunication) 석사 |

· 주요 전시 및 작품

2015	건축문화제 한강 건축상상전 기획, 서울시 건축기획부, 한국
2013	'미디어에서의 상호작용(INTER. Act Reciprocity in Media)', 브릭 미디어 박물관, 브루클린, 뉴욕, 미국
2012	가버너스 아일랜드 아트페어 아티스트 셀렉션, 가버너스 아일랜드, 뉴욕, 미국
2012	'상호 분할(Interconnected Segment)', 아트게이트갤러리, 뉴욕, 미국
2012	'한지 변형(Hanji Metamorphosis)', 스페이스 475, 뉴욕, 미국
2012	'동기화된 욕망(Desired SYNC), 뉴욕한국문화원, 뉴욕, 미국
2011	'불안과 욕망(Anxiety and Desire), 아트게이트갤러리, 뉴욕, 미국
2011	'모든-빛(All-Light)', 디지털미디어 전시, 서아트갤러리, 브루클린, 미국
2010	시그라프(SIGGRAPH) '공간-시간(Space-Time)' 전시, LA컨벤션센터, 미국
2009	Interactive VJ projection system; 'Fashion Victim' Fashion Show, 준스페이스, 뉴욕, 미국
2008	시그라프(SIGGRAPH) 아시아, 선텍 국제 컨벤션 센터, 싱가포르
2008	덤보 아트 페스티발, 브루클린, 미국

· 주요 약력

	아르후스 건축학과 부교수, 덴마크
	스튜디오 컨텍스트(CONTEXT) 건축소장, 덴마크, 이탈리아, 인디아
	도코모모(DOCOMOMO, Documentation and Conservation of buildings, sites and neighborhoods of the Modern Movement 근대운동에 관한 건물과 환경 형성의 기록조사 및 보존을 위한 조직) 부의장, 덴마크

GWANGJU
BIENNALE FOUNDATION

Honorary Chairman
Yoon, Jang Hyun

President
Kim, SunJung

Gwangju Folly Department
Director Kim, Eun Young
Staff
Lee, Bohyun
An, Mi Jeong
Kim, Do Kyun
Hwang, Myoung Jin

Curatorial Team of
the Gwangju Folly III
Director
Chun, Eui-Young
Curators
Yoo, Uoo Sang & Wee, Jinbok

Gwangju Metropolitan City
Lee, Eun Sang
Shin, Jung Ha
Yim, Dong Beom
Yang, Tae Young
Kim, Hyemi

Citizens Committee
for Gwangju Folly
Kang, PilSeo
Kim, Yongjun
Nam, SeungJin
Ryu, Youngguk
Park, Dongjoon
Park, Sangho
Park, Jeongyong
Yeo, Gyunsoo
Lee, KiHun
Jeon, Jinsuk
Cheon, Deukyoum

재단법인
광주비엔날레

명예이사장
윤장현

대표이사
김선정

광주폴리부
부장 김은영
직원 이보현, 안미정, 김도균, 황명진

광주폴리 III 기획진
총감독 천의영
큐레이터 유우상, 위진복

광주광역시
이은상
신정하
임동범
양태영
김혜미

광주폴리시민협의회
강필서
김용준
남승진
류영국
박동준
박상호
박정용
여균수
이기훈
전진숙
천득염

View Folly + Art Installation
'Architecture of Autonomy'
by Moon, Hoon and realities:united,
Jan Edler & Tim Edler
Project Name: View Folly
Project Team
– Moon, Hoon: Kang, Changsu,
Kim Sookhee, Tomasz Kisilewicz,
Cho, Guenyoung
– realities:united,
Jan Edler & Tim Eder
Johannes Fröhlich,
Christopher Gramer, Paula Oster,
Charlotte Popp
Construction
Cho, Dongjin (CL Engineering),
Green Wood Inc

THE I LOVE STREET
by Winy Maas (MVRDV)
Project Name:
GD (Gwangju Dutch) Folly
Project Team: Winy Maas,
Jacob van Rijs and Nathalie de
Vries with Wenchian Shi,
Lee, Kyo-suk, Lee, Dongmin,
Bowen Zhu, Sen Yang
Construction:
Gongjeong Construction co.
Sponsor: Creative Industries
Fund NL
Media Art: Jeroen Kooijmans
Additional thanks to
Executives and Staffs of
Seoseok Primary School,
Class No 1 & 2 at Grade 6 of
Seoseok Primary School,
Parent-Teacher Organisation
of Seoseok Primary School,
Resident's Association of
Seonam-dong & Dongmyeong-
dong, Urban Regenerations
of Dong-gu City Redevelopment
Department,
Jeon, Youngwon (Municipal
Assemblyman of Dong-gu),
Lee, KiHun (Executive Director of
Regional Cultural Exchange
Honam Foundation)

Dream House by Cho, ByoungSoo
Project Name:
GD (Gwangju Dutch) Folly
Project Team:
Cho, ByoungSoo
Architects Associates
Construction
Cho, Young Mook &
Kim, Soonho (CNO Construction)
Kim, Chun Hak
(Yang Jin Industrial Ltd)
Cho, Hyeong Hwan(Unitech Ltd)
Additional thanks to
Seo, SeongWon (Gwangju Dong-gu
City Redevelopment Department),
Cheon, Deukyoum
(Chonnam National University),
Ryu, Youngguk (Geocity Director),
Song, Joogwan (Media Art, Artist) ,
Gwangju Folly Department and
Gwangju Folly 3 curatorial team.

Chungmijang & Congzib
by Chang, Jinwoo
Project Name: Cook Folly
Project Team: Chang, Jinwoo,
Formative Architects
(Koh, Youngsung, Lee, SeongBum,
Kim, JeongEun), Jung, Gwangmin
(Seoro Archetects.Co.Ltd)
Construction
– Chungmijang: Jung, Minho
(Handeul Ltd)
– Congzib: Ha, Taihyun & Sin, Jinsuk
(SEA Design & Construction)
Gwangju Youth Cooperative

MEDIA CELL, INFINITY LIGHT,
MEDIA WALL and LIGHT PASSAGE
by Kim, ChanJoong & Jin, Siyon
Project Name: FuNPuN Folly
Project Team:
Siyon Media & The System Lab
Construction: O, Jaegon
(Sunjin Plus Ltd)
Additional thanks to
Choongjang-ro 4 -5 ga Cooperative

SPECTRUM
by Leif Høgfeldt Hansen
Project Name: Mini Folly
Project Team: Studio Context
 by Leif Høgfeldt Hansen
Co-workers
Paul Elliott, Mia Marker Marold
Bøhnke, Miriam Eugenie,
Karin Simone Hauser, Andy Hogan,
Johnny Huang, Lisa Marie Kolbinger,
Frederik Langhoff,
Frederik Kromann Laursen,
Florence Mareen, Lena Thomassen,
Anne Vingisar
External Supervisor:
Cho, ByoungSoo
Architects Associates
Main Adviser: Cho, ByoungSoo
Assistants: Eva Rosborg Aagaard,
Jeong, Yunseok
Additional thanks to Arhus School
of Architecture,
Cho, ByoungSoo Architects
Associates, Architect Student Tina
Tychsen Rasmussen, Henrik Søholt
Christensen's Travel Grant

Infinite Elements
by Kook, Hyoung-Gul &
Syn, Sue Gyeong
Project Name: Mini Folly
Project Team: Kook, Hyoung-Gul +
Syn, Sue Gyeong

문훈 + 리얼리티즈:유나이티드,
얀 에들러 & 팀 에들러의
‹뷰폴리 + 설치작품 '자율건축'›
프로젝트명: 뷰폴리
프로젝트팀
– 문훈: 강창수, 김숙희,
토마스 키실레비츠, 조근영
– 리얼리티즈:유나이티드,
얀 에들러 & 팀 에들러: 요하네스 프레리히,
크리스토퍼 그레이머, 파울라 오스터,
샬롯 포프
시공사: 조동진(씨엘 엔지니어링), 그린우드㈜

위니 마스(MVRDV)의 ‹아이 러브 스트리트›
프로젝트명: GD폴리
프로젝트팀: 판레이스와 나탈리 드프리스,
웬치안 쉬, 이교석, 이동민, 보웬 주, 센 양
시공사: ㈜공정건설
후원: 네덜란드창조산업기금
미디어아트: 예룬 코에이만스
또한 서석초등학교 임직원, 서석초등학교
6학년 1, 2반, 서석초등학교학부모위원회,
서남동 & 동명동 주민자치위원회,
동구청 도시재생과, 동구의회 전영원의원,
지역문화교류호남재단
이기훈 상임이사에게 감사드린다.

조병수의 ‹꿈 집›
프로젝트명: GD폴리
프로젝트팀: 조병수 건축연구소
시공사: 조영묵 & 김순호(CNO건설),
김춘학(㈜양진산업), ㈜유니테크(조형환)
서성원(광주동구청 도시재생과),
천득염 교수(전남대학교),
류영국(지오시티 대표이사),
송주관 작가(미디어 아티스트), 광주폴리부,
광주폴리 III 기획진에게 감사드린다.

장진우의 ‹청미장 & 콩집›
프로젝트명: 쿡폴리
프로젝트팀: 장진우,
포머티브 건축사(고영성, 이성범, 김정은),
정광민(서로건축사사무소)
시공사
– 청미장: 정민호(㈜한들)
– 콩집: 하태현 & 신진석
(SEA 디자인 & 컨스트럭션)
맛있는골목협동조합

김찬중 & 진시영의
‹미디어 셀, 무한의 빛, 미디어 월, 소통의 문›
프로젝트명: 뻔뻔폴리
프로젝트팀: 시연미디어 & 더시스템랩
시공사: 오재곤(㈜선진플러스)
또한 충장로 4~5가 상인번영회에
감사드린다.

라이프 호그펠트 한센의 ‹스펙트럼›
프로젝트명: 미니폴리
프로젝트팀: 라이프 호그펠트 한센의
스튜디오 컨텍스트
협력: 폴 엘리어트, 미아 마커 매럴드 번그 ,
마리암 유지니, 카린 시몬 하우저,
앤디 호건, 죠니 황, 리사 마리 콜비너,
프레드릭 랭호프, 프레드릭 크로만 라우젠,
플로렌스 마린, 레나 토마슨,
앤 빈지저
외부감독: 조병수 건축연구소
메인 어드바이저: 조병수
어시스턴트: 에바 로즈버그 마가드,
정윤석 또한 오르후스 건축학교,
조병수 건축연구소,
건축과 학생인 티나 틱슨 라스무센,
슈홀트 크리스텐슨의 여행단체에 감사드린다.

국형걸 & 신수경의 ‹인피니트 엘리먼츠›
프로젝트명: 미니폴리
프로젝트팀: 국형걸 + 신수경

Organisation & Host
Gwangju Metropolitan City
Gwangju Biennale Foundation
www.gwangjubiennale.org
www.gwangjufolly.org

Editorial team
Chun, Eui-Young
Yoo, Uoo Sang
Wee, Jinbok
Kim, Hongsung
Eleonoor Jap Sam

Production & Coordination team
Lee, Bohyun
Kim, Hongsung
Eleonoor Jap Sam

Authors
View Folly
Moon, Hoon + realities:united,
Jan Edler & Tim Edler
FunPun Folly
Kim, Chanjoong + Jin, Siyon
Mini Folly
Kook, Hyoung-Gul +
Syn, Sue Gyeong
Leif Høgfeldt Hansen
Cook Folly
Chang, Jinwoo
GD Folly
Winy Maas, MVRDV
Cho, ByoungSoo

Contributions
Formative
Jeroen Kooijmans
Lee, KiHun
Pirjo Sanaksenaho
HENG Chye Kiang
Ivan NASUTION
Mo, Jongryn
Mark Pimlott
Kas Oosterhuis
Harry den Hartog
Wim Nijenhuis

Translation
serenes lab
with Leam, Sooyoung,
Hong, Seunghae & Lim, Liwon

Proofreading
Richard Harris
(English proofreading)
KOH, Angela
(Korean proofreading)

Art Direction
Kim, Hongsung
(Kerb, Seoul)

Graphic Design & Illustrations
Jung, Sarok
(Kerb, Seoul)

Photography
Unreal Studio

Photo Credits
Unreal Studio
pp. 062~087, pp.126~150,
pp.197~207, pp.230~254

Image Editing
Jung, Sarok
(Kerb, Seoul)

Printing and Binding
CREIN

Publisher
Jap Sam Books
Heijningen, the Netherlands
www.japsambooks.nl

주최 및 주관
광주광역시 & 재단법인 광주비엔날레
www.gwangjubiennale.org
www.gwangjufolly.org

편집
천의영, 유우상, 위진복
김홍성, 엘레노어 얍 샘

제작 & 코디
이보현, 김홍성, 엘레노어 얍 샘

참여작가
뷰폴리
문훈 + 리얼리티즈:유나이티드,
얀 에들러 & 팀 에들러
뻔뻔폴리
김찬중 + 진시영
미니폴리
국형걸 + 신수경
라이프 호그펠트 한센
쿡폴리
장진우
GD폴리
위니마스, MVRDV
조병수

기고
포머티브
예룬 코에이만스
이기훈
피르요 사낙세나호
헹 치엥 키앙 + 이반 나수티온
모종린
마크핌롯
카스 오스터하위스
하리 덴 하르토흐
빔 네이엔하위스

번역
serenes lab
(협력: 임수영, 홍승해, 임리원)

교정교열
리처드 해리스(영문)
고윤희(국문)

아트 디렉션
김홍성(커브)

디자인 & 일러스트레이션
정사록(커브)

작품 사진 촬영
언리얼 스튜디오

사진 크레딧
언리얼 스튜디오
pp.062~087, pp.126~149,
pp.197~207, pp.230~254

이미지 편집
정사록(커브)

인쇄 및 제본
크레인

출판사
Jap Sam Books
www.japsambooks.nl

see play eat walk
Gwangju Folly III: Where
the Everyday and
the Unexpected Intersect
보고 놀고 먹고 걷고
광주폴리 III: 일상과 일탈의 교차점

© 2017 Gwangju Biennale Foundation,
the authors, the photographers
and Jap Sam Books

ISBN 978-94-90322-86-1

The Gwangju Biennale Foundation
and the publisher gratefully
acknowledge the permission
granted to reproduce the copyright
material in this book.
If any proper acknowledgement
has not been made, we encourage
copyright holders to notify
the Gwangju Biennale Foundation.
재단법인 광주비엔날레와 출판사는
저작권 사용에 대한 모든 허가를 받았으며
저작권 사용에 적절한 확인이 이루어지지
않았다면 재단법인 광주비엔날레에
문의하시길 바랍니다.

This publication has been made
possible with the generous support
of the Creative Industries Fund NL,
Crown-Haitai Confectionery &
Foods, Gwangju Metropolitan City,
and Gwangju Biennale Foundation.
이 책은 네덜란드창조산업기금, 크라운해태,
광주광역시, 재단법인 광주비엔날레의
도움으로 출판되었습니다.

**creative industries
fund NL**

GWANGJU CITY